ADVANCES IN THE STUDY OF GREEK

NEW INSIGHTS FOR READING
THE NEW TESTAMENT

CONSTANTINE R. CAMPBELL

ZONDERVAN®

ZONDERVAN

Advances in the Study of Greek
Copyright © 2015 by Constantine R. Campbell

This title is also available as a Zondervan ebook.
Visit www.zondervan.com/ebooks.

Requests for information should be addressed to:

Zondervan, 3900 *Sparks Dr. SE, Grand Rapids, Michigan 49546*

Library of Congress Cataloging-in-Publication Data

Campbell, Constantine R., author.
    Advances in the Study of Greek : New Insights for Reading the New Testament /
  Constantine R. Campbell.
      pages   cm
    ISBN 978-0-310-51595-1 (softcover)
    1. Greek language, Biblical — Syntax. 2. Greek language, Biblical. I. Title.
PA851.C36 2015
487'.4 — dc23   2014031678

Cover design: *Studio Gearbox*
Cover images: *CC by 3.0; Thinkstock*
Interior design: *Matthew Van Zomeren*

Printed in the United States of America

15 16 17 18 19 20 21 22 23 24 25 /DCI/ 20 19 18 17 16 15 14 13 12 11 10 9 8 7 6 5 4 3 2 1

For Nono, who took my advice and married Nona

Μικρό μου Καστελλόριζο είστε ένα μαργαριτάρι

CONTENTS

EXPANDED TABLE OF CONTENTS

ABBREVIATIONS

BDAG   W. Bauer, F. W. Danker, W. E. Arndt, and F. W. Gingrich, *Greek-English Lexicon of the New Testament and Other Early Christian Literature*. 3rd ed. Chicago, 2000.

BT   *The Bible Translator*

CBQMS   Catholic Biblical Quarterly Monograph Series

ConBNT   Coniectanea biblica: New Testament Series

EAGLL   *Encyclopedia of Ancient Greek Language and Linguistics*

JBL   *Journal of Biblical Literature*

JSNTS   *Journal for the Study of the New Testament*

JSNTSup   Journal for the Study of the New Testament Supplement Series

LBS   Linguistic Biblical Studies

LXX   Septuagint

Neot   *Neotestamentica*

NovTSup   Novum Testamentum Supplement

SBG   Studies in Biblical Greek

SNTSMS   Society for New Testament Studies Monograph Series

TJ   *Trinity Journal*

WUNT   Wissenschaftliche Untersuchungen zum Neuen Testament

FOREWORD

Almost twenty years ago, I found myself in a quiet discussion (perhaps I should say "debate") over aspect theory. I was arguing that, whatever its weaknesses, aspect theory enjoys stronger explanatory power than the regnant model, which in effect understands Greek verbs in the indicative to grammaticalize time, and Greek verbs in the other moods to grammaticalize *Aktionsart*. My interlocutor, well trained as a classical scholar as well as being an expert in the Greek New Testament, took the contrary position. We tossed examples back and forth, until he brought the discussion to a close by asserting, rather dismissively, that I was welcome to defend theories that had enjoyed only a few decades of life; he would prefer to stick with the understanding of the Greek verb that had enjoyed three millennia of life.

Two things were immediately obvious: he had read little in linguistics, and, fine scholar though he was, he knew little of the history of the study of the Greek verb. The grammarian Dionysius Thrax (second century BC) did not understand the Greek verb the same way that, say, Erasmus did. Erasmus, not to mention the Reformers, did not anticipate the rise of *Aktionsart* theory in the nineteenth century — so sweeping a development that for almost a century and a half one would be hard-pressed to find a bona fide Greek scholar who had not bought into such theory. Certainly *Aktionsart* theory had greater explanatory power than what it displaced. In other words, there had been some *advances* in the study of the Greek verb. The question now, however, is whether the large number of texts that *Aktionsart* explains poorly might be better served by aspect theory. In other words, can we speak of further "advances" in the study of Greek? Or should we apply the liturgical formula, "As it was in the beginning, is now, and evermore shall be, world without end"?

I have used aspect theory as my way of inviting reflection on Con Campbell's title: *Advances in the Study of Greek*. But the fact of the matter is that this book casts its net far more widely than aspect theory. Its range is broad: Campbell sets out to survey and evaluate the current topics in (primarily biblical) Greek where, in his view, recent advances have been made. In other words, this book is not a survey of the current state of affairs in Greek study, but a survey of those domains of study where, in Campbell's view, advances are being made.

Aspect theory is one part of the story, of course—indeed, a part of the story in which Campbell has been a key player. But along the way, Campbell carefully explains various linguistic theories, summarizes debates on deponency and the middle voice, probes idiolect and genre and register, and summarizes the approaches of Levinsohn and Runge. His summary of Runge's treatment of Greek particles is worth the price of the book. In his ninth chapter, Campbell engages in evenhanded discussion as to whether we should retain Erasmian pronunciation of Greek, or switch to modern pronunciation. In his last chapter, Campbell the teacher surfaces, as he offers a range of pedagogical reflections, largely drawn from his own experiences of learning and teaching Greek.

I cannot say that Con Campbell always convinces me—though he usually does. But I know no other book quite like this one. The range of coverage is hugely impressive. This book is not for beginners, but it will prove enormously useful in helping scholars, advanced students, and serious pastors to find out what is going on in the field of New Testament Greek studies—especially if they are tempted to think that advances cannot be made. That stance can be maintained only by those who are attracted to the delusion that three thousand years of scholarship have witnessed no paradigm shifts. It will also prove useful to the many New Testament scholars who would like to understand recent developments in linguistics and Greek, but whose distaste for linguistic jargon prevents them from breaking into these burgeoning fields. Here is a way in.

D. A. Carson

PREFACE

The origins of this book are found in a class I taught for several years at Moore Theological College, known as *Advanced Topics in Biblical Greek and Exegesis*. My purpose in teaching this course was to introduce Greek students to various issues within cutting-edge Greek scholarship and linguistics. First-year Greek programs are generally not able to discuss such topics in much depth (if at all), and while second-year programs may delve in to some extent, they leave plenty of room for further depth and interaction with scholarship.

It was never my intention to turn the course into a book. That idea came from some Moore College students. The first time a class raised the idea, I dismissed it. I didn't think it would be a book anyone would be interested in, and it would represent a lot of work! The following year's class raised the idea too, but pushed a little harder. I pushed back for some justification from the students. Then one student, Nick Moll, said something like, "I know I would have gone on to make exegetical mistakes in my sermon preparation for years to come if it were not for the principles and content of this course." That was the point at which I decided to try to turn my teaching material into the book you now hold in your hands.

I wish to thank my past students at Moore College, and my current students at Trinity Evangelical Divinity School, for their various contributions. I am grateful for their interest and enthusiasm, their questions and insights, and their commitment to Greek and to careful exegesis. They have inspired me; they have challenged my thinking and understanding; and they have even caused me to change my mind about a few things. I can honestly say this book would not exist if it were not for them.

I am grateful for the generous contributions of some learned friends. Stephen Levinsohn offered penetrating feedback with several suggestions for improvement, especially on linguistic matters. John Lee helped me with the tricky chapter on pronunciation in particular. Steve Runge, Josh Jipp, and Dana Harris also provided valuable insights. Special thanks go to Don Carson for contributing the foreword of the book. My gratitude goes to them all.

Thanks are due to Zondervan Academic for taking a chance on yet another out-of-the-box book idea. It is a privilege and a pleasure to work with this team. Particular thanks go to my editor, Verlyn Verbrugge, for his critical eye, attention to detail, and constant reminder to be *clear*.

Finally, this book is dedicated to my Nono and Nona—known to other people as Nick and Vasilo. They have contributed to my greekness as much as anyone. While I wish I could have written this preface on "our island," perhaps I will for a future edition.

Soli Deo Gloria

INTRODUCTION

Insofar as we love the gospel, to that same extent, let us study the ancient tongues.
                                                        —*Martin Luther*

This book is an introduction to issues of interest in the current world of New Testament Greek scholarship. Those within Greek scholarship often lament that students, pastors, professors, and New Testament commentators seem out of touch with what is going on in Greek studies. Those outside Greek scholarship often lament that they don't know what's going on, nor do they know how to get up to speed. Much of the scholarship is inaccessible to outsiders, since it is highly technical and laden with linguistic jargon and methodologies. Some of the debates about Greek make such topics seem contentious and overly complex. Moreover, it is not always clear what difference Greek scholarship really makes to reading and understanding the Greek New Testament. This book provides an accessible introduction for students, pastors, professors, and New Testament commentators to understand what are the current issues of interest in this period of paradigm shift(s) and why they matter. After all, the study of Greek ultimately affects everyone interested in the New Testament, whether they are Greek scholars or not.

My aim is that this book will be useful to anyone who is studying Greek at university or seminary level, to their professors, to pastors who use Greek, and to New Testament scholars and commentators. In short, anyone who engages with the Greek New Testament ought to benefit from this book, with the possible exception of Greek scholars themselves. However, I hope that even Greek scholars will benefit, since their expertise is often limited to two or three of the topics covered in the book; they too may profit from an introduction to issues outside their expertise.

0.1 What Is This Book About?

As mentioned above, this book aims to introduce issues of interest within Greek scholarship. This is a particular aim and requires some clarification. In colloquial terms, it could be seen as a presentation of the cutting edge. This cutting edge includes issues that have the potential to change the way we think about Greek. It includes issues that set new directions for Greek scholarship or that may overturn previously held ideas about Greek. It also includes issues that shape the way we think about language in general, and therefore how we should handle our questions and discussions of the Greek language. Some of the cutting-edge issues presented here are well known, perhaps due to (in)famous debates about them, and my readers will be looking to understand them and perhaps make some sort of adjudication, if possible. Others are issues that are not as widely known, but should be.

Such a focus on the cutting edge means that this book does *not* deal with issues that are relatively stable or have not yet been at the center of some kind of cutting-edge discussion. Uncontroversial issues, or areas that have not seen much development in recent years, are not included here. This book is not intended to be a general introduction to Greek, nor even a general introduction to Greek scholarship. The status quo of such consensuses can readily be ascertained through the consultation of informative Greek grammars and the like. Rather, the issues of contention, development, and even revolution are the focus here.

A final note about what this book is about concerns its limited scope. The book is deliberately focused on *New Testament* Greek because my ultimate aim is to equip those who read and expound the Greek New Testament (as the book's subtitle suggests). It will become clear (if it is not already), however, that the study of the Greek of the New Testament is inextricably tied to the study of Ancient Greek in general, since the New Testament is simply part of a wider corpus of ancient Greek literature. In fact, even the term *New Testament Greek* can be misleading if it is understood to mean that the Greek found in the pages of the New Testament is somehow a subcategory of Greek unto its own. It is not.

In this respect, the topics included are equally relevant to Koine Greek (c. 300 BC to AD 600),[1] and, indeed, most of it applies to the entire scope of Ancient Greek. So, why, then, is the book self-consciously focused on the Greek of the New Testament? As already mentioned, I have a particular readership in mind—those who engage with the Greek New Testament—though anyone else interested in Ancient Greek will also profit from the material set forth here. In addition to audience, the focus on New Testament Greek sets the parameters of application, since I have tried to point out how various issues may impact the exegesis and translation of the New Testament. Furthermore, most of the scholarship that is addressed here is limited to those scholars who are dealing with the Greek of the New Testament.

While there are occasional forays into wider Ancient Greek scholarship, and the contributions of some scholars working within that wider field, my intention is not to cover everything in the world of Greek scholarship. That would result in quite a different book and would not serve my aims as clearly. In any case, it is probably fair to say that a great deal of the controversy within Greek studies of late has taken place within New Testament Greek circles. This may be due to the unruly nature of the scholars within such circles (!), or, more likely, it is due to the level of devotional commitment to the New Testament. Such commitment has focused research on the New Testament in a way that no other small corpus within Greek literature has ever received.

0.2 How Is This Book Unique?

There is currently no other volume that attempts to bring together modern advances in the study of New Testament Greek. Over the past thirty years, Greek scholarship has undergone a series of paradigm shifts, the likes of which have not been seen in the preceding century. The application of modern linguistic methodologies, lexical and lexicographical advances, the rejection of deponency, the rise of discourse analysis, verbal aspect, and idiolect, register, and genre studies have all changed the face of the study of Greek. No other single source gathers these issues together.

Moreover, there are currently no other *accessible* treatments of such issues that present recent scholarly consensuses, debates, and inquiries at

---

1. Some scholars prefer the dates c. 300 BC to AD 300.

a level that is appropriate for nonspecialists (with the exception of verbal aspect and one school of discourse analysis). Thus, there are at least two characteristics that make this book unique: its scope of interest and its accessibility. This book gathers together the most important areas of discussion in an accessible manner, so that all students, pastors, and teachers of the New Testament might understand and apply these advances in Greek studies.

0.3 Why Is This Book Needed?

Some readers will require no explanation as to why they should read this book. They are reading it because the answer is obvious to them. Others may require some persuasion. Whether one knows it or not, everyone interested in the Greek New Testament needs to become familiar with the discussions that are included here. These issues are important. They are not esoteric discussions about linguistic mumbo jumbo that have no connection to the interests of normal people. Rather, I have been careful to select discussions that have some kind of direct bearing on the way we read the New Testament. If you think reading the Greek New Testament is important, then you should regard these issues as important.

The matters discussed in these pages exhibit two types of relevance to reading the Greek New Testament. First, genuine advances in Greek linguistics can lead to new insights into text. These may not be earth shattering, nor will they necessarily revolutionize the exegesis of certain passages or theological formulations. But they will add nuance, depth of understanding, and increased precision. They may open up fresh exegetical possibilities here or there, or clarify which existing possibilities are most likely from a linguistic standpoint. Greek linguistics develops an awareness of whole texts and of how Greek is used to structure them and to create coherence within them. Linguistic awareness also aids our *discussions* about the Greek New Testament; as we become clearer about methodological principles and certain terminology, we are better able to talk with one another about Greek and about Greek texts.

Second, advances in Greek linguistics can correct long-held errors. Such errors might be methodological; others may result from false information; and still other errors might involve wrong readings of certain texts. Regardless, such errors are far too common. Surely it is incumbent on interpreters of the New Testament to correct errors of method or practice as they become evident.

Nor are these topics just passing fads. Within New Testament circles, there seems to exist an inherent suspicion about the "new" when it comes to Greek (though, interestingly, other areas of New Testament research welcome the "new" and are sometimes even preoccupied with it). A common attitude is one that wonders, if we've understood Greek the same way for two thousand years, why do we now think we've finally understood it? Can a few scholars over a few years overturn two millennia of agreement?

Such an attitude reveals a serious ignorance of history—no offense, if that was you—and all the more underscores the need to read this book! It will be clear from chapter 1 that it is certainly *not* the case that Greek scholarship has been settled for two thousand years and only now is being unsettled. In fact, prior to the nineteenth century, there was comparatively little Greek scholarship, and what did exist was deeply incoherent. After the ancient Greek grammarians Dionysius Thrax (170–90 BC) and Apollonius Dyscolus (2nd century AD), the Renaissance period initiated major steps forward, followed by gradual advances until the nineteenth century. From the nineteenth century onward, many advances have taken place— including the overturning of some common beliefs about Greek, the results of which are assumed today. They have not existed since the first century; they're only 150 years old at best. And yet they are treated as the "traditional" understanding that we've always had. Part of the burden of this book is to familiarize the reader with the historical contours of discussion, so that you can appreciate that modern scholarship has not just plucked its ideas and conclusions out of the air. Several cutting-edge issues represent the culmination of more than a hundred years of reflection and debate.

0.4 Why Include *These* Topics?

Mention has already been made of some of the considerations in choosing the topics of discussion in this book. Allow me now to be more specific. The first chapter offers a short history of Greek studies from the nineteenth century to the present day. It combines some of the advances in the wider study of Ancient Greek generally, New Testament Greek specifically, and key movements within modern linguistics. The purpose of the first chapter is to set the scene for the following discussions. By grasping something of the historical development of Greek scholarship, we are better able to assess current trends, understand where they have come from, and gain an appreciation for the contours and trajectory of the scholarship in general. A key part of that trajectory is the delineation of clear periods or epochs of scholarship, each imbued with its own interests, methodologies, and conclusions.

The second chapter addresses linguistics. For some readers, linguistics is the dirty word that has muddied the study of Greek. No doubt the incorporation of linguistic methodology and terminology has in large part enhanced the inaccessibility of Greek scholarship. So, this chapter aims to explain and clarify some important concepts and major figures in linguistics. Chapter 2, however, has another purpose. It is placed near the beginning of the book because some grasp of linguistic methodology and terminology is essential for several of the discussions that follow. I want my readers to have the necessary linguistic keys to unlock the doors of debate.

Chapter 3 treats lexical semantics and lexicography. The issues pertaining to the former are nothing new, but they are explored for two reasons. First, they are necessary for a proper engagement of the issues in lexicography, concerning which there are several new insights affecting our use of standard lexicons. Second, the unfortunate truth is that the field of biblical studies has yet to fully absorb the lessons of lexical semantics. Its principles affect every word study, all lexical analysis, and all exegesis in which certain words matter.

The fourth chapter may well be seen to be the most explosive, as it addresses the issue of deponency within Greek's voice system. Though it has one of the highest levels of consensus among scholars, the proposal to abandon deponency altogether means reconfiguring the middle voice and restructuring the structure of the Greek voice system.

Chapter 5 deals with verbal aspect and *Aktionsart*. This has been the most controversial area of discussion within Greek scholarship, and yet there are many common points of agreement that need to be adopted by New Testament interpreters. Some of the key issues of debate are discussed as well as useful exegetical implications of aspect.

The sixth chapter addresses a lesser-known area of discussion, dealing primarily with idiolect and its relationship to register and genre. Idiolect, genre, and register have exegetical implications for the language choices made by individual authors in particular text-types. They are especially relevant to synoptic studies.

The next two chapters introduce various approaches to discourse analysis, which is a burgeoning and highly significant field in Greek studies. Of all the topics explored, this is probably the one with most exegetical potential as it offers tools for examining texts through ever-larger units of meaning.

Chapter 9 explores debates about Greek pronunciation. Though not completely irrelevant for exegesis, pronunciation is considered for other reasons, including historical accuracy, textual criticism, and respect for the language and its heritage.

The final chapter discusses Greek pedagogy and some of the developments that may affect Greek teaching and learning. Though not a study of the Greek language per se, pedagogy has obvious implications for anyone who wants to learn the language or teach it to others.

0.5 How Should This Book Be Used?

This book can be used for personal study or classroom use. In fact, much of the material originated in a class I have taught over several years, so it was originally designed with the student in mind and for class interaction. It may be set as a class text, depending on the nature of the class, or used as an ancillary resource to supplement other Greek textbooks.

For personal use, the book should be accessible to students, pastors, and scholars alike. Students may read it in order to understand the currents in Greek scholarship and develop their own grasp of language and language use. It will be especially helpful to anyone engaging in New Testament postgraduate studies, since an awareness of these scholarly trends is essential. Pastors will, I hope, find much here that will sharpen and refine their handling of the Greek New Testament. New Testament scholars also need to be aware of scholarly trends, of course, and this book will be the easiest way to come to grips with current Greek scholarship.

In part, the book presents a series of literature surveys. This is obviously a necessary component of introducing scholarship. Some such surveys are focused on a particular author or two (such as in chapter 8), while others are more wide-ranging. Whatever the case, I have sought a balance between two desires. On the one hand, I want to provide enough of a summary of key scholars that this book will be independently useful, as the reader can immediately begin to absorb and apply various methods and practices. On the other hand, I do not want to give so much away that the reader feels it unnecessary to pursue the summarized works for themselves. That would be counterproductive, since a central goal is to promote the work of important scholars and widen the level of engagement with them. Nothing would please me more than if my book were to be quickly forgotten because the reader has become so engrossed in following it up with further reading.

To that end, each chapter concludes with a list for further reading. All works listed are introduced throughout their respective chapters, but they are collated in one place for ease of reference. Not every work mentioned is listed, but only those regarded immediately useful for further reading.

Finally, the reader should consider debated issues carefully for themselves. I have tried to present the material objectively for this purpose (though occasionally my bias comes through). Nevertheless, I have not refrained from making my own opinions and conclusions known. I trust this too will be of some use to the reader, though of course you should not feel beholden to them.

0.6 What Is the Intended Outcome of This Book?

I hold hope for several possible outcomes. First, I hope the reader will be properly introduced to the issues of greatest importance for current Greek studies. Second, the reader will become better equipped to handle Greek text with linguistic sophistication, both on a methodological and practical level. Third, the reader will feel competent to engage further with Greek scholarship. Fourth, the reader will engage further with Greek scholarship. Fifth, the teaching of Greek will be well informed of current issues. Sixth, the wider world of New Testament scholarship will become more engaged with Greek scholarship. Seventh, some readers will be inspired to become Greek scholars themselves. Eighth, I hope that future editions of this book will need to include the contributions of some of those aforementioned readers.

CHAPTER 1

A SHORT HISTORY OF GREEK STUDIES: THE NINETEENTH CENTURY TO THE PRESENT DAY

It is hardly possible for the student of the present day [early twentieth century] to enter into sympathy with the inanities and sinuosities that characterized the previous treatises on the N. T. idiom.
—*A. T. Robertson*

1.1 Introduction

"What's past is prologue." So wrote Shakespeare,[1] and so it is for the study of Greek. In order to understand current Greek scholarship, we require an understanding of its past trajectory—its prologue.

This chapter outlines the history of Greek studies over the last two hundred years, paying attention to the study of Ancient Greek in general, Biblical (Koine) Greek in particular, and the rise of modern linguistics. The chapter will provide a context for the rest of the book, as well as demonstrate how and why certain discussions have taken shape.[2]

---

1. William Shakespeare, *The Tempest*, Act 2, Scene 1.
2. This chapter represents a selective survey, and the informed reader may think of several names and

The following historical outline is not restricted to Greek studies, but includes major movements within the field of linguistics. The influence of linguistics in Greek studies has become important, both for Koine Greek and Ancient Greek generally.[3] Rather than offer two separate surveys—one for Greek, the other for linguistics—I have attempted to blend them so that the reader can understand how the currents of one have affected the other.

1.2 The Nineteenth Century

The nineteenth century saw dramatic advances in the study of Greek, many of which would reverberate well into the twentieth century. Two of the most significant achievements of this century were the analysis of Greek through comparative philology and breakthroughs in understanding the Greek verbal system. A brief survey follows, drawing on Robertson's summary of the period in particular.[4]

1.2.1 The Pre-Winer Period

A. T. Robertson notes that prior to G. B. Winer's grammatical study *Grammatik des neutestamentlichen Sprachidioms*,[5] "it is hardly possible for the student of the present day to enter into sympathy with the inanities and sinuosities that characterized the previous treatises on the N. T. idiom."[6] This period was characterized by weak methodology, misunderstanding of the nature of language, and internal self-contradiction.

1.2.2 Georg B. Winer (1822)

Winer regarded the current state of affairs absurd, and instead insisted on a methodological order of interpretation: grammatical, historical, theolog-

---

movements that are not here included. Such omissions are not intended to render a negative value judgment in any way, but rather those included are so included in order to serve the particular purpose of the chapter. This purpose is not to provide an encyclopedic history of Greek studies, but rather to set the stage for the various discussions included in the remainder of this book.

3. The survey of linguistics presented here is even more curtailed than that of Greek. A full survey of modern linguistics takes (at least) a whole book of its own, and is not needed here in any case. The linguists and linguistic schools included are those that have most shaped the advances in the study of Greek.

4. A. T. Robertson, *A Grammar of the Greek New Testament in the Light of Historical Research* (4th ed.; Nashville: Broadman, 1934), 3–7.

5. Georg Benedict Winer, *Grammatik des neutestamentlichen Sprachidioms* (Leipzig: Friedrich Christian Wilhelm Vogel, 1822).

6. Robertson, *Grammar*, 3.

ical. The publication of his *Grammatik des neutestamentlichen Sprachidi-oms* in 1822 marked a new epoch in New Testament grammatical study. Two translations of Winer's *Grammatik*—one by Thayer and the other by W. F. Moulton—became standards for English-speaking Greek students and scholars.

1.2.3 Franz Bopp (1833)

Franz Bopp was the founder of comparative philology, publishing on the subject from as early as 1816. The second edition of his *Vergleichende Grammatik* popularized the term "Indo-European," and his work is regarded as the beginning of Indo-European studies as an academic discipline.[7] According to Delbrück, before Bopp "in all grammars the mass of 'irregular' words was at least as great as that of the 'regular' ones, and a rule without exception actually excited suspicion.'"[8]

1.2.4 Georg Curtius (1846ff.)

The chief significance of Curtius's scholarship was as the father of Greek verbal aspect studies. He was the first to argue that the Greek verbal system differs from Latin, and that temporal reference is limited to the indicative mood and is *not* a feature of the other moods (a fact taken for granted today). He also argued that the key difference between tenses was the *type of time* they express (*Zeitart*).[9] Brugmann later changed the term *Zeitart* to *Aktionsart*, since the notion of *type of action* was regarded to be more accurate.[10]

1.2.5 Brugmann and Delbrück (1886–1900)

Robertson regards Brugmann and Delbrück's *Grundriß der vergleichenden Grammatik der indogermanischen Sprachen* as the high-watermark in

---

7. Franz Bopp, *Vergleichende Grammatik des Sanskrit, Zend, Griechischen, Lateinischen, Litthauischen, Altslavischen, und Deutschen* (2nd ed.; Berlin: Ferd. Dümmler's Verlagsbuchhandlung, 1857). The first edition was published in 1833. See also E. F. K. Koerner, *Practicing Linguistic Historiography: Selected Papers* (Amsterdam: John Benjamins, 1989), 164.

8. Berthold Delbrück, *Introduction to the Study of Language: A Critical Survey of the History and Methods of Comparative Philology of the Indo-European Languages* (trans. E. Channing; Leipzig: Breitkopf and Härtel, 1882), 25.

9. Georg Curtius, *Die Bildung der Tempora und Modi im Griechischen und Lateinischen sprachvergleichend dargestellt* (Berlin: Wilhelm Besser, 1846), 148–53. See also his *Erläuterungen zu meiner griechischen Schulgrammatik* (Prague: F. Tempsky, 1863); *Das Verbum der griechischen Sprache* (Leipzig: S. Hirzel, 1873).

10. According to Gustav Herbig, "Aktionsart und Zeitstufe: Beiträge zur Funktionslehre des indogermanischen Verbums," *Indogermanische Forschungen* 6 (1896): 185–88.

comparative grammar.[11] He comments that "it is impossible to write a grammar of the Greek N. T. without taking into consideration this new conception of language."[12] The account of Proto-Indo-European syntax presented in this five-volume work is still regarded as unsurpassed.

1.2.6 Friedrich Blass (1896)

The publication of *Grammatik des neutestamentlichen Griechisch* by Blass in 1896 marked a significant new addition to Greek grammar in this period.[13] It remained one of the most widely used grammars for decades, with its latest iteration in English being produced in 1961, through the additional contributions of Debrunner and Funk.[14] In this way, Blass's grammar remains the most potent injection of nineteenth-century Greek scholarship into modern times.

1.2.7 Ernest de Witt Burton (1898)

Burton's *Syntax of the Moods and Tenses in New Testament Greek* was one of the few significant nineteenth-century contributions to Greek scholarship written in English.[15] Burton preempted the distinction that Saussure made famous (see §1.4.1) between historical and synchronic analyses of language, describing his own approach as "exegetical," which is in fact synchronic: "Exegetical grammar ... takes the forms as it finds them, and defines the function which at a given period each form discharged."[16] Though he does not use the term, half of Burton's *Syntax* (dealing with "The Tenses") is a study of *Aktionsart* in the usage of verbs in the Greek New Testament. Burton's treatment of the Greek verbal system remained influential well into the twentieth century.

1.3 The Early Twentieth Century

The significance of the early twentieth century is seen through two important legacies. The first, beginning just prior to the turn of the century, saw great

---

11. Robertson, *Grammar*, 11; Karl Brugmann and Berthold Delbrück, *Grundriß der vergleichenden Grammatik der indogermanischen Sprachen* (Strassburg: Karl J. Trübner, 1886–1900).
12. Robertson, *Grammar*, 12.
13. Friedrich Blass, *Grammatik des neutestamentlichen Griechisch* (Göttingen: Vandenhoeck & Ruprecht, 1896).
14. Friedrich Blass, Albert Debrunner, and Robert W. Funk, *A Greek Grammar of the New Testament and Other Early Christian Literature* (Chicago: University of Chicago Press, 1961).
15. Ernest de Witt Burton, *Syntax of the Moods and Tenses in New Testament Greek* (3rd ed.; Grand Rapids: Kregel, 1976 [orig. Edinburgh: T&T Clark, 1898]).
16. Ibid., 2.

advances in understanding the Greek of the New Testament through careful examination of papyrological evidence, as well as inscriptions and ostraca. The second was the production of two of the greatest Greek grammars to be written in the English language—those by Moulton and Robertson. Both of these legacies have powerfully shaped all subsequent study of Greek.

1.3.1 Adolf Deissmann (1895ff.)

In light of the remarkable papyri discoveries in Oxyrhynchus and other regions within Egypt, Adolf Deissmann's *Bibelstudien, Neue Bibelstudien,* and *Licht vom Osten* set the ground for a new era in Greek grammatical studies.[17] Deissmann condemned the idea of "biblical" Greek, which he demonstrated is no different from "profane" Greek; the language of the New Testament is simply that of popular Greek language of the time. He summarized the significance of the papyri, ostraca, and inscriptions for understanding New Testament Greek:

> New Testament philology is at present undergoing thorough reconstruction; and probably all the workers concerned, both on the continent and in English-speaking countries, are by this time agreed that the starting point for the philological investigations must be the language of the nonliterary papyri, ostraca, and inscriptions.[18]

1.3.2 Albert Thumb (1901)

A clear picture of Koine Greek was provided by Albert Thumb's *Die griechische Sprache im Zeitalter des Hellenismus*.[19] Like Deissmann, Thumb drew on contemporaneous Hellenistic literature to discuss and illustrate the character and historical evolution of Koine Greek. Thumb was able to distinguish between literary and colloquial forms of Koine and designated at least five dialects within it.

---

17. G. Adolf Deissmann, *Bibelstudien: Beiträge, zumeist aus den Papyri und Inschriften, zur Geschichte der Sprache, des Schrifttums und der Religion des hellenistischen Judentums und des Urchristentums* (Marburg: N. G. Elwert, 1895); *Neue Bibelstudien: Sprachgeschichtliche Beiträge, zumeist aus den Papyri und Inschriften, zur Erklärung des Neuen Testaments* (Marburg: N. G. Elwert, 1897); *Licht vom Osten. Das Neue Testament und die neuentdeckten Texte der hellenistisch-römischen Welt* (Tübingen: Mohr, 1908).
18. Adolf Deissmann, *Light from the Ancient East: The New Testament Illustrated by Recently Discovered Texts of the Graeco-Roman World* (trans. Lionel R. M. Strachan; New York: Hodder & Stoughton, 1910), 55.
19. Albert Thumb, *Die griechische Sprache im Zeitalter des Hellenismus: Beiträge zur Geschichte und Beurteilung Der ΕΙΕΙÇ* (Strassburg: Karl J. Trübner, 1901).

1.3.3 Jakob Wackernagel (1904)

Jakob Wackernagel coined the term *resultative perfect* (*Resultativ-perfektum*), which would go on to become a widely accepted category of usage for the Greek perfect indicative form. He argued that the so-called "present result" of the action expressed by the perfect was attributed to the *object*, rather than the *subject*, of the verb.[20] This understanding developed out of the increasing use of the perfect with transitive verbs through the Hellenistic period. In fact, Wackernagel's solution to the growing use of the perfect with transitive verbs reveals a crack in the traditional understanding of the perfect, in which it is necessary to split the perfect in two; "the aoristic action is carried out by the subject of the verb, while the present result is associated with the object."[21] This problem led to significant discussions about verbal aspect, beginning with McKay in 1965.

1.3.4 James Hope Moulton (1906)

One of the first great contributions to New Testament Greek grammar to be written in English was James Hope Moulton's *Prolegomena*, volume 1 of *A Grammar of New Testament Greek*.[22] Taking his cue from Deissmann, Moulton utilized insights from the papyri to enhance grammatical understanding of the language of the New Testament. The Greek of the New Testament is consonant with the vernacular Koine of the papyri.

1.3.5 A. T. Robertson (1914)

In 1914, A. T. Robertson produced the greatest of all New Testament Greek grammars, *A Grammar of the Greek New Testament in the Light of Historical Research*.[23] As with Deissmann and Moulton, Robertson drew on the evidence of papyri, but he also employed the comparative method where appropriate. The most distinct feature of Robertson's grammar is that even today, a century later, it seems remarkably modern. This can

20. Jakob Wackernagel, "Studien zum griechischen Perfectum," in *Programm zur akademischen Preisverteilung* (n.p. 1904), 3–24; repr. in *Kleine Schriften* (Göttingen: Vandenhoeck & Ruprecht, 1953), 1000–1021.
21. Constantine R. Campbell, *Verbal Aspect, the Indicative Mood, and Narrative: Soundings in the Greek of the New Testament* (SBG 13; New York: Peter Lang, 2007), 164.
22. James Hope Moulton, *A Grammar of New Testament Greek: Prolegomena* (vol. 1; Edinburgh: T&T Clark, 1906).
23. A. T. Robertson, *A Grammar of the Greek New Testament in the Light of Historical Research* (1st ed.; New York: Hodder & Stoughton, 1914).

only be explained by Robertson's carefully nuanced sense for the language, such that even prior to the dawn of modern linguistics, Robertson handles Greek in a way that is not (on the whole) overturned by modern linguistic principles and methodology. While the comparative method fell on hard times after Saussure (see §1.4.1), Robertson's employment of it has not greatly affected the enduring value of his contribution to Greek grammar.

1.4 Modern Linguistics

It is impossible to overstate the magnitude of change ushered in with the dawn of the new epoch known as modern linguistics. Linguistics shifted the study of language to such an extent that "much nineteenth-century work in the subject has become relatively remote from the concerns of the linguist in recent years."[24] The nineteenth century had been dominated by philology—more commonly referred to as historical linguistics today—and comparative philology in particular. That is, most scholarly interest had involved the history of language development and the relationships between languages. The new era moved toward synchronic linguistics, namely, "the analysis of languages as communicative systems as they exist at a given point of time (often the present), ignoring (as their speakers ignore) the route by which they arrived at their present form."[25]

The age of modern linguistics has forever changed the study of Greek. This section will trace some of the major movements within modern linguistics while also including some of the ongoing advances within Greek linguistics. This approach is preferred over trying to separate the history of modern linguistics and that of twentieth century Greek studies, since they have become inherently entwined—even if regrettably late.

1.4.1 Ferdinand de Saussure (1916)

The Swiss Mongin-Ferdinand de Saussure was trained as a historical linguist, and most of his career dealt with historical rather than synchronic linguistics, though the latter is responsible for his stature now as the father of modern linguistics.[26] His *Cours de linguistique générale* was published posthumously in 1916 (Saussure died in 1913) by his colleagues Charles

---

24. Geoffrey Sampson, *Schools of Linguistics: Competition and Evolution* (London: Hutchison, 1980), 13.
25. Sampson, *Schools of Linguistics*, 13.
26. Ibid., 35.

Bally and Albert Sechehaye, who constructed the book from Saussure's lecture notes and from notes taken by students.[27]

Fundamentally, Saussure stressed the importance of viewing language as a living phenomenon, of studying speech, of analyzing the underlying system of a language to demonstrate its structure, and of seeing language within its social milieu.[28] As David Crystal states, the tradition of the study of Saussure has been to focus on various theoretical dichotomies extracted from his work; these will be laid out next.[29]

The Saussurean dichotomy that most marks his work out from nineteenth-century emphases is that between *synchronic* and *diachronic* points of view. Synchronic linguistics examines language as it exists at a certain point in time.[30] Diachronic linguistics considers the evolution of language over time.[31]

A second dichotomy advanced by Saussure is that between *langue* and *parole*. *Langue* refers to the language system itself—its morphemes, grammar, structure, and so forth, as defined corporately and socially.[32] *Parole* refers to the performance of the language user—the way in which an individual speaks the language.[33] *Langue* is, in fact, an abstraction since it has no reality apart from the actual use of individuals, and yet *parole* is controlled by the social and communal expectations that are incorporated in the abstract *langue*.

A third dichotomy is that between the *signifié* and *signifiant*. The *signifié* refers to "the thing signified," while the *signifiant* refers to "the thing which signifies."[34] The relationship of the thing signified and the thing that signifies it is a linguistic *sign*.[35] Thus, there are three terms here: the signified, the signifier, and the sign. An item in the world is the thing signified, while a word may be the device used to refer to that thing. It is the *relationship* between these two things that Saussure calls a sign. For

27. Ibid., 36.
28. David Crystal, *Linguistics* (Middlesex: Penguin, 1971), 159.
29. Ibid., 159.
30. Ferdinand de Saussure, *Course in General Linguistics* (ed. Charles Bally and Albert Sechehaye; trans. Wade Baskin; New York: Fontana, 1974), 101–37.
31. Ibid., 140–89.
32. Ibid., 9–11.
33. Ibid., 14–15.
34. Ibid., 65–67.
35. Ibid., 67.

Saussure, the sign is the basic unit of communication, within the *langue* of the community; the *langue* is, in fact, is a system of signs.[36]

Through all these dichotomies (and others) runs the common notion that a language is a system of mutually defining entities. Saussure employs the illustration of a chess game at various points in *Cours de linguistique générale* to elucidate this point. First, the internal game of chess can be separated from its external facts. The game passed from Persia to Europe, but the history of chess makes little difference to the internal interrelationships of the pieces on the board.[37] Second, one move within a chess game "has a repercussion on the whole system," and yet one need not know the history of the game to be able to understand the state of play at any given moment, because "the route used in arriving there makes absolutely no difference."[38] Third, a chess piece only has meaning when it takes a position on the board, in relation to all other pieces. By itself, or off the board, the piece is meaningless.[39] Thus Saussure demonstrates that linguistic items, or signs, only have meaning in relation to other signs; by themselves they are meaningless. Additionally the history of the language makes little difference on the internal dynamics of language use as it currently stands; how the language got there does not affect how it works in real time.

Saussure marks the dawn of modern linguistics in at least two respects: first, by establishing a clear break with previous language methodologies, and second, by establishing the principles that are now foundational to all subsequent linguistic schools. His influence can be seen in all corners of linguistics through the twentieth century to the present day.

1.4.2 The Prague School (1920s)

The so-called "Prague School" was a circle of like-minded linguists who met for regular discussion, centered around the Czech Vilém Mathesius. The Prague School was characterized by a concern for synchronic linguistics, as was Saussure, and saw language in terms of function, in that "they analysed a given language with a view to showing the respective functions played by

---

36. Crystal, *Linguistics*, 164.
37. Saussure, *General Linguistics*, 22–23.
38. Ibid., 89.
39. Ibid., 110.

the various structural components in the use of the entire language."[40] This concern for function set the Prague School apart from their contemporaries in that they went beyond description to explanation, "saying not just *what* languages were like but *why* they were the way they were."[41]

Mathesius was concerned with the notions of *theme* and *rheme*. In relation to a conversation, theme refers to something the hearer already knows from the context, while the rheme is any new information contributed to the conversation. Generally, theme precedes rheme to create a context in the hearer's mind before anything new is established.[42]

The Prague School remains influential today, with several leading linguists of the twentieth century being shaped by their interests. For example, Roman Jakobson's phonological theory is recognizably consonant with the Prague School's approach to phonetics.[43] William Labov developed the school's interest in language use within different social settings into his sophisticated theory of sociolinguistics.[44]

1.4.3 Pierre Chantraine (1927)

Chantraine's monograph, *Histoire du parfait grec*, remains an authoritative contribution to the study of the diachronic development of the Greek perfect.[45] Together with Wackernagel (see §1.3.3), Chantraine represented the most sophisticated account of the so-called traditional view of the perfect and would become part of the impetus for McKay's work on aspect, which in turn led to the modern era of aspect studies. Chantraine had already defined the Greek perfect in terms of verbal aspect as a state, though it was understood to be a state resulting from a past action.[46]

1.4.4 The Decline of Greek Studies

For nearly half a century, beginning with the rise of modern linguistics, there was little activity in the world of Greek scholarship. In fact, it would be fair to say that Greek linguistics became comparatively stagnant. At

---

40. Sampson, *Schools of Linguistics*, 103.
41. Ibid., 104.
42. Ibid.
43. Ibid., 118.
44. Ibid., 127.
45. Pierre Chantraine, *Histoire du parfait grec* (Collection linguistique; Paris: Champion, 1927).
46. Ibid., 4–8.

the risk of evoking the fallacy *post hoc, ergo propter hoc*,[47] it seems that this inactivity in Greek studies was *due* to the rise of modern linguistics. As we have seen, Greek scholarship before Saussure was focused on comparative and historical philology. After Saussure, linguistics was preoccupied with synchronic linguistics rather than diachronic, thus making the direction of nineteenth-century Greek philology suddenly almost irrelevant.

Related to this fact is the noticeable lack of Greek scholarship produced by Germans after Wackernagel. While the nineteenth century had been unquestionably dominated by German scholarship—they being the masters of comparative philology—it seems that modern linguistics effectively ended their influence.[48] It would take some time to fill the vacuum left by German scholarship.[49]

1.4.5 J. R. Firth (1957)

J. R. Firth is credited with making linguistics a recognized academic discipline in Britain in a movement now known as the London School of linguistics.[50] Firth focused on phonology, semantics, and syntax—the latter being of most interest here.[51] On semantics, "meaning," or "function in context," "is to be interpreted as acceptability or appropriateness in that context: an utterance or part of an utterance is 'meaningful' if, and only if, it can be used appropriately in some actual context."[52]

The analysis of syntax in the London School is often called "systemic grammar," in which "system" refers to "a set of mutually exclusive options that come into play at some point in a linguistic structure."[53] The London

---

47. This fallacy assumes that because one thing follows another, the latter thing is caused by the prior thing.
48. Admittedly, social factors no doubt also had a negative effect on German scholarship from 1914 on.
49. While works in English eventually filled the space left by the nineteenth-century German scholars, there has also been an increase in French scholarship in recent times, with particular focus on the Greek verbal system. See, for example, André Sauge, *Les degrés du verbe: Sens et formation du parfait en grec ancient* (Bern: Peter Lang, 2000); Yves Duhoux, *Le verbe grec ancient: Éléments de morphologie et de syntaxe historiques* (2nd ed.; Bibliothèque des cahiers de l'Institut de linguistique de Louvain 114; Leuven: Peeters, 2000); Paula Lorente Fernández, *L'aspect verbal en grec ancien: le choix des themes verbaux chez Isocrate* (Bibliothèque des cahiers de l'Institut de linguistique de Louvain 111; Bern: Peeters, 2003).
50. Sampson, *Schools of Linguistics*, 214.
51. His most significant publication is *Papers in Linguistics 1934–1951* (Oxford: Oxford University Press, 1957).
52. John Lyons, "Firth's Theory of 'Meaning,'" in *In Memory of J. R. Firth* (ed. C. E. Bazell et al.; London: Longmans, 1966), 290.
53. Sampson, *Schools of Linguistics*, 277.

School is interested in the nature and significance of various choices that the language user makes in crafting a particular sentence or utterance. Significant British linguists to emerge from the London School following Firth are John Lyons and M. A. K. Halliday, the latter featuring below (see §1.4.8).

1.4.6 Noam Chomsky (1957ff.)

After Saussure, the most influential figure in twentieth-century linguistics is Avram Noam Chomsky.[54] Sometimes touted the Einstein of linguistics, Chomsky's central claim is that there are linguistic universals in syntax. In several of his publications, Chomsky argued that "the general principles which determine the form of grammatical rules in particular languages ... are to some considerable degree common to all human languages."[55] The existence of universal principles means that all language shares an underlying common structure. This means that all language iterations may be analyzed in terms of their *surface structure* and their *deep structure*.[56]

The surface structure is the way in which a language encodes its information with its own phonemes and morphemes. The deep structure consists of the underlying semantic principles shared by all languages (or, linguistic universals), which are expressed on the surface level by differing features, depending on the language. The problem with prior grammatical analyses, according to Chomsky, is that they only dealt with the surface level of language—what the Greek genitive case means, for example—rather than the deep structure, which would demonstrate how Greek is inherently the same as all other languages at their core. Thus, while the genitival relationship between two nouns in Greek is conveyed by a set of case endings, genitival relationships in other languages will be conveyed through different means, such as the word "of" in English. The Greek genitive case endings are simply the surface level encoding of the universal notion of "genitive."

The domain of linguistics associated with Chomsky is known as generative grammar (or transformational grammar) and posits that the universal principles seen in all languages point to a biological factor in language

---

54. Some important early works include *Syntactic Structures* (The Hague: Mouton, 1957); *Current Issues in Linguistic Theory* (The Hague: Mouton, 1964); and *Aspects of the Theory of Syntax* (Cambridge: M.I.T., 1965).
55. John Lyons, *Chomsky* (rev. ed.; Glasgow: Fontana, 1977), 11.
56. Chomsky, *Aspects*, 16.

generation: languages are structured by the way in which our brains are wired for linguistic competency.

> The problem for the linguist ... is to determine from the data of performance the underlying system of rules that has been mastered by the speaker–hearer and that he puts to use in actual performance. Hence, in the technical sense, linguistic theory is mentalistic, since it is concerned with discovering a mental reality underlying actual behavior.[57]

Especially dominant in North America, Chomskyan linguistics has redeemed the value of nineteenth-century comparative philology, since the comparison of different languages is not viewed as irrelevant. In fact, if all languages are related at the level of deep structure, then comparative approaches are actually useful. Chomsky sought to undo the separation between linguistics and classical language approaches that had begun with Saussure: "It is commonly held that modern linguistic and anthropological investigations have conclusively refuted the doctrines of classical universal grammar, but this claim seems to me very much exaggerated."[58]

1.4.7 James Barr (1961)

We see the worlds of linguistics and biblical studies collide in James Barr's famous *The Semantics of Biblical Language*, in which he strongly criticized the tendency of many biblical scholars to endorse linguistically flawed arguments.[59] Being influenced by Saussurean principles, Barr demonstrated the problems of establishing meaning through etymology (the etymological fallacy), the misunderstanding of verbs, and the construction of theology through word studies, such as is seen in Kittel's *Theological Dictionary*, among other things.[60]

While mainly focused on Hebrew, Barr's critique of the linguistic state of affairs within biblical scholarship applied equally well to Greek. The underlying problem was that the practitioners were all too ignorant of linguistics. The theories of language, methodology, and linguistic principles all growing out of Saussure's influence were simply not applied, leading to a number of

---

57. Ibid., 4.
58. Ibid., 118.
59. James Barr, *The Semantics of Biblical Language* (Eugene, OR: Wipf & Stock, 2004 [orig. Oxford: Oxford University Press, 1961]).
60. Ibid., 46–88, 107–60, 206–62.

erroneous conclusions in exegesis and theology based on the language of the Bible. The problems indicated by Barr have taken decades to rectify within biblical studies; unfortunately they have not yet been fully expunged.

1.4.8 M. A. K. Halliday (1961ff.)

The best-known student of the London School of linguistics is the "neo-Firthian," Michael Halliday. He is the founding figure of *Systemic Functional Linguistics* (*SFL*), taking his cues primarily from Firth and the Prague School. His seminal paper on this topic was published in 1961, but his most influential publications are *Cohesion in English* (with Ruqaiya Hasan) and *Halliday's Introduction to Functional Grammar*.[61] *SFL* is currently one of the dominant linguistic schools in Britain and Australia and is seen as a functional alternative to generative linguistics.[62]

SFL approaches language as a social semiotic system — as a tool for communication within the variety of contexts of human interaction. Any act of communication involves choices from within a series of options within the language system. In addition, languages do what they do through three *metafunctions*: ideational, interpersonal, and textual. These metafunctions, and *SFL* in general, are explored further in the next chapter.

1.4.9 Joseph H. Greenberg (1963ff.)

The American linguist Joseph H. Greenberg pioneered the study of linguistic typology, which is intended to identify generalizations across languages for the purpose of discovering universal structures underlying all human language. Greenberg's approach differs from Chomsky, however, in that it is functional rather than generative. He examined several languages from a wide geographic distribution, leading him to propose a set of "linguistic universals" based on his study of thirty languages.[63] Greenberg's work spawned a major interest in typology, with recent exponents such as

61. M. A. K. Halliday, "Categories of the Theory of Grammar," *Word* 17 (1961): 241–92; M. A. K. Halliday and Ruqaiya Hasan, *Cohesion in English* (London: Routledge, 1976); M. A. K. Halliday and Christian M. I. M. Matthiessen, *Halliday's Introduction to Functional Grammar* (4th rev. ed.; London: Routledge, 2014).

62. *SFL* is arguably *the* dominant school in Australian universities, largely due to Halliday's influence as Professor of Linguistics at the University of Sydney during the years 1976–1987. In Britain, the linguistics scene has diversified to a great extent since the 1990s, but *SFL* remains one of the popular schools.

63. Joseph H. Greenberg, ed., *Universals of Language: Report of a Conference Held at Dobbs Ferry, New York, April 13–51, 1961* (Cambridge, MA: MIT Press, 1963).

Matthew S. Dryer and Timothy Shopen.[64] Typology is also a significant influence on Stephen H. Levinsohn, whose work is discussed in chapter 8.

1.4.10 Kenneth L. McKay (1965ff.)

If Curtius was the father of Greek aspect studies, McKay was the father of *modern* aspect studies in Greek. His first essay was on the Greek perfect,[65] but his interest spanned across the entire verbal system over the next three decades, culminating in the volume that summarized his settled conclusions.[66] McKay rejected the notion of the resultative perfect, championed by Wackernagel and Chantraine, instead arguing that the Greek perfect is stative in aspect (which he called *perfect aspect*), without necessary reference to a past action.[67] While McKay began by asserting the priority of aspect over tense in the Greek verbal system, he concluded in the end that "the tenses of ancient Greek do not signal time except by implication from their relationship to their context."[68]

Both Porter and Fanning (§§1.5.1–2) were strongly indebted to McKay, and in this way, McKay became one of the most important figures leading to the creation of the so-called Modern Era of the study of New Testament Greek.

1.4.11 Kenneth L. Pike (1967ff.).

The American Kenneth L. Pike was one of the earliest members of the Summer Institute of Linguistics (SIL), an association of linguists devoted to Bible translation (see §7.2.1). In his volume, *Language in Relation to a Unified Theory of Structure of Human Behavior*, Pike developed *tagmemic linguistics.*[69] In tagmemics, the *tagmeme* is the smallest functional element in the grammatical structure of a language. Tagmemes are stringed together

---

64. Matthew S. Dryer and Martin Haspelmath, *The World Atlas of Language Structures Online*, http://wals.info; Timothy Shopen, *Language Typology and Syntactic Description* (3 vols.; 2nd ed.; Cambridge: Cambridge University Press, 2007).
65. K. L. McKay, "The Use of the Ancient Greek Perfect Down to the Second Century A.D.," *Bulletin of the Institute of Classical Studies* 12 (1965): 1–21.
66. K. L. McKay, *A New Syntax of the Verb in New Testament Greek: An Aspectual Approach* (SBG 5; New York: Peter Lang, 1994).
67. Ibid., 31.
68. Ibid., 39.
69. Kenneth L. Pike, *Language in Relation to a Unified Theory of Structure of Human Behavior* (2nd ed.; The Hague: Mouton, 1967). See also his *Linguistic Concepts: An Introduction to Tagmemics* (Nebraska: University of Nebraska Press, 1982).

to form constructions known as *syntagmemes*. Grammatical units are organized hierarchically into levels: morphemes, words, phrases, clauses, sentences, and so forth.[70] Tagmemics has been highly influential in the work of SIL and has been applied to the Greek New Testament by Robert E. Longacre.

1.4.12 Louw & Nida (1989)

Johannes Louw and Eugene Nida's major contribution to the study of the Greek of the New Testament was the production of their *Greek-English Lexicon of the New Testament Based on Semantic Domains* in 1989.[71] This lexicon differs from all previous Greek lexicons in that lexical entries are arranged by "semantic domain" rather than by alphabet. In delineating semantic domains, Louw and Nida drew on three classes of semantic features:

> The basis for the various semantic domains and subdomains consists of three major classes of semantic features: shared, distinctive, and supplementary. The shared features are those elements of the meaning of lexical items which are held in common by a set of lexical items. The distinctive features are those which separate meanings one from another, and the supplementary features are those which may be relevant in certain contexts or may play primarily a connotative or associative role.[72]

Another major distinguishing feature of their lexicon is that Louw and Nida offered *definitions* for each lexical entry rather than *glosses*. This was a significant advance from a linguistic standpoint, since "the definitions are based upon the distinctive features of meaning of a particular term, and the glosses only suggest ways in which such a term with a particular meaning may be represented in English."[73] The lexicon therefore focuses on the meaning of Greek words, rather than the English words with which they may be translated.

---

70. David Crystal, *A Dictionary of Linguistics and Phonetics* (6th ed.; Malden: Blackwell, 2008), 476.
71. Johannes P. Louw and Eugene A. Nida, *Greek-English Lexicon of the New Testament Based on Semantic Domains* (New York: United Bible Societies, 1989).
72. Ibid., vi. They offer the following example: "In Domain 19 *Physical Impact*, for example, κολαφίζω (19.7), ῥαβδίζω (19.8), and μαστίζω and μαστιγόω (19.9) all share the features of physical impact involving hitting or striking. They differ, however, in certain distinctive features in that κολαφίζω designates striking or beating with the fist, ῥαβδίζω designates beating or striking with a stick or rod, and μαστίζω and μαστιγόω designate beating with a whip. The terms μαστίζω and μαστιγόω also differ from κολαφίζω and ῥαβδίζω in that they normally refer to officially sanctioned punishment."
73. Ibid., vii.

The roots of Louw and Nida's work go back to the 1970s and 1980s as they developed their approach to lexical semantics.[74] Subsequent to the lexicon's publication, however, they offered the most detailed explanation of their methodological approach in the separate volume, *Lexical Semantics of the Greek New Testament*, published in 1992.[75]

1.5 The Modern Era (1989–)

This leads us to consider what I will refer to as the "Modern Era" of the study of the Greek of the New Testament. Beginning with Porter and Fanning, this Modern Era has ushered in a significant increase in activity, debate, and genuine advances in New Testament Greek scholarship. The renewed activity of the Modern Era did not, however, come from nowhere; its heritage can be traced at least as far back as McKay in 1965, with important voices such as Louw and Nida, James Voelz, Moisés Silva, and James Boyer contributing to the growing groundswell that finally led to this new period in the study of Greek.

1.5.1 Stanley E. Porter (1989)

The publication of Stanley Porter's *Verbal Aspect in the Greek of the New Testament* in 1989 is significant for at least three reasons.[76] First, along with the work of Buist Fanning published shortly after, it (re)launched verbal aspect as a subject of discussion (and debate) within Greek studies. Though there was a flowering of aspect studies in the period 1890–1910, the topic became more or less dormant in the interim with a few important exceptions, such as McKay. Porter and Fanning remain the founding fathers of modern aspect scholarship in Greek.

Second, as a consequence of relaunching the study of Greek verbal aspect, Porter (and Fanning) also relaunched Greek scholarship in general. After great activity in the nineteenth century and early twentieth, Greek

---

74. See, e.g., Johannes P. Louw, "A Semantic Domain Approach to Lexicography," in *Lexicography and Translation: With Special Reference to Bible Translation* (ed. J. P. Louw; Cape Town: Bible Society of South Africa, 1985), 157–97.

75. Eugene A. Nida and Johannes P. Louw, *Lexical Semantics of the Greek New Testament: A Supplement to the Greek-English Lexicon of the New Testament Based on Semantic Domains* (Atlanta: Scholars, 1992).

76. Stanley E. Porter, *Verbal Aspect in the Greek of the New Testament with Reference to Tense and Mood* (SBG 1; New York: Peter Lang, 1989).

scholarship as a whole became relatively quiet after the rise of modern linguistics. It had begun to gain some momentum again in the second half of the twentieth century, but was given a significant injection of energy from 1989 on.

In addition to aspect, Porter has addressed a variety of other topics in Greek linguistics, including discourse analysis, diglossia, and prominence. And Porter has effectively established his own "school" for Greek studies, having produced several doctoral graduates from McMaster Divinity College in Canada.

Third, Porter's work was marked by a serious engagement with linguistic method, notably Halliday's systemic functional linguistics. While the principles and methodology of modern linguistics already had a presence in the study of Greek, this was on the whole focused in the area of lexical semantics, such as in the work of Louw and Nida, Moisés Silva, and others. Since Porter, one of the most important elements of the modern period of Greek studies is its engagement with linguistics in all areas of investigation, not just lexical semantics and verbal aspect.

1.5.2 Buist M. Fanning (1990)

Fanning's major publication on Greek verbal aspect followed soon after Porter's, both the fruit of British doctoral theses written independently.[77] Fanning's work equally contributed to the relaunching of the study of Greek verbal aspect and, indeed, the relaunching of Greek studies in general. Though the disagreements between Fanning and Porter are perhaps better known, the reality is that there is a remarkable level of agreement between their two approaches to Greek verbal aspect. Areas of agreement include their understanding of what aspect *is* (which, in general, is not a foregone conclusion), the endorsement of the distinction between semantics and pragmatics, and the allocation of the same aspectual values for a good number of Greek tense-forms.[78]

In fact, the disagreement and agreement between Fanning and Porter has served Greek scholarship well. The disagreements created an aspect debate that helped to make Greek once again an area of controversy and,

---

77. Buist M. Fanning, *Verbal Aspect in New Testament Greek* (Oxford Theological Monographs; Oxford: Clarendon, 1990).

78. Further discussion of their views is offered in chapter 5.

therefore, an area of interest to the wider New Testament world. The agreements meant that there was established a relatively stable foundation for future aspectual research. From this point on, Greek aspect scholars would necessarily position their own views in relation to Fanning and Porter.

1.5.3 Further Developments

Moving out from Porter and Fanning on verbal aspect, the Modern Era has witnessed several more studies on Greek aspect, from Olsen, Decker, Evans, Campbell, Mathewson, Cirafesi, Huffman, and, most recently, Crellin.[79] Beyond verbal aspect, there have been significant contributions on the following topics, to name a few: discourse analysis from the likes of Levinsohn and Runge;[80] lexicography from Danker and Lee;[81] voice from Allan and Taylor;[82] corpus linguistics from Brook O'Donnell;[83] the imperative mood from Fantin and Huffman;[84] the article from Wallace and Peters;[85] prepositions from Bortone and Harris;[86] and Greek diachronics from Caragounis.[87]

As will be clear from the bibliography and footnotes throughout the book, two important academic monograph series are home to much of the cutting-edge research on the Greek of the New Testament. *Studies in Biblical Greek* is published by Peter Lang and edited by D. A. Carson; *Linguistic Biblical Studies* is published by Brill and is edited by Stanley E. Porter. While these two series do not exhaust the recent monograph-length literature on the subject, a large portion of it is found here. No doubt they will be the home of several forthcoming publications.

---

79. See chapter 5 for more on these authors.
80. See chapter 8 for more.
81. See chapter 3.
82. See chapter 4.
83. Matthew Brook O'Donnell, *Corpus Linguistics and the Greek of the New Testament* (New Testament Monographs 6; Sheffield: Sheffield Phoenix, 2005).
84. Joseph D. Fantin, *The Greek Imperative Mood in the New Testament: A Cognitive Approach* (SBG 12; New York: Peter Lang, 2010); Douglas S. Huffman, *Verbal Aspect Theory and the Prohibitions in the Greek New Testament* (SBG 16; New York: Peter Lang, 2014).
85. Daniel B. Wallace, *Granville Sharp's Canon and Its Kin: Semantics and Significance* (SBG 14; New York, Peter Lang, 2009); Ronald D. Peters, *The Greek Article: A Functional Grammar of ὁ-items in the Greek New Testament with Special Emphasis on the Greek Article* (LBS 9; Leiden: Brill, 2014).
86. Pietro Bortone, *Greek Prepositions from Antiquity to the Present* (Oxford: Oxford University Press, 2010); Murray J. Harris, *Prepositions and Theology in the Greek New Testament: An Essential Reference Resource for Exegesis* (Grand Rapids: Zondervan, 2012).
87. Chrys C. Caragounis, *The Development of Greek and the New Testament: Morphology, Syntax, Phonology, and Textual Transmission* (Grand Rapids: Baker, 2006 [Mohr Siebeck, 2004]).

As for essay-length publications, a new journal devoted to Greek has appeared, called *Biblical and Ancient Greek Linguistics* (*BAGL*). Edited by Stanley E. Porter and Matthew Brook O'Donnell, it is in its early development with two volumes having been published as of 2014. Another journal that is so dedicated is *Filologia Neotestamentaria*, which currently spans thirty-two volumes, but has not issued a publication since 2010.

Most of the content of this book is concerned with the advances that have taken place, and are currently taking place, within this so-called Modern Era. While many of these developments have their roots in earlier scholarship, the Modern Era has seen various issues come under vigorous treatment, discussion, and in some cases, resolution.

1.5.4 Encyclopedia of Ancient Greek Language and Linguistics (2014)

A major new resource of relevance to all students of Ancient Greek is Brill's *Encyclopedia of Ancient Greek Language and Linguistics* (*EAGLL*), edited by a team led by Georgios K. Giannakis.[88] The *EAGLL* is a powerful research tool for scholars and students of Greek, of linguistics, as well as of biblical literature. Available in online and print editions, and with over five hundred entries, the *EAGLL* aims to become *the* recognized reference work on the subject. It treats various aspects of the history and study of Ancient Greek, offering descriptions of the language from Proto-Greek to Koine. The *EAGLL* addresses the linguistic subjects of history, structure, biographical references, schools of thought, technical metalanguage, sociolinguistic issues, dialects, didactics, translation practices, generic issues, Greek in relation to other languages, and on all levels of analysis including phonetics, phonology, morphology, syntax, lexicon, semantics, and stylistics.

The encyclopedia is not focused on the language of the New Testament, but it nevertheless takes Biblical Greek into frequent consideration and engages with some of the scholarship that has focused on it. While the exponents of New Testament Greek linguistics might prefer to see their contributions feature more prominently, the New Testament (and LXX) is but a small corpus within the whole sweep of Ancient Greek. From

---

88. Georgios K. Giannakis et al., eds., *Encyclopedia of Ancient Greek Language and Linguistics* (Brill Online, 2014)

that perspective, there is probably disproportionate attention given to our guild. For example, there are two articles authored by Porter ("New Testament" and "Septuagint") and several others that discuss New Testament Greek scholarship. Some of the articles that feature the discussions of New Testament Greek linguistics include "Tense and Aspect from Hellenistic to Early Byzantine" (by Klaas Bentein), "Discourse Analysis and Greek" (by Helene Perdicoyianni-Paleologou), "Compound Tenses (Hellenistic Greek)" (by Vit Bubenik), "Lexical Aspect (Aktionsart)" (by Coulter George), "Text Linguistics and Greek" (by Gerry Wakker), and "Null Anaphora" (by Eirik Welo).

The encyclopedia is also evidence that the movement of modern linguistics has penetrated classical Ancient Greek studies. The likes of Saussure, Jakobson, Chomsky, Lyons, and Halliday feature throughout. The topics addressed reveal that many authors have engaged the Greek language with the tools and methodologies of modern linguistics.

1.6 Conclusion

A history of New Testament Greek scholarship over the past two centuries has its own independent importance, but this chapter serves to set the stage for what is to follow. It provides context for the discussions of the next nine chapters by introducing the general trajectory of Greek scholarship, as well as some of the key figures who feature in those discussions. It has not been my intention to cover everyone and everything in this chapter, but rather to provide some necessary "scaffolding." The figures included are those who have shaped the ongoing trajectory of scholarship in significant ways.

It is also important to recognize the ways in which modern linguistics has influenced the study of the Greek of the New Testament. The depth of its impact will become more evident in subsequent chapters, and for that reason the next chapter will focus entirely on linguistic theories. Also, while general Ancient Greek scholarship and New Testament Greek scholarship have trammelled fairly separate paths for some time — though having begun together — their paths are intersecting once more, as reflected in the *EAGLL*. Both have been redefined by their engagement with linguistics.

1.7 Further Reading

Barr, James. *The Semantics of Biblical Language*. Eugene, OR: Wipf & Stock, 2004 [Oxford: Oxford University Press, 1961].

Chomsky, Noam. *Aspects of the Theory of Syntax*. Cambridge: M.I.T., 1965.

Deissmann, Adolf. *Light from the Ancient East: The New Testament Illustrated by Recently Discovered Texts of the Graeco-Roman World*. Translated by Lionel R. M. Strachan. New York: Hodder & Stoughton, 1910.

Fanning, Buist M. *Verbal Aspect in New Testament Greek*. Oxford Theological Monographs. Oxford: Clarendon, 1990.

Giannakis, Georgios K., et al., eds. *Encyclopedia of Ancient Greek Language and Linguistics*. Brill Online, 2014.

Halliday, M. A. K., and Christian M. I. M. Matthiessen. *Halliday's Introduction to Functional Grammar*. Fourth revised edition. London: Routledge, 2014.

Porter, Stanley E. *Verbal Aspect in the Greek of the New Testament with Reference to Tense and Mood*. SBG 1. New York: Peter Lang, 1989.

Robertson, A. T. *A Grammar of the Greek New Testament in the Light of Historical Research*. Fourth edition. Nashville: Broadman, 1934.

Saussure, Ferdinand. *Course in General Linguistics*. Edited by Charles Bally and Albert Sechehaye. Translated by Wade Baskin. New York: Fontana, 1974.

CHAPTER 2

LINGUISTIC THEORIES

A grammar is an attempt to crack the code.

—*M. A. K. Halliday*

2.1 Introduction

This chapter explores the need for linguistic theory within New Testament Greek studies. It goes on to explore the broad shape of modern linguistics, sketching out key differences between generative and functional linguistics, with a focus on *Systemic Functional Linguistics*, which has become significant within Greek studies. The chapter explains some of the linguistic terminology that frequently blocks the access of nonexperts to recent discussions.

To begin, it is worth rehearsing the essential distinction between the study of *language* and the study of *linguistics*. When the student begins her journey with Greek—learning vocabulary, paradigms, and Greek grammar—she has embarked on the long road of *language* learning. Language study is simply the study of the "content" of a particular language. Linguistics, on the other hand, is not necessarily about the study of any particular language, but is the study of the *phenomenon* of language. It pays attention to methodological issues related to the study of language, the principles of how languages work, and how to articulate various language phenomena. In other words, a linguist is interested in language per se, but not necessarily any individual language, though linguistics does include the study of individual languages too, but from an analytical point of view. As David

Alan Black points out, a linguist may, in fact, know only his own language; being fluent in French, German, or Greek is not the point. Black uses the illustration of a musicologist:

> A musicologist could analyze a piano concerto by pointing out its themes, movements, meter, and tempo. But he need not be able to play the concerto himself. He leaves that to the concert pianist.[1]

Just as the musicologist is interested in the *theory* of music while the musician *performs* the music, so the linguist is interested in the theory of language, while the language student learns to understand and use a particular language.

2.2 Linguistics and New Testament Greek

The long tradition of studying the Greek of the New Testament has been strong on the language-learning side of things, but relatively weak on the linguistic front. Greek students are better equipped to recite paradigms than to articulate what a *paradigmatic opposition* is. This situation must be redressed for the simple reason that the principles of linguistics have direct bearing on exegesis and translation. Students and teachers of the Greek New Testament ignore linguistics at their own peril.

Several factors complicate the relationship between linguistics and the study of New Testament Greek. First, linguistics is a massive, evolving field of study in its own right. It is difficult enough for a professional linguist, let alone the Greek scholar or student, to keep abreast of all its developments. Second, several linguistic schools exist, each with its own literature, complex terminology, and differing sets of principles and methodologies. This means that the Greek scholar or student is faced with a bewildering set of alternatives for consideration, even before engagement with a particular linguistic school is attempted.

David Alan Black lists some other common objections that students of the Greek New Testament raise about linguistics:

> The terms used in linguistics are too difficult for me to understand.
> I could never hope to master all of the topics covered in linguistics.

---

1. David Alan Black, *Linguistics for Students of New Testament Greek: A Survey of Basic Concepts and Applications* (2nd ed.; Grand Rapids: Baker, 1995), 4.

Linguists themselves seem uncertain about their conclusions, and the entire discipline is in a state of flux. Why, then, should I enter this jungle?[2]

Clearly, there are many possible objections that people may entertain in order to ignore linguistics—but at what cost?

2.2.1 The Need for Linguistic Theory

In Moisés Silva's *God, Language, and Scripture*, he offers a humorous example of some of the problems of biblical interpretation that are caused by a misconception of how language normally works.[3] Silva imagines that in the year 2790, the most powerful nation in the world speaks Swahili, and English-speaking countries have ceased to exist, as has most of their literature written before 2012. Archaeologists discover a short text written in English and seek to interpret it:

> Marilyn, tired of her glamorous image, embarked on a new project. She would now cultivate her mind, sharpen her verbal skills, pay attention to standards of etiquette. Most important of all, she would devote herself to charitable causes. Accordingly, she offered her services at the local hospital, which needed volunteers to cheer up terminal patients, many of whom had been in considerable pain for a long time. The weeks flew by. One day she was sitting at the cafeteria when her supervisor approached her and said: "I didn't see you yesterday. What were you doing?" "I painted my apartment; it was my day off," she responded.

The discovery is rushed to one of the finest philologists in their country, who publishes the following commentary on it.

> We are unable to determine whether this text is an excerpt from a novel or from a historical biography. Almost surely, however, it was produced in a religious context, as is evident from the use of such words as *devoted, offered, charitable*. In any case, this passage illustrates the literary power of twentieth-century English, a language full of wonderful metaphors. The verb *embarked* calls to mind an ocean liner leaving for an adventuresome cruise, while *cultivate* possibly alerts the reader to Marilyn's botanical interests. In those days North Americans compared time to a bird—probably the eagle—that flies.
>
> The author of this piece, moreover, makes clever use of word associations. For example, the term *glamorous* is etymologically related to

---

2. Black, *Linguistics for Students*, 1–2.
3. Moisés Silva, *God, Language, and Scripture: Reading the Bible in the Light of General Linguistics* (Grand Rapids: Zondervan, 1990), 11–13.

grammar, a concept no doubt reflected in the comment about Marilyn's "verbal skills." Consider also the subtleties implied by the statement that "her supervisor approached her." The verb *approach* has a rich usage. It may indicate a similar appearance or condition (*this painting approaches the quality of a Picasso*); it may have a sexual innuendo (*the rapist approached his victim*); it may reflect subservience (*he approached his boss for a raise*). The cognate noun can be used in contexts of engineering (e.g., access to a bridge), sports (of a gold stroke following the drive from the tee), and even war (a trench that protects troops besieging a fortress).

Society in the twentieth century is greatly illumined by this text. The word *patient* (from *patience*, meaning "endurance") indicates that sick people then underwent a great deal of suffering: they *endured* not only the affliction of their physical illness, but also the mediocre skills of their medical doctors, and even (to judge from other contemporary documents) the burden of increasing financial costs.

A few syntactical notes may be of interest to language students. The preposition *of* had different uses: causal (*tired of*), superlative (*most important of all*), and partitive (*many of whom*). The simple past tense had several aoristic functions: *embarked* clearly implies determination, while *offered* suggests Marilyn's once-for-all, definitive intention. Quite noticeable is the tense variation at the end of the text. The supervisor in his question uses the imperfect tense, "were doing," perhaps suggesting monotony, slowness, or even laziness. Offended, Marilyn retorts with a punctiliar and emphatic aorist, "I painted."

Sound familiar?

Silva makes the point well. Sadly, such misunderstanding of language and its resultant misleading exegesis can be found in many commentaries and sermons that make language-based observations from the Greek text.

Moreover, much of the literature concerning New Testament Greek is linguistically uninformed, such that it is not possible to discern the methodological principles at work (if any). Without a considered methodological approach, even the best grammatical studies are potentially flawed. Additionally, many grammatical works that *are* linguistically informed do not explicitly reveal their methodological commitments and presuppositions. And so, as Dennis Stamps comments, "New Testament interpreters face a pluralism in grammatical theory."[4] The diversity of methodologies and presuppositions within linguistics adds to the complexity of grammatical studies.

---

4. Dennis L. Stamps, "Interpreting the Language of St Paul: Grammar, Modern Linguistics and Translation Theory," in *Discourse Analysis and Other Topics in Biblical Greek* (ed. Stanley E. Porter and D. A. Carson; JSNTSup 113; Sheffield: Sheffield Academic, 1995), 131.

Before it can be suggested, however, that Greek grammar therefore would be better off without adding the complications of linguistics, this solution should be seen as naïve, not to mention impossible. The fact is that Greek grammarians are subject to linguistic theory, whether or not they are aware of it and whether or not they are explicit about it. Even "no theory" is, in fact, a theoretical position. The only question is whether it is a good one. There is no way to avoid the concerns of linguistics when studying grammar (of any language). Thus, Stamps warns, "The biblical critic needs to understand the options before using a 'look-up and footnote' approach to grammars when interpreting a text."[5] We cannot consult Greek grammars without consideration of their linguistic presuppositions and methodologies. And so we turn to the practice and theories of linguistics.

2.3 Branches of Linguistics

Before exploring some of the distinctions within linguistic theory, it is worth noting some of the different tasks that define linguistics. The practice of linguistics is broad, with different fields being interested in different goals. Often these practices are complementary rather than competitive, but it helps to distinguish between them for the sake of functional clarity.

According to John Lyons, the broadest distinction within linguistics is that between *general* and *descriptive* linguistics. General linguistics is interested in the study of language itself, asking the question, "What is language?" Its inquiries, however, remain general rather than specific to any particular language. Descriptive linguistics, by contrast, is the study of particular languages.[6] Descriptive linguistics differs from *language study* (mentioned above) in that it is an analytical study of the mechanics of a particular language—its structure and the ways in which it performs various functions—whereas language study is concerned with gaining proficiency in a language (to speak, read, and write it). The descriptive linguist may study a language without necessarily being able to speak it.

---

5. Ibid., 133.
6. John Lyons, *Language and Linguistics: An Introduction* (Cambridge: Cambridge University Press, 1981), 34.

Lyons points out that general and descriptive linguistics depend on each other:

> ... general linguistics supplies the concept and categories in terms of which particular languages are to be analysed; descriptive linguistics, in its turn, provides the data which confirm or refute the propositions and theories put forward in general linguistics.[7]

Of course, descriptive linguists are not necessarily interested in providing data for general linguistics, but wish to analyse a particular language for the sake of advancing understanding of that language.[8] The study of the Greek of the New Testament is obviously an exercise in descriptive linguistics for the sake of improving our understanding of it, and therefore of the texts in which Greek is used.

Another broad distinction within linguistics is that between diachronic and synchronic study of language. Historical linguistics is characterized by a diachronic approach, which traces the historical development of language. It can be interested in language in general (i.e., general linguistics), or in a particular language (descriptive linguistics).[9] In addition to its comparative methodology, much nineteenth-century Greek scholarship was diachronic in nature, being interested in the changes in the Greek language from Proto-Indo-European through to the Koine period and beyond. A synchronic description of a language, however, is nonhistorical; "it presents an account of the language as it is at some particular point in time."[10] Most studies of New Testament Greek today are synchronic in nature, though classical Greek scholarship (or, more accurately, Ancient Greek scholarship) often employs diachronic approaches.

A third distinction that Lyons discusses is that between theoretical and applied linguistics. Theoretical linguistics is interested in constructing a theory of the structure and functions of language (or languages), but without any attention given to their practical applications. Applied linguistics, however, is concerned with the application of linguistic theory to a variety of practical tasks, including language teaching.[11]

---

7. Ibid., 34.
8. Ibid., 35.
9. Ibid.
10. Ibid.
11. Ibid.

Finally, Lyons draws a distinction between microlinguistics and macrolinguistics. This distinction has to do with the scope of the subject. On the one hand, microlinguistics adopts a narrower view of the task of linguistics, while macrolinguistics takes a broader view.[12] The narrower view sees the concerns of linguistics to be limited to the structure of language(s):

> without regard to the way in which languages are acquired, stored in the brain or used in their various functions; without regard to the interdependence of psychological mechanisms that are involved in language-behaviour; in short, without regard to anything other than the language system, considered in itself and for itself.[13]

Macrolinguistics, on the other hand, "is concerned with everything that pertains in any way at all to language and languages."[14] Macrolinguistics therefore gives rise to several interdisciplinary branches of inquiry, such as sociolinguistics, psycholinguistics, ethnolinguistics, stylistics, and so forth.[15]

In practice, there are various combinations of these sets of distinctions at work within the world of linguistics. Lyons points out, however, that the dominant combination in modern linguistics is theoretical, synchronic, microlinguistics.[16] This is certainly the dominant approach to the study of New Testament Greek today. It is theoretical rather than applied, though there are some applications of interest, such as Bible translation and teaching Greek (see chapter 10). It is synchronic, being interested in the Greek of the Koine period, though there is also a continuing interest in diachronics within Ancient Greek scholarship generally. And it is generally microlinguistic in the sense that the language is the focal point, not its role in sociolinguistics or psycholinguistics. However, most Greek scholars are interested in the intersection of Greek language with exegesis—indeed, that is often the impetus for the study of Greek in the first place—and in that sense, Greek scholarship can be quite "multidisciplinary."

Having traced the major distinctions within the practice of linguistics, we turn now to the major distinctions within linguistic theory. These distinctions are summarized in 2.4.

---

12. Ibid., 36.
13. Ibid.
14. Ibid.
15. Ibid.
16. Ibid., 37.

Branches of Linguistics	
General Linguistics Language in general	**Descriptive Linguistics** Specific language(s)
Diachronic Linguistics Language development through history	**Synchronic Linguistics** Language at a specific point in history
Theoretical Linguistics Pure linguistic theory	**Applied Linguistics** Linguistics applied to various functions
Microlinguistics Monodisciplinary	**Macrolinguistics** Multidisciplinary

2.4 Linguistic Theories

There is no single linguistic theory that binds the field of linguistics together, though many linguists working today would recognize a range of basic linguistic principles on which all agree—mostly derived from Saussure. Nevertheless, it is most accurate to say that linguistics consists of a collection of theories. As such, it is important to have a basic grasp on the shape of the terrain in order to understand where various linguistic approaches "fit," and what methodological principles govern the major linguistic schools. On the broadest scale, there are two major divisions within linguistic schools, known as generative linguistics and functional linguistics.

2.4.1 Generative Linguistics

The term *generative* was derived from mathematics and introduced to linguistics by Chomsky in his book *Syntactic Structures*.[17] The narrow use of the term *generative linguistics*, or *generative grammar*, refers to a language's ability to generate sets of grammatical sentences. As Lyons summarizes, "A generative grammar is a mathematically precise specification of the grammatical structure of the sentences that it generates."[18] The broader use of the term refers to a whole field of linguistics that shares certain theoretical and methodological assumptions originating with Chomsky (see §1.4.6). We are primarily interested in the broader use of the term.

Generative linguistics is characterized by the core assumption that all

---

17. Chomsky, *Syntactic Structures*; David Crystal, *A Dictionary of Linguistics and Phonetics* (6th ed.; Malden: Blackwell, 2008), 208.
18. Lyons, *Language and Linguistics*, 126.

languages are ultimately shaped by a universal grammar, or universals of linguistic structure. Chomsky, and the generativist school that formed around him, views individual languages as expressions of these linguistic universals. On the surface level, each language is different, with its own characteristics, but the generative linguist seeks to understand how this surface-level language encodes the "deep-structure" that is common to all.

Ultimately, the commitment to the existence of such a deep-structure, or linguistic universals grammar, leads generative linguists to an interest in the human mind. Again following Chomsky, these linguistic universals are what they are because of the way the brain is wired for language production and comprehension. If linguistic universals provide the common deep-structure for all surface-level languages, their universality strongly suggests a universal origin: the human brain. The brain is the source of all language. This is not simply about the brain acquiring and retaining the "content" of particular languages. It is directly related to the shape of linguistic universals. Linguistic universals are a product of biology and neurology: the structure of the human brain determines the structure of all language. So Sampson summarizes:

> Chomsky argues that the explanation for the fact that all languages of the world are cut to a common pattern (assuming that they are) is that the inherited structure of Man's mind forces him to use languages of that particular type.[19]

Chomsky holds a rationalist view of the human mind, believing it to be of fixed structure with preexisting potentialities.[20] He even suggests that "if one tried to teach a child a language not conforming to that plan ... then no matter how 'simple' the language might otherwise be, the child would be innately incapable of mastering it."[21]

Generative linguistics has been enormously influential throughout the world of linguistics, but particularly in North America, and also within the fields of philosophy and psychology.[22] But Chomsky and his followers have also seen criticisms of some of the very core principles of generative linguistics. Geoffrey Sampson, for example, states:

---

19. Sampson, *Schools of Linguistics*, 147.
20. Ibid.
21. Ibid., 148.
22. See Noam Chomsky, *Language and Mind* (Cambridge: Cambridge University Press, 1968); idem, *New Horizons in the Study of Language and Mind* (Cambridge: Cambridge University Press, 2000).

the existence of linguistic universals is, for Chomsky and his followers, not so much a finding which has emerged from their research despite their expectations, but rather a guiding assumption which determines the nature of hypotheses they propose in order to account for data.[23]

If the core principle of generative theory is the existence of linguistic universals, it can be viewed as a precarious endeavor based on an unproven assumption.[24] Though Sampson is perhaps too harsh in his assessment, we can therefore understand his claim that "the ascendency of the Chomskyan school has been a very unfortunate development for the discipline of linguistics."[25]

2.4.2 Functional Linguistics

Functional linguistics is concerned to account for how language is *used*, and how the use of language informs us as to its structures. "It is characterized by the belief that the phonological, grammatical and semantic structure of languages is determined by the functions that they have to perform in the societies in which they operate."[26] Two of the best-known functional linguistic schools are the Prague School (see §1.4.2) and the school of *Systemic Functional Linguistics* (see §1.4.8).

Unlike generative linguists, most functional linguists are not interested in elucidating a universal grammar or linguistic universals, but they seek to treat each language on its own terms. This is not to deny, however, the existence of common features and similarities across languages. In fact, functional typology (see §1.4.9) is interested in the different mechanisms that languages use to perform functions that are universal to languages.[27] While the creation of rhythm is a universal function of all musical genres, *how* rhythm is created may differ from one genre to the next. Nevertheless, functional linguists are primarily focused on how individual languages function to convey meaning.

---

23. Sampson, *Schools of Linguistics*, 148.
24. "The Chomskyans are always eager to suggest an explanation in 'universalist' terms for data which might well have some 'non-universalist' explanation if one were willing to look for it. When such explanations are false they can, of course, be refuted by counter-evidence from other languages, but to find and publish such counter-evidence takes time. For this reason ... at any given time the Chomskyan school tends to believe in a much richer system of universalist hypotheses than are really warranted" (ibid., 148–49).
25. Ibid., 163.
26. Lyons, *Language and Linguistics*, 224.
27. See Alice Caffarel, J. R. Martin, and Christian M. I. M. Matthiessen, eds., *Language Typology: A Functional Perspective* (Amsterdam: Benjamins, 2004).

Functional linguists also share the conviction "that the structure of utterances is determined by the use to which they are put and the communicative context in which they occur."[28] In these ways, functionalism is firmly opposed to generativism, since the latter seeks to analyze languages as systems of formal rules rather than according to their varied functions.[29]

Consequently, functional linguistics emphasizes the social element of language. Language is a "social-semiotic" tool—it is a tool of social interaction, which is the obvious (but sometimes overlooked) wider context through which to understand what language is all about. That is probably why we regard someone talking to himself as humorous—if not inherently strange. Language is therefore best studied as the tool that it is, within the contexts of social interaction.

Such a focus on functionality may help to account for the similarities that *do* pertain across various languages. The parallel operations that language is expected to perform across all cultures and their various social situations means that we ought not be surprised to discover some parallels in the structure of certain languages. As Lyons says,

> in all societies, we may assume, there are occasions when it is necessary to make descriptive statements, to ask questions and to issue commands; it is not surprising therefore that most languages, if not all, should distinguish grammatically between declarative, interrogative and imperative sentences.[30]

This means that apparent similarities between languages need not be attributed to a set of linguistic universals that are hardwired in the human mind, as generative linguistics assumes, but can be accounted for through the common needs of social interaction across human cultures and languages.

By the same token, Lyons points out, the social needs of differing cultures help to explain the differences between languages. "In so far as the more specific semiotic needs of one society differ from those of another,

---

28. Ibid., 227.
29. Having said that, Lindsay J. Whaley has sought some middle ground through discussion of the differences between the generative and typological-functional approaches and concludes: "In all likelihood, the unity of language, and consequent language universals, arises from a slate of interacting factors, some innate, others functional" (*Introduction to Typology: The Unity and Diversity of Language* [Thousand Oaks, CA: SAGE, 1997], 5–6).
30. John Lyons, *Semantics: Volume I* (Cambridge: Cambridge University Press, 1977), 249.

languages will tend to differ one from another in their grammatical and lexical structure."[31] Function, then, is a useful way in which to understand both the similarities and differences across various languages.

2.5 Systemic Functional Linguistics

While there are many useful insights derived from formal linguistics, it is argued below (see §2.6) that a functional approach is ultimately most suited to the study of Biblical Greek. There are several functional linguistic schools, including the Prague School, Simon Dik's Functional Grammar, Foley and Van Valin's Role and Reference Grammar, and Danish Functional Grammar, but it is not possible to survey them all here.[32] Instead, we will explore just one of the prominent schools within the field of functional linguistics — *Systemic Functional Linguistics*. This is offered by way of example to demonstrate the inner workings of a functional approach to linguistics, but also because systemic linguistics has had considerable impact on the study of Ancient Greek in recent years.

Particularly prominent in England and Australia, *Systemic Functional Linguistics* was developed by M. A. K. Halliday, influenced by the work of J. R. Firth.

2.5.1 Functional

The functional nature of language is emphasized within Systemic Functional Linguistics, and, as with other functional schools, it is the key to unlocking what language is and how it works. Halliday and Matthiessen expand:

> We use language to make sense of our experience, and to carry out our interactions with other people. This means that the grammar has to interface with what goes on outside language: with the happenings and conditions of the world, and with the social processes we engage in. But at the same time it has to organize the construal of experience, and the enactment of social processes, so that they can be transformed into wording.[33]

---

31. Ibid. It follows, then, that the more divergent the social operations of two cultures are from each other, the more differences we may detect in the structures of their respective languages.
32. For a guide and comparison of three major functional schools — Functional Grammar, Role and Reference Grammar, and Systemic Functional Grammar — see Christopher S. Butler, *Structure and Function: A Guide to Three Major Structural-Functional Theories* (2 vols.; Amsterdam: Benjamins, 2003).
33. Halliday and Matthiessen, *Functional Grammar*, 24.

It is the functionality of language that causes Halliday and Matthiessen to reflect on the nature of the human brain. While they share this interest with Chomsky, their approach and conclusion is the exact opposite. While Chomsky argued that linguistic universals are derived from the hardwired structure of the human brain, Halliday and Matthiessen see it the other way around. They say that the development of language had immense significance in the evolution of the human species: "it is not an exaggeration to say that it turned *homo*...into *homo sapiens*." The power of language "created the modern human brain."[34] By construing our experiences in the world, language creates categories and structures within the mind that are not predetermined but come into being through this construal of experience.

2.5.2 Systemic

The term *systemic* points to the understanding of language as a system of choices; "Systemic theory gets its name from the fact that the grammar of a language is represented in the form of system networks."[35] Meaning is created through meaningful choices within a system of options. When a language user chooses a certain word, she is also "unchoosing" other options that might have been chosen. It's like picking your teammates in gym class—each choice says as much about those *not* chosen as those who *are*. Whatever has been "unchosen" helps to convey what is meant by what is chosen, because meaning is elucidated as much by what a word *doesn't* mean as by what it does. Each set of systemic choices contributes to the overall meaning of a text: "A text is the product of ongoing selection in a very large network of systems—a system network."[36]

Since language is a network of interlocking options, to understand how meaning is encoded in the wording of a language, a linguist needs to understand the systemic structure of options within the language. As Halliday says,

> The system network is a theory about language as a resource for making meaning. Each system in the network represents a choice: not a conscious decision made in real time but a set of possible alternatives, like

---

34. Ibid., 25.
35. Ibid., 23.
36. Ibid.

"statement/question" or "singular/plural" or "falling tone/level tone/rising tone".... The system includes (1) the "entry condition" (where the choice is made), (2) the set of possible options, and (3) the "realizations" (what is to be done—that is, what are the structural consequences of each of the options).[37]

For example, the meaning of the aorist tense-form in Greek is sharpened when we understand how it differs from the imperfect tense-form. When we understand the differences between the two tense-forms, they become mutually defining. Thus, when an author chooses to use the aorist, he has unchosen the imperfect. In that choice and unchoice, meaning is conveyed. Furthermore, if we have understood properly the differences between the two tense-forms, we ought to be able to predict when one will be used rather than the other.

2.5.3 Metafunction

In addition to its systemic nature, language has three *metafunctions*—ideational, interpersonal, and textual.[38] The term *metafunction* is to be distinguished from the common linguistic term *function* in that the latter "simply means purpose or way of using language, and has no significance for the analysis of language itself."[39] *Metafunction*, on the other hand, is intrinsic to language: "the entire architecture of language is arranged along functional lines."[40] Halliday's term is adopted "to suggest that function was an integral component within the overall theory."[41] These metafunctions are, quite literally, the grand functions of language. The three metafunctions of language are summarized below.

2.5.3.1 **Ideational metafunction.** Halliday and Matthiessen say that "language provides a theory of human experience," and certain grammatical resources of every language are dedicated to that function. This function of language is called the *ideational metafunction*.[42] We use language to encode our experience of the world. When someone describes a sunset,

---

37. M. A. K. Halliday, *An Introduction to Functional Grammar* (2nd ed.; London: Edward Arnold, 1994), xxvi.
38. Halliday and Matthiessen, *Functional Grammar*, 361.
39. Ibid., 31.
40. Ibid.
41. Ibid.
42. Ibid., 30.

or talks about nuclear physics, or writes about jazz, she is encoding her understanding or experience of these things through language.

The ideational metafunction is divided into two components, the *experiential* and *logical* metafunctions. The experiential metafunction is the most basic of all human language in that it refers to the choices speakers make in order to make meanings about the world.

While the experiential metafunction describes our linguistic organization of experience, there is also a logical aspect to it—"language as the expression of certain very general logical relations."[43] The *logical metafunction* creates combinations of words that are connected through a logical relation. A clause, for instance, is not simply a group of words; a *meaningful* clause is a group of words that bear a logical relation to each other. To describe a sentence simply by the "words-in-sentences" model ignores their relationship to each other. Halliday and Matthiessen employ the following analogy, "Describing a sentence as a construction of words is rather like describing a house as a construction of bricks, without recognizing the walls and the rooms as intermediate structural units."[44]

2.5.3.2 Interpersonal metafunction. Language not only describes our experience, it also *enacts*. Enacting takes place within our personal and social relationships with people around us.[45] The *interpersonal metafunction* refers to the way in which we use language to "act on" others. When we ask questions, issue instructions, offer encouragement, or just share news with each other, we are using language to affect others in some way. This metafunction is more "active" than the ideational metafunction: "if the ideational function of the grammar is 'language as reflection,' this is 'language as action.'"[46]

2.5.3.3 Textual metafunction. The *textual metafunction* has to do with turning all of this into a coherent message. It "can be regarded as an enabling or facilitating function, since both the others—construing experience and enacting interpersonal relations—depend on being able to build up sequences of discourse, organizing the discursive flow and creating cohesion and continuity as it moves along."[47] The term "textual" does not here refer to written text, but to the "text" of a message, whether it be

---

43. Ibid., 362.
44. Ibid.
45. Ibid., 30.
46. Ibid.
47. Ibid., 30–31.

written or spoken. For any successful communication to occur, information must be encoded into a coherent "text."

These three metafunctions—ideational, interpersonal, and textual—"are realized throughout the grammar of a language."[48] They are part of the architecture of language, and every utterance can be analysed with respect to them.

2.5.4 Semantics and Grammar

Like many linguistic schools, *Systemic Functional Linguistics* is interested in the relationship between semantics and grammar. That is, it seeks to unpack how "meaning" (semantics) is related to "wordings" (grammar, or lexicogrammar).[49] In fact, semantics and grammar are two out of the three "strata" of language, the third being phonology. These three strata are layered vertically, so to speak. The bottom layer is phonology: the sound system of a language. The stratum above phonology is lexicogrammar: words and their relationships to each other within a clause. The stratum above lexicogrammar is semantics: the meaning intended by lexicogrammatical (and phonological) wordings.[50] These three strata are understood in an interlocking fashion, and together they enable a language to perform its metafunctions.

The connection between semantics and grammar in any given language is never straightforward and, indeed, this presents the major challenge for linguistic investigation: how does a language encode meanings through its wordings? According to systemic functional linguists, this relationship between semantics and grammar is one of realization, such that the wording "realizes," or encodes, the meaning. In keeping with the presuppositions of functional linguistics, each language has its own semantic code. Thus, Halliday comments, "stated in other terms, a grammar is an attempt to crack the code."[51] This can only be attempted one language at

---

48. Ibid., 361.
49. Though he is happy to use the term *grammar* as a shorthand expression, Halliday prefers the term *lexicogrammar* in order to view grammar and vocabulary as part of the same stratum; "they are the two poles of a single continuum, properly called lexicogrammar" (ibid., 24). By the same token, syntax and morphology are both part of lexicogrammar. The middle stratum of lexicogrammar therefore includes grammar, vocabulary, syntax, and morphology, which covers most of the interest of traditional Greek scholarship.
50. Ibid., 24–27, 660.
51. Halliday, *Functional Grammar* (2nd ed.), xxx.

a time, since there is no "universal code" that will unlock all languages at once (contra generative linguistics). In the case of Greek, for instance, we are obliged to crack its own code rather than rely on the codes of other languages.

This means that a systemic functional approach to language would be highly skeptical of interpreting Greek grammar through the instrument of comparative philology—understanding Greek through the lens of Latin, for example. Latin has its own code: semantic meanings are encoded in Latin's lexicogrammatical wordings. By the same token, Greek has its own code, with its semantic meanings being encoded in the lexicogrammatical wordings of Greek, and Greek alone. This principle has wide-ranging application for current discussions about Greek.

2.5.5 Syntagmatic Chains and Paradigmatic Choice

Within the lexicogrammatical stratum, systemic linguists analyze language choices through "horizontal" and "vertical" planes. The horizontal plane is described as *syntagmatic* and concerns the combination of wordings in a clause or sentence. Syntagmatic ordering involves "patterns, or regularities, in what *goes together with* what."[52] Belonging to the realm of syntax, a syntagmatic chain is the linear relation of given linguistic items—how each word in a phrase, clause, or sentence relates to the other words in its phrase, clause, or sentence. In a jazz trio, this would be the way that piano, bass, and drums interact with each other. Each musician has a role to play with respect to the other two, and the three are mutually dependent.

The vertical plane is described as *paradigmatic* and concerns the choice of a single linguistic item as distinct from other items of the same class. Paradigmatic ordering involves "patterns in what *could go instead of* what."[53] In the jazz trio, this would be like replacing the drummer with another drummer and considering what difference that would make to the trio. For instance, when one chooses an aorist tense-form, this choice is analyzed with reference to all the other possible choices that might have occupied the verb "slot" in the sentence. Each choice is meaningful against the set of paradigmatic options that are unchosen. It is the paradigmatic axis that most clearly connects to the *systemic* nature of language (see

---

52. Halliday and Matthiessen, *Functional Grammar*, 22.
53. Ibid.

§2.5.2): any set of paradigmatic alternatives "constitutes a system in this technical sense."[54]

2.6 Functional Linguistics and New Testament Greek

The foregoing section (§2.5) outlines some of the characteristics of Systemic Functional Linguistics. It is only a sketch of this functional linguistic school at the broadest level, yet includes some key methodological principles that are useful to the Greek scholar and student.

While a plethora of linguistic approaches abound within Greek grammatical studies, it is worth reflecting on the question of which approaches are most useful for our purposes. It is reasonable to conclude that a functional linguistic approach is most suited to the enterprise of Greek grammatical study. As we've seen, there are several schools within the field of functional linguistics (*Systemic Functional Linguistics* being just one of many), but it's not necessary to push further here. It is enough to recognize the benefits of functional analysis for the reasons stated by Porter:

> It is prima facie much more reasonable and potentially promising to approach a "dead" language from a functional paradigm, in which instances of real language are cited, than from a "formal" (psychological) model which must test user competence against an already finite set of sentences, with no possible recourse to native speakers for verification.[55]

In other words, the approach and presuppositions of functional linguistics are inherently better suited to the study of an ancient language—of which there are no native speakers—than those of formal, or generative, linguistics. Since generative linguistic approaches ultimately seek to understand how language coheres with the human mind, they are better suited to "live" languages with living native speakers. But since ancient languages only exist now in the texts in which they are preserved, we must utilize tools that suit the examination of such empirical evidence. These are found most readily in the realm of functional linguistics.

There are already some excellent tools available that marry functional linguistics and New Testament Greek. Perhaps the alarming fact is that

---

54. Ibid.
55. Porter, *Verbal Aspect*, 7.

they have been in print for quite some time, and yet most Greek students remain ignorant of linguistics. As such, it is worth drawing attention to them here for future study.[56]

Peter Cotterell and Max Turner's *Linguistics and Biblical Interpretation* is an excellent, fulsome guide to various intersections between linguistics and biblical language (not restricted to Greek).[57] It covers such themes as the relationship between language and exegesis, semantics and hermeneutics, lexical semantics, sentence structure, discourse analysis, and nonliteral language.

Moisés Silva's *God, Language, and Scripture* is a highly accessible work that most likely provides the quickest and easiest way into the relationship between linguistics and biblical languages (also not restricted to Greek). As well as covering basic principles of linguistics and their application to the biblical languages, Silva includes helpful theological and biblical perspectives on language and an appendix on the biblical languages in theological education.

David Alan Black's *Linguistics for Students of New Testament Greek* finds middle ground between the aforementioned works, with Cotterell and Turner offering the most demanding treatment of the three, and Silva the most accessible. Black's treatment will be spot on for many second year (and above) Greek students. He answers objections raised about linguistics, treats phonology, morphology, syntax, and semantics, and offers a chapter on the historical development of Greek and a chapter on discourse analysis.

2.6.1 An Example Relating to the Greek Verbal System

One of the major areas of innovation and development in the study of Ancient Greek is the verbal system, and verbal aspect in particular. This topic will be explored in more detail in chapter 5, but for now it provides an apt example of the kind of difference that linguistic methodology can make to academic discussion.

One of the debated facets of the discussions about Greek verbal aspect is whether or not temporal reference ("time" or "tense") is encoded in the indicative verb forms. While it used to be accepted that temporal reference

---

56. At least two of these works exhibit traces of generative linguistics, especially Black (see his *Linguistics for Students*, 114–18), but on the whole their methodology is in line with functional linguistics.

57. Peter Cotterell and Max Turner, *Linguistics and Biblical Interpretation* (Downers Grove, IL: InterVarsity Press, 1989).

was encoded in *all* Greek verb forms (including nonindicative verbs), this was narrowed to the indicative mood in the nineteen century because of the observations of Georg Curtius. Through the work of McKay, Porter, Decker, and myself, the claim that the indicative mood encodes temporal reference has also been challenged (though I accept future temporal reference for the future indicative form).

In the debate between Porter and Fanning on this issue, it is clear that a linguistic principle lies at the heart of the discussion. While both scholars recognize the importance of the functional linguistic distinction between semantics and pragmatics, they differ on how strictly this distinction is to be held.

Porter claims that temporal reference is not a semantic category of indicative verbs, since there are so many examples of indicatives expressing actions that are not set in the time frame in which they are supposed to be. Many present indicatives convey past action, some aorists convey present and future activity, and so on. Thus, for Porter, temporal expression must be a pragmatic category—it is a function of the verb in context, rather than a constant, permanent feature of the verb. Fanning, however, disagrees. While he acknowledges that not all indicative verbs behave "according to the rules," temporal reference is nevertheless a semantic feature of indicative verbs.

All of this is to be unpacked in a subsequent chapter, but for now it is safe to say that the disagreement between Porter and Fanning on this issue rests largely on how strictly the linguistic distinction between semantics and pragmatics is to be held. Porter holds the distinction tightly, such that uses "against the rules" means that the rules are wrong. Fanning holds the distinction less tightly, such that uses "against the rules" are exceptions that prove the rule. These uses are created by various factors impinging on the verb, but they do not overthrow the verb's overall semantic meaning.

Suffice to say, if one prefers a tight distinction between semantics and pragmatics, Porter will appear to be correct. If, however, one is happy for a certain "fuzziness" to exist between semantic and pragmatic categories, Fanning will seem the more sensible option. Thus, in the end, the debate about "tense" in the Greek indicative system depends on methodological, presuppositional distinctions. These are *linguistic* distinctions.

2.7 Further Reading

Black, David Alan. *Linguistics for Students of New Testament Greek: A Survey of Basic Concepts and Applications*. Second edition. Grand Rapids: Baker, 1995.

Cotterell, Peter, and Max Turner. *Linguistics and Biblical Interpretation*. Downers Grove, IL: InterVarsity Press, 1989.

Crystal, David A. *A Dictionary of Linguistics and Phonetics*. Sixth edition. Malden: Blackwell, 2008.

Halliday, M. A. K., and Christian M. I. M. Matthiessen. *Halliday's Introduction to Functional Grammar*. Fourth revised edition. London: Routledge, 2014.

Lyons, John. *Language and Linguistics: An Introduction*. Cambridge: Cambridge University Press, 1981.

Silva, Moisés. *God, Language, and Scripture: Reading the Bible in the Light of General Linguistics*. Grand Rapids: Zondervan, 1990.

CHAPTER 3

LEXICAL SEMANTICS AND LEXICOGRAPHY

Scholars' tasks are not for sissies.   *—Frederick W. Danker*

3.1 Introduction

Louw and Nida lament, "In no area of New Testament studies is there such a dearth of valid information and such a wealth of misinformation as in lexical semantics."[1] This chapter focuses on the methodology of lexical semantics (drawing particularly on the work of Moisés Silva) and issues in Greek lexicography (drawing on John A. L. Lee). It will be demonstrated that several exegetical mistakes and fallacies can be avoided by a better understanding of the theory of lexemes. Furthermore, certain problems inherent to our current lexicons will be addressed, with a view to using such tools in a responsible manner.[2]

Lexical semantics, or lexicology, is concerned with the meanings of words.[3] Lexicography aims to produce a lexicon—the collected results of lexical semantics for all words of a language. A key distinction between lexical semantics and lexicography is at the level of theory versus practice. While both are concerned with the meanings of words, lexical semantics

---

1. Nida and Louw, *Lexical Semantics*, 1.
2. It is worth noting that some of the following discussion is not "new" in the sense that it has arisen during the Modern Era of New Testament Greek studies—and, in fact, much of it can be traced at least as far back as James Barr in 1961—but the issues addressed represent perennial problems that seem not to go away. Thus, lexical semantics and lexicography remain pertinent topics for modern discussions.
3. Moisés Silva, *Biblical Words and Their Meaning: An Introduction to Lexical Semantics* (rev. ed.; Grand Rapids: Zondervan, 1994), 10.

includes thinking through theoretical issues related to words (lexemes). It provides the framework and methodology for the work of lexicography, which is "the art and science of dictionary-making, carried out by lexicographers."[4] Both lexical semantics and lexicography seek to determine the meaning of lexemes, how lexemes differ from each other, and what the semantic range of each word is. A book such as Moisés Silva's *Biblical Words and Their Meaning* deals with the theoretical issues of lexical semantics. A lexicon such as BDAG is a product of lexicography.

3.2 Lexical Semantics

This section will treat some of the key theoretical issues in the work of lexical semantics, drawing in particular on the helpful overview of such issues offered by Moisés Silva's book. Pertinent examples from the Greek New Testament will demonstrate the importance of these theoretical topics.

3.2.1 Symbol-Sense-Referent

One of the most important distinctions in the theory of lexical semantics, made famous by Ogden and Richards in 1945, is that between *symbol, sense*, and *referent*.[5] A *symbol* is a word (either spoken or written); the *sense* is the image or concept evoked in the mind by the symbol; the *referent* is the actual thing in the real world that is denoted by the symbol.[6] The so-called Ogden-Richards triangle demonstrates the indirect relationship between a word and the thing it points to:

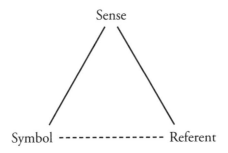

Sense

Symbol ---------------- Referent

---

4. Crystal, *Linguistics and Phonetics*, 278.
5. C. K. Ogden and I. A. Richards, *The Meaning of Meaning* (New York: Harcourt, Brace & Co., 1945). Silva uses the term *sense* in place of Ogden and Richards's terms *thought* and *reference*, which are unnecessarily confusing (Silva, *Biblical Words*, 102).
6. Silva, *Biblical Words*, 102.

As the Ogden-Richards triangle illustrates, there is no direct relationship between the symbol and its referent. In fact, different languages will each have different symbols for the same referent.[7] A cat may be referred to as *cat* in English, *chat* in French, *Katze* in German, or *kass* in Estonian. They are different symbols and yet share the same referent. Conversely, the referent of a particular symbol can be changed too, so that *nice* used to mean *stupid* in Middle English, but now means something else entirely.

The key to such changes in referent on the one hand, or symbol on the other, is the fact that a symbol only has meaning because it signals something in the mind of the language-user. When the word *cat* is used, most hearers will picture a domestic feline. But others may picture a lion, and some may even picture a jazz musician! In fact, the symbol can point to any of those referents, but only because the symbol evokes a thought or image or concept in the mind first. If normal people have never associated the word *cat* with *jazz musician*, then they will not immediately understand the intended referent in the sentence, *That horn player is a nice cat.*

Additionally, if the *sense* is changed over time in the minds of a language community, so then the symbol's referent will change. Thus, eight hundred years ago the word *nice* caused people to think of the characteristic of stupidity; but now it causes people to think of the characteristic of pleasantness. *That horn player is a nice cat* must have meant something entirely different in the thirteenth century!

3.2.2 Synonymy

Silva discusses synonymy under the topic of *sense relations*.[8] The *sense* concept is represented by the middle apex of the Odgen-Richards triangle (see above), and does not involve symbol or referent.[9] As Cotterell and Turner explain:

> Synonymy is a relationship of identity of *sense* between two linguistic expressions.... Because lexemes usually have a variety of senses (polysemy), it is to be expected that lexemes may be truly synonymous for one or even several of their senses (partial synonymy), but much less probable that they will be synonyms in all of their senses and habitual collocations.[10]

---

7. Ibid., 103–4.
8. Ibid., chapter 5.
9. Ibid., 121.
10. Cotterell and Turner, *Linguistics*, 159.

While it is probably true that no two words are fully interchangeable in all contexts,[11] proper synonymy exists when two words overlap enough so that they may be exchanged in certain contexts. Silva's example is the synonymous use of πνεῦμα and ψυχή; both words are capable of evoking the sense of the immaterial aspect of a person. So, in certain contexts, the two words can be used interchangeably.[12] This overlap is a case of proper synonymy (or, in Cotterell and Turner's terminology, *partial synonymy*).

However, Silva notes popular-level misuses of the term *synonymous*, which can afflict biblical interpreters. Often when the term *synonymous* is misused, what is actually meant is that two words have the same *referent*. But it is not correct to say that the two words are synonyms, which refers to two words that overlap in *sense*, not referent. To say that *the beloved disciple* and *the author of the fourth Gospel* are synonyms is a mistake; these two terms do not overlap in their *sense* relations, but in their referent (John).[13] This type of mistake about synonymy commonly afflicts biblical interpreters.

3.2.3 Context

An obvious principle of lexical semantics is that context is extremely important for uncovering lexical meaning. Indeed, linguists assign a *determinative* function to context; "the context does not merely help us understand meaning — it virtually makes meaning."[14] Cotterell and Turner state:

> Whereas most words are polysemous (capable of multiple sense meanings), it cannot be emphasized too strongly that this should not be taken to mean that a word is normally capable of a full range of meanings in its use in any one utterance. The context of the utterance usually singles out the *one* sense, which is intended, from amongst the various senses of which the word is potentially capable.[15]

What is not always appreciated, however, is the complexity of context. Literary context (called "co-text" by some linguists) is the type of context that is normally the first port of call for students of the New Testament. For lexical semantics, this involves understanding the meaning of a word

---

11. Silva, *Biblical Words*, 121, n, 6.
12. Ibid., 122.
13. Ibid., 121.
14. Ibid., 139.
15. Cotterell and Turner, *Linguistics*, 175.

in light of its surrounding text. What light can be shed on a word through appreciating the sentence in which it belongs, but also the paragraph or pericope, chapter, and book? Indeed, the fact that literary context can range as widely as the sentence through to the chapter or book reveals the phenomenon of "contextual circles." If we begin with the most immediate context—the sentence—we can move out through a series of concentric circles of context: the paragraph, the section, the chapter, the whole book. All of these levels of context can help to establish the meaning of a word, but which level should have priority? If, for example, the general function of a word throughout a book stands in apparent contrast to its use in a particular sentence, should we allow the sentence-level context to trump the wider context?[16]

Differing answers to this question alone can yield quite different exegetical results. For instance, debate about the meaning of the δικαιοσύνη – δικαιόω word group in Paul's usage will sometimes involve this methodological issue. Should we try to determine Paul's meaning in a particular passage by first establishing how he uses a word everywhere else, or should we just read the word in its immediate context and go from there? Assuming we seek to do both, which level of context takes priority when they are in apparent conflict?

Take Romans 6:7 for example. Most English translations render this verse something like, "For one who has died has been set free from sin" (ESV). Readers of English translations, therefore, may be completely unaware that Paul has used the word δικαιόω in this verse, which is rendered "set free." But since that word is elsewhere in Romans understood to mean "to justify" or "to declare righteous," why is it here rendered "to set free"? No doubt this unusual translation of the word is due to its immediate context, which translators have privileged over the wider context in this case.

Speaking of Paul and Romans, another type of literary context is authorial context. The example above is not only related to the use of δικαιόω in Romans, but to Paul's use overall. It is a common practice to consider a particular author's use of a lexeme across books, and while this could be understood as a type of theological method, it is properly regarded another

16. See Silva, *Biblical Words*, 156–59.

type of literary context. It constitutes another contextual circle—wider than a book, it includes all literature authored by the same person. This category belongs to *literary* context because it considers an author's literary use of a word; it is just not restricted to one piece of literature.

In addition to literary context, or co-text, lexical semantics takes into account context of situation. Context of situation can be divided into at least two further types of context: situation proper and historical context. The former subdivision refers to the situation into which a document is written. If we consider 1 Corinthians, for example, it is clear that Paul is addressing certain problems within the Corinthian congregation. Working out Paul's purpose in writing 1 Corinthians not only tells us about his purpose, but relates to contextual issues too. For example, when considering the use of the lexeme εἰδωλόθυτον in 1 Corinthians 8, the situation into which Paul writes may have some bearing on its meaning and function.

The latter subdivision involves understanding the cultural, religious, and sociological backgrounds that relate to a text. For 1 Corinthians, understanding what food sacrificed to idols is about, for example, has direct bearing on our understanding of the text and, in turn, on our understanding of εἰδωλόθυτον. On this word, Louw and Nida state:

> Part of the sacrifice was normally burned on the altar, part was eaten during a ritual meal in a temple, and part was sold in the public market. According to Jewish tradition this meat was unclean and therefore forbidden.[17]

Obviously, the Jewish tradition associated with this meat offered to idols is essential background for understanding Paul's argument in 1 Corinthians 8. Thus, context of situation considers extra-textual issues that inform our reading of the text and, therefore, our ability to comprehend the usage of lexemes.

One more type of context is pertinent for lexical semantics. This context, as with context of situation, is also extra-textual. Sometimes referred to as "reception history," this context considers contextualizations that occur *subsequent* to the writing of the original document.[18] While we might be tempted to think that "reception context" is not relevant for

---

17. Louw and Nida, *Greek-English Lexicon*, 5.15.
18. Silva, *Biblical Words*, 147–48.

understanding an author's use of a particular lexeme, such an attitude is naïve. The reason that reception context matters is that certain words will be "heard" by modern readers through the lens of how others have understood them in the past.

The δικαιοσύνη–δικαιόω word group is again a classic example of this. Do we simply read these words through the lens of the Protestant Reformation? Does the Reformation skew what these words actually mean? In large part, the so-called New Perspective on Paul argues exactly along such lines—that reception history has caused us to misunderstand Paul. Whether or not such is the case, the point here is that the ways in which others throughout history have understood texts—and particular words in them—affect our reading. Lexical semantics must take this fact into account as we seek to understand words accurately.

3.2.4 Lexical Choice

A principle of lexical semantics is that every lexeme represents a choice that the author has made. While there are certain idiomatic and linguistic restraints that delimit lexical choice, nevertheless it is significant that an author chooses to use one word when another might have been chosen instead. This relates to the issue of synonymy, addressed earlier in this chapter. It also relates to the principle of paradigmatic choice, explored in chapter 2. In fact, lexical choice is a subset of paradigmatic choice; whenever a lexeme is used, its choice is meaningful against other possible options. To choose one lexeme is to "unchoose" another.

There are a couple of types of lexical choice to consider. One type represents the choice of one referent over another. That is, the choice is determined by what object, person, or action the author wishes to specify. For example, the choice between the words "cat" and "dog" is entirely related to the referent—if the author wants to refer to a dog, she cannot use the word "cat" because it is the wrong sign for the referent. This type of lexical choice sheds some light on the meaning of these two words as we contrast them.

Another type of lexical choice is more nuanced. Rather than a choice that reflects a different referent, this type of lexical choice involves different options for speaking of the same referent. For example, instead of the choice between "cat" and "dog," this choice is between "canine" and "dog."

In a sentence, the referent would be the same if either word is used, so the difference between them is much more subtle. In fact, this type of lexical choice normally involves synonymous lexemes. For lexical semantics, a choice between synonyms can be difficult to analyze, and yet it is often highly instructive.

3.2.5 Lexical Fields

A distinguishing feature of Saussure's legacy is his observation that words are mutually defining, in the sense that they limit each other reciprocally: "The value of a word is first known when we mark it off against the value of neighboring and opposing words. Only as part of the whole does the word have sense; for only in the field is there meaning."[19] Silva points to some scholars who have used this concept for analysis of biblical vocabulary, such as James Barr on "the image of God" and John Sawyer on Hebrew "salvation" terminology.[20]

For the student of the Greek New Testament, study of lexical fields is greatly assisted through the use of Louw and Nida's lexicon, since all vocabulary is already arranged according to semantic domains. This means that synonyms and non-synonymous-yet-related words can be compared with relative ease. While such comparisons are not difficult to arrange (with the use of Louw and Nida), the practice is still not standard among interpreters. Rather than simply trying to ascertain which sense of a lexeme is most likely in a particular context, it is worth asking how the use of a different lexeme in its place might have changed the meaning of the utterance. That contrast can illuminate the use of the original lexeme in question.

3.2.6 Ambiguity

Lexical ambiguity is a problem for lexical semantics. Exegetes often encounter instances in which the use of a word in a particular text is unclear because it is capable of different meanings. The first issue to work through is whether or not the use of the word is genuinely ambiguous. In other words, it is possible that only *one* meaning is truly plausible in the context, but this conclusion has yet to be reached. The exegete must study the text and its context carefully, and research the lexeme's meaning and function,

---

19. Saussure, *General Linguistics*, 116.
20. Silva, *Biblical Words*, 161–63.

with the expectation that such study will yield a compelling conclusion to the problem. Most of the time, apparent ambiguity is just that — *apparent*.

In other instances, however, ambiguity is genuine. If such is the case, we must consider two types of ambiguity — *deliberate* ambiguity and *unintended* ambiguity. Deliberate ambiguity refers to an author's choice of a word that is deliberately used in order to convey more than one meaning, or even to keep the meaning slightly vague. As Silva reflects,

> It may well be that a great mind occasionally and deliberately uses vague language for specific purposes. In view of the nature of language and communication, however, we should assume *one* meaning unless there are strong *exegetical* (literary, contextual) grounds to the contrary.[21]

Silva thus acknowledges the possibility of deliberate ambiguity, yet helpfully sets parameters for its use. Our default expectation ought to be that there is a nonambiguous solution, unless there are strong reasons to think otherwise.

One possible case of intended ambiguity would be Acts 17:26, in Paul's Areopagus discourse. So Joshua Jipp says that,

> when Paul states that God ἐποίησέν τε ἐξ ἑνὸς πᾶν ἔθνος ἀνθρώπων κατοικεῖν ἐπὶ παντὸς προσώπου τῆς γῆς (17:26a), the interpreter may take ἐξ ἑνός as referring to the biblical story of God's creation of humanity in Genesis 1.... Or the interpreter may interpret the phrase in the Stoic sense whereby all humanity originates in and is a part of, Zeus.[22]

After suggesting the same type of double meaning in 17:26b, Jipp concludes, "Luke has crafted this sentence in such a manner as to resonate with both biblical and philosophical traditions."[23] If Jipp's assessment is correct, Acts 17:26 certainly ought to be regarded as an instance of intended ambiguity.

Unintended ambiguity is that which results from the imprecise nature of language and, in particular, the imprecision of exegesis and translation of texts written in a foreign, and ancient, language. The author does not deliberately cause this type of ambiguity; in fact, it might not be the author's "fault" at all. While language is sometimes ambiguous because a

---

21. Silva, *Biblical Words*, 151.
22. Joshua W. Jipp, "Paul's Areopagus Speech of Acts 17:16–34 as *Both* Critique *and* Propaganda," *JBL* 131 (2012): 581–82.
23. Ibid., 582.

communicator has not given enough concern to clarity, at other times it is due to a lack at the recipient's end. This is particularly pertinent for us as we wrestle with unintended ambiguity in the New Testament. The author may have been perfectly clear to his original readers and hearers, but less so to us. We are removed from the original context by two thousand years and we are not native speakers of the chosen language. It should not be surprising, therefore, that unintended ambiguity exists. We should be surprised, rather, that there is not more of it!

Sorting through ambiguity remains a difficult task for lexical semantics. Once we have availed ourselves of all the resources and tools at our disposal, there is not much more to be done. We simply must live with the reality that some ambiguity exists. Nevertheless, it is also possible that certain ambiguities will be cleared up through further discovery. For example, the monumental discovery of *The Oxyrhynchus Papyri* over a hundred years ago has had a dramatic impact on our understanding of Greek in general and on certain lexemes in particular. Ongoing discoveries—though extremely rare at that magnitude—continue to shed light. So, at least in that respect, the further we move away from the time of the New Testament, the closer we get to a complete understanding of its details.

3.2.7 Implications of Lexical Semantics

The foregoing is a simple overview of some key issues within the methodology of lexical semantics. All of these principles are crucial for reading the Greek New Testament with any level of linguistic sophistication. Whenever one wishes to construct a "word study," or to investigate certain vocabulary related to some theological theme, or simply to understand the use of one word in its context, careful consideration of these lexicological insights will help to avoid common—and unhelpful—pitfalls in interpretation.

Cotterell and Turner offer a list of implications of lexical semantics for theological word studies, which is worth summarizing here.[24]

> Etymology cannot be counted on for determining meaning of words,
> but only synchronic analysis of the language will aid accurate
> interpretation.

---

24. Cotterell and Turner, *Linguistics*, 178–81.

A lexical form will have several senses, and we must allow for the full diversity of those senses. However, in any one context, a word will only carry *one* of its possible senses.

A key way to determine the meaning of a word in context is to compare and contrast the sense of the word with other words with related senses.

3.3 New Testament Greek Lexicography

Having discussed some of the key methodological issues of lexical semantics, we turn now to the application of theory as it relates to New Testament Greek. Lexicography is the study of words with a view to their collection in a dictionary. While the New Testament is the corpus we are interested in, the language of the New Testament should not be understood apart from its historical context. That is, the New Testament employs language that is naturally found in the first century, and in that sense our interest in this corpus is artificial. "New Testament Greek" is no different from the Greek used throughout the Koine period (see §1.3.1), and thus any practice of lexicography must take into account the use of words outside the New Testament as well as their use within it. This means that "New Testament Greek Lexicography" is the study of words that appear in the New Testament, without claiming that there is something special about the language of the New Testament. It may be special to us because it is in the New Testament, but it is not special from a linguistic point of view.

3.3.1 Difficulties in Practice

New Testament Greek Lexicography is a difficult and arduous task. First, the practice of understanding words in context is complex and involves careful study of each word as it appears in ancient literature. This task alone can take a lifetime. Second, whenever advances in lexical semantics occur, the task of lexicography is altered. This means that lexicographers are required to update their methods and nuance their results according to the best theoretical advances. It also means that previous results may need adjustment or correction. Third, the language of the New Testament is overlaid with special challenges—not because the language itself is any different from standard first-century Greek, but because of the nature of the New Testament. This corpus has a history of interpretation spanning two thousand years, which will affect the way we read it. There are a myriad of theological issues that play into how we understand the language. Furthermore, new evidence is coming to light even now that requires to be factored in to our conclusions. As the great New Testament lexicographer Frederick Danker once said, "Change spells pain, but ... scholars' tasks are 'not for sissies.' "[25]

One of the challenges of lexicography is that there are two languages of concern, not just one. Greek lexicography does not simply involve the matter of understanding Greek; it also involves English (in our case, at least) and the way that the "receptor" language continues to change. In other words, a lexicon will only make sense to its reader if it is up to date with respect to the reader's own language. Because English is changing at an incredibly fast rate at the moment, lexicons from a hundred years ago are rendered nearly useless (except for the purpose of studying the history of lexicography). One of the obvious difficulties of lexicography, then, is that it is never finished. As long as the receptor language continues to change, lexicons will require updating.

Another challenge for lexicography is the issue that a word in English may have nuances or connotations that are not shared with the Greek word it translates. Consider this comment from Danker:

> Because an expression may be either semantically designative or associative (connotative), it is particularly important that terms used to translate a given expression do not have an associative aspect that distorts the meaning of a term in the source language. The frequent use of "preach" for the term κηρύσσω is a case in point. In English, "preach" suggests a moralistic or didactic mode of communication, whereas "proclaim" may be what a NT writer expresses with the word κηρύσσω, especially when focusing on the distinctive and unique character of a message that comes with divine authority.[26]

As Danker points out, a problem with the translation "preach" for the Greek word κηρύσσω is that there is a nuance to "preach" that is not implied by the Greek word. This is just one example of a complex problem that lexicographers face for several Greek words. It also highlights the

---

25. Frederick William Danker, "Review of *Lexical Semantics of the Greek New Testament*, by E. A. Nida and J. P. Louw, 1992," *JBL* 113 (1994): 533.
26. Frederick William Danker, "Lexical Evolution and Linguistic Hazard," in *Biblical Greek Language and Lexicography: Essays in Honor of Frederick W. Danker* (ed. Bernard A. Taylor et al.; Grand Rapids: Eerdmans, 2004), 23.

danger of trusting a one-word "gloss" definition for Greek words. We will return to this issue below.

Related to this problem is another that Danker calls the "stained glass" connotation. Due to the long history of New Testament interpretation, there are English words that lexicographers and translators may use that are really only used because of a historical understanding of such English words. The problem here is that the English word no longer has any real currency in contemporary English (or, in fact, means something else entirely). Danker's example is the English word "grace":

> Associated with the foregoing concerns is the common practice of lexi-cographers to convey what can be termed a "stained glass" connotation to certain words, with the result that numerous texts take on a patina of exclusiveness not really present in the text. Thereby certain terms lose almost all connection with the socio-cultural context that made them meaningful for their primary audiences. Thus the rendering "grace" for χάρις is not especially meaningful to modern audiences, since the ancient word χάρις was used at numerous levels or registrations to express "gen-erosity." "Saved through God's generosity" may not sound churchly, but it expresses the truth: not a theological preference, but a semantic reality that can steer one away from the hazard of dogmatic presuppositions.[27]

Danker's phrase "'saved through God's generosity' may not sound churchly" captures the sentiment well: "grace" is a "churchly" word, and in normal usage today does not mean what those in the church mean by it. This is obvious by the fact that it nearly always needs to be explained. For someone not used to the "churchly" meaning of "grace," it must be explained as "unmerited favor," or, as Danker acknowledges, simply as "generosity."

Should we keep using English words that do not mean to our con-temporaries what they mean to us? Perhaps it can be argued that this is precisely what the early church did with certain technical terms. It could also be argued that a word like "grace" connects us to important historical discussions about salvation, such as those that define the Protestant Refor-mation. These points are worth considering, but it is clear that from a pure lexicographical standpoint, the English word "grace" is not a great option for translating χάρις.

---

27. Ibid., 24.

Yet another problem besetting lexicographers is the practice of illegitimate totality transference. While James Barr famously critiqued this decades ago (also having coined the term), the problem persists.[28] This practice refers to reading too much into every use of a particular word. If we collate a full picture of the possible uses of a word and then read that "full picture" into every use of the word, we have illegitimately transferred the "totality" of possible meanings into every use. As Danker explains,

> In the case of a term like βλασφημέω, a range of synonyms is possible, but this does not mean that all the meanings we bring to these terms in our receptor language are semantically present in the lexical term and therefore exist in any and every usage of the term in the source language. Context in the source text determines what specific word in the receptor language is adequate to express what the source speaker nuanced through the syntagmatic structure that colored the lexeme.[29]

A good example is the word σάρξ. This is often used in the New Testament to refer to the fallen, sinful nature, such as in Romans 8:6, "The mind governed by the flesh [σαρκός] is death, but the mind governed by the Spirit is life and peace." But to assume that *every* use of σάρξ therefore refers to the sinful nature is to commit the error of totality transference. In Luke 24:39, for example, Jesus says, "Look at my hands and my feet. It is I myself! Touch me and see; a ghost does not have flesh [σάρκα] and bones, as you see I have." Clearly, Jesus simply refers to his physical body here, not the "sinful nature."

It is not that the full picture of possible uses of the word is necessarily incorrect; the problem lies in seeing that full picture in every use of the word instead of understanding the particular use of the word as conditioned by its context. Context serves to narrow the possible meanings of a word in use.

All these difficulties illustrate the complexity of the task of lexicography. They also serve to warn us of the dangers of blindly relying on the results of lexicography. It is easy to make mistakes, and the New Testament interpreter must be aware of the potential pitfalls. This leads to the methodological problems inherent to our New Testament Greek lexicons.

---

28. Barr, *The Semantics of Biblical Language*, 217–18. See also Silva, *Biblical Words*, 25–26; D. A. Carson, *Exegetical Fallacies* (2nd ed.; Grand Rapids: Baker, 1996), 60–61.
29. Danker, "Lexical Evolution," 26–27.

3.3.2 Methodological Problems

No one has drawn more attention to the methodological issues and, well, let's face it, flaws, in our New Testament Greek lexicons than John A. L. Lee. In a good summary statement of the state of affairs for our lexicons, Lee says, "The concise, seemingly authoritative statement of meaning can, and often does, conceal many sins—indecision, compromise, imperfect knowledge, guesswork, and, above all, dependence on predecessors."[30]

Some may be gratified to note that New Testament lexicons are not the only targets of Lee's critique. Regarding the standard lexicon for Ancient Greek—Liddell-Scott-Jones—Lee is unreserved: it "has no coherent definition method, but relies on glosses; its basic material is derived from predecessors, in some cases descending from the ancient lexicographers; and the organization is chaotic as a result of piecemeal revisions."[31]

The situation for New Testament lexicons, however, is further complicated by issues related to the nature of the New Testament. Lee raises these in his third and fourth points below.

> First, there is the legacy of the long tradition of indicating meaning by glosses rather than definitions, which leads to many problems (as Louw and others have shown). Secondly, there is the fact that even the latest lexicons derive their material from their predecessors, and a great deal of it has been passed on uncritically over the course of centuries. Thirdly, there is an aspect that I think is not well known: meanings given in the NT lexicons are contaminated by glosses from the standard translations, going back as far as the Vulgate. There is a fourth tendency which has become evident to me lately: NT lexicons are unsystematic in their control of other discussions, and may or may not take up useful contributions to the understanding of the meaning.[32]

In his important monograph, *A History of New Testament Lexicography*, Lee acknowledges the widespread accessibility of New Testament lexicons, yet also their failure to achieve their purpose.

---

30. John A. L. Lee, "The Present State of Lexicography of Ancient Greek," in *Biblical Greek Language and Lexicography: Essays in Honor of Frederick W. Danker* (ed. Bernard A. Taylor et al.; Grand Rapids: Eerdmans, 2004), 66.
31. Ibid., 68.
32. Ibid., 69.

There has hardly been a time in four centuries when a recently published New Testament lexicon has not been available for purchase. Yet New Testament lexicography has failed to deliver the results one might expect from such long-sustained attention. Instead of a commodity that provides accurately described meanings and a reliable summation of the relevant data, we have haphazard coverage of the latter and a considerably flawed treatment of the former.[33]

There are, however, some helpful innovations to be seen in recent contributions to New Testament lexicography. Louw and Nida's *A Greek-English Lexicon of the New Testament Based on Semantic Domains* takes the approach of arranging lexical entries through semantic domains (as the title indicates), rather than via alphabetical arrangement. The chief benefit of such arrangement is that words may be compared to each other according to their similarity or synonymy. Since words are defined in relation to each other, their arrangement based on semantic domains is in itself a useful contribution. Having said that, however, Louw and Nida are open to the critique that their arrangement based on semantic domains is not entirely objective: there is a fair degree of subjective assessment involved in delineating said semantic domains.[34]

A second innovation of Louw and Nida is to use definitions to indicate meaning, rather than to rely on glosses. This is a major advance that moves us away from problematic reliance on gloss translations that are susceptible to many of the difficulties raised in §3.3.1, above.

The latest edition of Bauer's lexicon, BDAG — the chief modern lexicon under Lee's scrutiny — also embraces the significant advance of adding definitions for the majority of words. As with Louw and Nida, this helps to alleviate the traditional problem of reliance on glosses. While Lee acknowledges that there is still a place for glosses — especially for the purpose of learning vocabulary — caution is needed: "It is quite clear that they must not be used as the primary tool for determining meaning ... nor must the definitions be generated from existing glosses."[35]

While the innovations of Louw and Nida and BDAG are encouraging, especially in comparison to other Greek lexicographical traditions, there

---

33. John A. L. Lee, *A History of New Testament Lexicography* (SBG 8; New York: Peter Lang, 2003), 177.
34. However, see their discussion of the methodology involved in this; Nida and Louw, *Lexical Semantics*, 107–14.
35. Lee, *History*, 185.

is much more to be desired. Lee concludes, "Nevertheless, the NT lexical tradition, although it is in an advanced state compared with other areas, would benefit from a thorough rethinking."[36]

Subsequent to John Lee's study of New Testament lexicography, Frederick Danker produced *The Concise Greek-English Lexicon of the New Testament*.[37] In response to critiques of previous methodology, Danker's concise lexicon redressed some of the problems that afflict BDAG. The most significant advance in this regard is the inclusion of extended definitions for many lexical entries—alongside glosses. This volume is useful for students, being less encumbered by detail that they rarely need—and being much less expensive—but it cannot replace BDAG for scholars and many pastors, who will require a more fulsome treatment of lexemes.

3.3.3 Conclusion

John Lee's critiques of Greek lexicography are not presented without hope for the future. The two major innovations of Louw and Nida's lexicon (addressed above) set the direction to be followed.

> By the adoption of the domain arrangement it has brought into focus lexical structure as a vital element of the vocabulary. The full description of how a word is used requires sensitivity to its place in the complex web of sense-relations of which it is a part. This will need to be one of the concerns of future work. Secondly ... by rejecting the gloss method and adopting definition as the means of describing meaning, Louw and Nida have blazed a trail to follow.[38]

Lee also envisages a future for lexicography that is redefined by electronic media. We no longer need to wait for major editions of Greek lexicons to be published in print now that unlimited data can be stored and updated easily by electronic means.[39] Lexicographers could create an exhaustive electronic database, which "should be a collection of *all* the data relevant to the lexicography of the New Testament."[40] Such a project would be a cooperative effort and would be an ongoing, cumulative task so that new data and developments could be incorporated immediately. Lex-

---

36. Lee, "Present State," 70.
37. Frederick William Danker with Kathryn Krug, *The Concise Greek-English Lexicon of the New Testament* (Chicago: University of Chicago Press, 2009).
38. Lee, *History*, 180.
39. Ibid., 182.
40. Ibid., 183.

ical information, then, would always be up to date and could be accessed rapidly for exhaustive searching and analysis.

In the meantime, students of the Greek New Testament ought to be grateful that our lexicons are in better shape than those for Ancient Greek generally—and, indeed, for most (if not all) ancient languages. But we need also to be aware of the several problems that have been outlined by John Lee. While we have little choice but to continue to make use of the reference tools at our disposal, we ought to develop a critical engagement of them, rather than imagining that their conclusions have descended from on high.

BDAG remains enormously useful in pointing out ancient sources in which lexemes are found and for outlining the range of senses for each lexeme. However, it is not necessary to agree with the sense that BDAG allocates for each particular use of the lexeme in question. For example, in my monograph *Paul and Union with Christ*, I made frequent use of BDAG in the study of certain Greek prepositions.[41] The range of senses and functions identified for each preposition was enormously useful. However, I found myself regularly disagreeing with the sense attributed to certain prepositions in particular texts. Accordingly, the best approach is to make use of the range of senses outlined in the lexicon, but to examine the use of the lexeme in its context to establish which sense is most likely in that instance. Many times, BDAG will prove to be correct in its sense allocation, but it should not be assumed thus.

Louw and Nida is likewise a helpful tool. The chief advantage here, as anticipated above, is that lexemes can be compared to synonymous or otherwise related words. Since words are mutually defining, Louw and Nida's work represents a great advance in our ability to understand Greek vocabulary with precision.

3.4 Further Reading

Barr, James. *The Semantics of Biblical Language.* Oxford: Oxford
    University Press, 1961. Reprint: Eugene, OR: Wipf & Stock, 2004.
Black, David Alan. *Linguistics for Students of New Testament Greek: A*
    Survey of Basic Concepts and Applications. Second edition. Grand

---

41. Constantine R. Campbell, *Paul and Union with Christ: An Exegetical and Theological Study* (Grand Rapids: Zondervan, 2012).

Rapids: Baker, 1995.

Danker, Frederick William. "Lexical Evolution and Linguistic Hazard." Pages 1–31 in *Biblical Greek Language and Lexicography: Essays in Honor of Frederick W. Danker*. Edited by Bernard A. Taylor, John A. L. Lee, Peter R. Burton, and Richard E. Whitaker. Grand Rapids: Eerdmans, 2004.

————. "Review of *Lexical Semantics of the Greek New Testament*, by E. A. Nida and J. P. Louw, 1992." *JBL* 113 (1994): 532–33.

Lee, John A. L. *A History of New Testament Lexicography*. SBG 8. New York: Peter Lang, 2003.

————. "The Present State of Lexicography of Ancient Greek." Pages 66–74 in *Biblical Greek Language and Lexicography: Essays in Honor of Frederick W. Danker*. Edited by Bernard A. Taylor, John A. L. Lee, Peter R. Burton, and Richard E. Whitaker. Grand Rapids: Eerdmans, 2004.

Roberts, Terry. "A Review of BDAG." Pages 53–65 in *Biblical Greek Language and Lexicography: Essays in Honor of Frederick W. Danker*. Edited by Bernard A. Taylor, John A. L. Lee, Peter R. Burton, and Richard E. Whitaker. Grand Rapids: Eerdmans, 2004.

Silva, Moisés. *Biblical Words and Their Meaning: An Introduction to Lexical Semantics*. Revised edition. Grand Rapids: Zondervan, 1994.

CHAPTER 4

DEPONENCY AND THE MIDDLE VOICE

For Greek, then, what needs to be laid aside is the notion of
deponency. —*Bernard A. Taylor*

4.1 Introduction

A paradigm shift is taking place in our understanding of Greek voice, with particular reference to the concept of deponency. A small but powerful movement is calling for the displacement of deponency, and the arguments put forth require careful consideration. The purpose of this chapter is to provide a brief review of the discussion thus far, since an awareness of the development of ideas aids our comprehension and assessment of the current state of affairs. Most of the chapter surveys the contributions of key scholars, with space given toward the end for assessment of the central arguments, remaining challenges, and some suggested ways forward.[1]

4.2 A Brief History

To understand why the validity of deponency is being questioned—or outright rejected—it is helpful to see that this trend has grown slowly over the course of the twentieth century, beginning with some well-known grammarians who raised question marks about the category, and climaxing with the

---

1. Much of this chapter originates from my conference paper, "Defective Deponency? A Review of the Discussion So Far," presented at the 2010 SBL conference in Atlanta.

Greek Language and Linguistics Unit of the 2010 SBL conference in Atlanta, at which the presenters uniformly rejected the legitimacy of deponency.

4.2.1 James Hope Moulton

In the 1908 third edition of his grammar, Moulton begins his discussion of the middle voice with verbs that are found with active only or middle only forms, both of which should be given the "unsatisfactory name 'deponent,'"[2] if that name is retained for either. In other words, why call middle-only verbs *deponent* and not also active-only verbs?

On the relation between middle and passive voices, Moulton believes that there is little that distinguishes them: "the two voices were not differentiated with anything like the same sharpness as is inevitable in analytic formation such as we use in English."[3] "The dividing line is a fine one at best."[4] This virtual indistinguishability between middle and passive voices will have implications for the following discussion.

4.2.2 A. T. Robertson

In the 1934 fourth edition of Robertson's grammar, his initial discussion of deponency is found in the section ominously entitled "The So-Called 'Deponent' Verbs."[5] He agrees with Moulton's assertion that the term should be applied to all three voices if any, but goes a step further by saying that "the truth is that it should not be used at all."[6]

Drawing on the parallel of Sanskrit, Robertson points out that in Greek "some verbs were used in both active and middle in all tenses ... some verbs in some tenses in one and some in the other ... some in one voice only."[7] Consequently, such verbs are better regarded as "defective" rather than "deponent." Thus, Robertson concludes that "the name 'deponent' is very unsatisfactory. It is used to mean the laying aside of the active form in the case of verbs that have no active voice. But these verbs in most cases never had an active voice."[8]

---

2. Moulton, *Grammar*, 153.
3. Ibid., 162.
4. Ibid.
5. Robertson, *Grammar*, 332.
6. Ibid.
7. Ibid., 332–33.
8. Ibid., 811–12.

4.2.3 Neva F. Miller

After Robertson, there were a few voices of discontent with the term "deponency," such as K. L. McKay, who described the label as "not entirely necessary in terms of ancient Greek itself."[9] In an appendix on deponent verbs in Friberg's lexicon,[10] published in 2000, Neva Miller did not set out to challenge the notion of deponency in an explicit fashion, yet her analysis nevertheless drives in that direction. Miller's main concern was to revitalize our understanding of the middle voice, which has been neglected because of the assumption that verbs without active voice forms are deponent rather than properly middle.

By exploring a representative selection of so-called deponent verbs, Miller demonstrated that these could be understood as middle in voice, which thus suggests "an alternate way of thinking about them,"[11] in which "the self-involvement of the subject in the action or state expressed in the verb is highlighted."[12] While Miller did not attempt an exhaustive study, and she put her conclusions tentatively,[13] nevertheless she suggests that "if the verbs in the above classes are understood as true middles—and if active forms could not have expressed such concepts—then it may be that categorizing such verbs as deponent is no longer relevant."[14]

4.2.4 Bernard A. Taylor

It was not until 2001 that Bernard Taylor issued a direct challenge to the concept of deponency. Taylor's paper presented at the 2001 SBL conference challenged not only the term "deponency" but also the phenomenon it supposedly describes, and his arguments reached fuller expression in his contribution to the 2004 Danker Festschrift.[15]

Taylor points out that the label "deponent" is a Latin term, which arose

---

9. McKay, *A New Syntax*, 25.
10. Neva Miller, "A Theory of Deponent Verbs," Appendix 2, in *Analytical Lexicon of the Greek New Testament* (ed. Barbara Friberg, Timothy Friberg, and Neva F. Miller; Grand Rapids: Baker, 2000), 423–30.
11. Ibid., 426.
12. Ibid.
13. Ibid., 430; "I do not claim that all the dust surrounding the issue of deponency is settled.... Much study remains to be done on the matter of deponency."
14. Ibid., 429.
15. Bernard A. Taylor, "Deponency and Greek Lexicography," in *Biblical Greek Language and Lexicography: Essays in Honor of Frederick W. Danker* (ed. Bernard A. Taylor et al.; Grand Rapids: Eerdmans, 2004), 167–76.

from the fact that "by the Renaissance, Latin grammar and terminology had become the norm and were used to describe and delimit other languages."[16] Taylor contends that deponency was a Latin notion transferred to Greek and had not existed in that language before.[17]

Taylor also points out that with the importation of the Latin category, an assumption about the nature of the Greek verbal system is smuggled in, namely, that a verb is not "normal" unless its forms occur in the active voice.[18] Thus he objects that "the subject of middle verbs is still the doer of the action, even if the subject bears a different relation to the result of the action than a verb in the active voice."[19] These middle verbs have not "laid aside" a form, since the middle is as old as the active. "Nor have they laid aside meaning, since the middle shares with the active having the subject perform the action."[20]

4.2.5 Carl W. Conrad

In 2002, classical Greek scholar Carl Conrad argued that "the conception of deponency is fundamentally wrong-headed and detrimental to understanding the phenomenon of 'voice' in ancient Greek."[21] The key to Conrad's discussion is that "the fundamental polarity in the Greek voice system is not *active-passive* but *active-middle*."[22] As such, the middle voice needs to be understood in its own right and ought to regain the significance that the artificial category of deponency took from it.

In fact, in somewhat of a reversal of standard thinking, Conrad argues that it is a mistake to understand the *passive* voice as an independent category with its own morphological paradigms. Instead, the distinction between "middle" and "passive" was not "sufficiently important to require distinct morphoparadigms to indicate the distinct notions."[23] In light of this, so-called "middle/passive" forms should be viewed as one set of forms that are secondarily capable of conveying passive function.[24]

---

16. Ibid., 170–71.
17. Ibid., 171.
18. Ibid., 173.
19. Ibid.
20. Ibid.
21. Carl Conrad, "New Observations on Voice in the Ancient Greek Verb." Unpublished paper, 2002. www.artsci.wustl.edu/~cwconrad/docs/NewObsAncGrkVc.pdf, 1–2.
22. Ibid., 3.
23. Ibid., 7–8.
24. Ibid., 8.

This inevitably raises the question of the aorist stem that has separate "middle" and "passive" forms. To this, Conrad argues that "the -θη- endings were *never* essentially passive, even if they were often used and understood as indicating a passive sense to the verb in question; rather the -θη- endings are forms developed in the course of the history of ancient Greek to function for the *middle-passive* in the aorist and future tenses."[25] In other words, the paradigms currently labeled "middle-passive" *and* those labeled "passive" should *both* bear the label "middle-passive,"[26] and context will determine whether a middle or passive sense is meant in each instance.[27]

4.2.6 Rutger J. Allan

Also in 2002, Ancient Greek linguist Rutger Allan's dissertation on the middle voice was completed.[28] The dissertation treats the middle voice, not deponency per se, but his conclusions have major implications for the discussion about deponency. Moreover, Allan explicitly rejects the label of deponency:

> *Media tantum* (or *middle-only* verbs) are middle verbs that do not have active counterparts. They are sometimes called *deponentia*, a term borrowed from Latin grammar. This term is less adequate since it suggests that these verbs have "laid off" (i.e. lost) their active forms. There is no historical evidence that this is what actually happened.[29]

The burden of Allan's dissertation is to uncover a semantic element common to all uses of the middle voice (including those middles normally designated "deponent").[30] His conclusion is that "the middle voice expresses the presence of the semantic property of *subject-affectedness*."[31] This means that all Greek middle verbs—regardless of whether they are "middle-only" verbs (*media tantum*) or also have an active form—indicate that the grammatical subject of the verb is involved in the action somehow. This does not imply that active voice verbs indicate an *absence* of subject-affectedness; instead, "the active voice must be considered as

---

25. Ibid., 3.
26. Ibid., 11.
27. Ibid., 13.
28. Rutger J. Allan, "The Middle Voice in Ancient Greek: A Study in Polysemy," Dissertation presented to the University of Amsterdam, 2002. Allan's thesis is available for download at http://dare.uva.nl/record/108528.
29. Ibid., 2, n. 4.
30. Ibid., 3.
31. Ibid., 185 [italics are original].

neutral to the element of subject-affectedness."[32] Thus, active verbs *may* indicate subject-affectedness, but middle verbs are *marked* for it — they will always indicate subject-affectedness.

In a way, Allan's position with regard to deponency is similar to Neva Miller's conclusions, in that the category becomes unnecessary if a comprehensive understanding of the middle voice can be achieved. Allan is more forthright than Miller in rejecting deponency, but the logic is similar in that a cohesive understanding of the middle voice will render deponency irrelevant.

4.2.7 Jonathan T. Pennington

Following Taylor and Miller, Jonathan Pennington, first publishing on this topic in 2003 then again in 2009,[33] points to the importation of the Latin concept of deponency and a weak understanding of the middle voice as the factors leading to the current situation. Moving beyond their lead, however, Pennington develops a defense against two potential problems for the "anti-deponency" position: the existence of active verbs that take middle future forms (i.e., "partial deponents") and so-called "passive deponents."

On the issue of middle future forms, Pennington refers to the cross-linguistic phenomenon in which there is a close affinity between the middle voice and future tense.[34] Since the future tense can only present an event as a "mental disposition or intention," the middle voice serves well to communicate that sense.[35] This does not mean that all futures will be middle, of course, but it explains why some are.

On the issue of passive deponents, Pennington regards these as middle in voice but with passive forms.[36] The reason these middle verbs have passive forms is that "the middle voice form was losing ground to the passive," such that the passive forms are gradually replacing the older middle forms.[37] Labeling this phenomenon as a "slipping of register," Pennington

---

32. Ibid., 19 [italics are original].
33. Jonathan T. Pennington, "Deponency in Koine Greek: The Grammatical Question and the Lexicographical Dilemma," *TJ* 24 (2003): 55–76; Jonathan T. Pennington, "Setting Aside 'Deponency': Rediscovering the Greek Middle Voice in New Testament Studies," in *The Linguist as Pedagogue: Trends in the Teaching and Linguistic Analysis of the Greek New Testament* (ed. Stanley E. Porter and Matthew Brook O'Donnell; New Testament Monographs 11; Sheffield: Sheffield Phoenix, 2009), 181–203.
34. Pennington, "Setting Aside 'Deponency,'" 194–95.
35. Ibid., 194.
36. Ibid., 195.
37. Ibid.

suggests that in such cases, the aorist middle should have been employed, but because such forms are disappearing, "it is not uncommon for authors to accidentally utilize the more common aorist passive forms."[38]

4.2.8 Stratton L. Ladewig

In his dissertation completed in 2010, Stratton Ladewig has spoken in *defense* of the term "deponency."[39] Since his is the only work that gives an up-to-date defense of deponency at a serious level, it is necessary to engage his key theses. While Taylor has pointed out that the term "deponency" was not applied to Greek until the Latinization of the Renaissance period, Ladewig argues that, while the *term* is not found in the earliest Greek grammars, the *concept* is.[40] If this claim were to be substantiated, it would, of course, offer a powerful argument in defense of deponency.

In his reading of Dionysius Thrax and Apollonius Dyscolus, Ladewig detects their wrestling with the middle voice. Dionysius says: "There are three voices: active, passive, middle; active such as τύπτω, but passive such as τύπτομαι, but middle representing at one time active and at another time passive."[41] Ladewig interprets this statement to mean that Dionysius here acknowledges a discrepancy between form and function; in other words: a verb may be middle in form, but active or passive in meaning.[42] This apparent mismatch between form and function is what the later term "deponency" addresses.

However, I would suggest that this is a misreading of Dionysius Thrax. It is more likely that he is acknowledging that the middle voice is very broad in its meaning, capable of active and passive functions and everything in between. The same can be said about Apollonius Dyscolus.[43] Thus, Ladewig's most powerful argument—that while the term did not exist, the concept of deponency was understood by the Greeks—is not, in my opinion, successful.

The most serious problem with Ladewig's work, however, is that he assumes a narrow understanding of the middle voice that is largely limited

---

38. Ibid., 195–96.
39. Stratton, L. Ladewig, "Defining Deponency: An Investigation into Greek Deponency of the Middle and Passive Voices in the Koine Period." Unpublished doctoral dissertation, Dallas Theological Seminary, 2010.
40. Ladewig, "Defining Deponency," 36, 41.
41. Thracis, *Ars Grammatica*, 46–53. The English translation is produced by Ladewig, 27.
42. Ladewig, "Defining Deponency," 28–30.
43. Ibid., 32–33.

to reflexive and reciprocal functions. If one assumes such a narrow set of functions for the middle voice, then it is natural that one would detect deponency ubiquitously, since middle forms are *apparently* active in many instances. If, however, one accepts the possibility that the middle voice is much broader in its meaning—as Allan asserts, and as I suggest Dionysius and Apollonius assert—then there is no need for the category (nor the term) of deponency, and in fact it proves to be a mistaken understanding of Greek voice.

4.2.9 The 2010 SBL Conference

In November of 2010, a session of SBL's Biblical Greek Language and Linguistics Unit was devoted to the question of deponency. The four presenters (Stanley Porter, Bernard Taylor, Jonathan Pennington, and I) each argued that the category of deponency ought to be abandoned. Notably, Taylor provided a history of the term "deponency," proving its genesis in the Renaissance period.[44] And Pennington revised his views about passive deponents, falling in line with Conrad.

It is rare at SBL to find four presenters who completely agree on a controversial topic, and the session seemed to have historic importance. So uniform were the conclusions, in fact, that two years later an SBL session was dedicated to the middle voice, playfully entitled "We Killed Deponency. Now What?" While not all Greek professors are yet convinced that deponency should be abandoned, there is a consensus among most scholars working in the field that it should.

4.3 "Setting Aside" Deponency

Since a survey of several different scholarly contributions can become confusing, especially when the developments between them do not proceed in a linear fashion, it is worth drawing out a few threads from the previous discussion.

---

44. Taylor's paper is being published as "Greek Deponency: The Historical Perspective," in *Biblical Greek in Context* (ed. T. V. Evans and J. K. Aitken; Leuven: Peeters, 2015).

4.3.1 Terminological Reservations

First, there are those who take issue with the *term* "deponency," but do not necessarily offer a comprehensive alternative for the *category* that the term represents. Moulton, Robertson, and McKay fit here, and while the former two scholars press the category hard, they do not go so far as to abandon it.

4.3.2 Reconstituting the Middle Voice

Second, Miller comes close to displacing the category of deponency simply by allowing the possibility that verbs that are middle in form may be middle in meaning. By reading so-called deponent verbs as genuine middles, she witnesses the category of deponency virtually vanish before her eyes. She does not, however, formulate a reconstruction of the voice system in the wake of deponency's disappearance but simply demonstrates that a reconstituted appreciation of the middle voice seems to make deponency redundant.

4.3.3 Categorical Rejection

Third, there is the group of scholars who wholly reject the label and category of deponency. Taylor, Conrad, Allan, and Pennington wish to see the term disappear and require the reformulation of our understanding of the voice system to better reflect the history and usage of the language. This latter requirement is noteworthy, since displacing deponency is not quite as simple as removing the concept from our reconstructions of the voice system.

4.3.4 Evaluation

In evaluating these strands, all three have merit, but the final solution can only be found via the third. It is not enough simply to dislike the term "deponency," nor is it sufficient simply to reconstitute the middle voice, though of course that will be part of the solution. If we are persuaded by these challenges to deponency, we must rethink our entire approach to voice.

In light of these critiques, we should seriously consider abandoning the category of deponency, notwithstanding Ladewig's arguments in its defense. The questions that remain, however, will be how to assimilate the problems of so-called "mixed deponents" and "passive deponents," and how to make responsible assertions about voice, given that the matter appears to be more complex than simply recognizing morphology.

4.4 Remaining Challenges

4.4.1 "Mixed Deponents"

It remains an open question as to why some active verbs have middle future forms. Pennington and Egbert Bakker have made similar attempts at a solution, linking the future tense with volitionality and intention, thus explaining why some verbs become middle in their future forms.[45] While this seems possible, it is not overly compelling.

This kind of solution makes philological assumptions related to philosophical reflections about futurity. Just because—when we stop to think about it—the future is unknown and our speaking about it must, in the end, be speculative or volitional, this reality does not necessarily correspond with our use of language. The fact is that people often *do* speak of the future as certain, even if it is not. If I say that I will finish writing this chapter in a few minutes, my use of language does not reflect any uncertainty about this future reality, even though it is possible that an earthquake, a heart attack, or a raging bull might prevent it from coming to pass. Consequently, a solution that relies on the volitional nature of the future tense to explain why some verbs revert to the middle voice in the future is unlikely, since volition is not inherent to the future tense.

4.4.2 "Passive Deponents"

A more serious problem is the existence of so-called "passive deponent" verbs, and the solutions offered by Conrad and Pennington both have vulnerabilities. Pennington's original solution is simplest,[46] relabeling "passive deponent" forms as middles that employ passive endings. A problem here is that the suggestion is speculative and therefore may be a little too convenient. Having said as much, Moulton does come to Pennington's aid when he acknowledges that "the -θην aorist was originally developed, according to Wackernagel's practically certain conjecture, out of the old aorist middle."[47] However, Pennington's diachronic solution runs in the opposite direction: while Moulton and Wackernagel have middle forms

---

45. Egbert J. Bakker, "Voice, Aspect and Aktionsart Middle and Passive in Ancient Greek," in *Voice: Form and Function* (ed. Barbara Fox and Paul J. Hopper; Amsterdam: John Benjamins, 1994), 29.
46. He later changed his approach to this question; see §4.2.9, above.
47. Moulton, *Grammar*, 161.

becoming passives, he sees passives (effectively) becoming middles again. Pennington's solution may also create another type of deponency, in which the middle form has been laid aside and the passive form has taken its place, thus getting us back on to that merry-go-round.

Conrad argues that "passive" forms are really an alternate set of middle-passive forms, so that both sets of middle-passive forms can express either middle or passive meanings, depending on lexeme and context. His understanding of the Greek voice system is that there is a paradigm for the active voice (A) and two paradigms for the middle-passive voice (MP1 and MP2), as opposed to the standard configuration of paradigms as Active, Middle, Passive. MP1 and MP2 are therefore two paradigms for the same semantic meaning, analogous to first and second aorist forms. This finds some support in Moulton's observation of the virtual indistinguishability between middle and passive voices, and Wackernagel's conjecture that passive forms developed out of the middle.[48]

While this is a bold suggestion that holds some promise, two questions come to mind. First, what do we make of verbs that have middle *and* passive forms (traditionally understood)? Does not the existence of both forms for the same lexeme suggest a meaningful semantic difference between them?[49] Second, is it true that some middle forms are actually passive in meaning? This may be the case, but if it cannot be established, then Conrad's framework could be threatened.

It is possible that Pennington or Conrad is correct, or that some other approach will solve the problem, but that is unclear at this point. What remains clear is that the phenomenon of so-called "passive deponents" currently presents a challenge to the anti-deponency movement.

4.4.3 Lexical Complexities

A more positive challenge remains in which the relationship between lexeme and voice requires further investigation. As Bakker and Conrad have acknowledged, there is a complex interweaving between lexeme and voice, perhaps parallel to that between lexeme and verbal aspect. If voice is not simply determined through morphological realization but is dependent upon lexeme and context, then there is much more work to be done here.

---

48. See §4.2.1, above, and ibid., 162.
49. This question was posed by my former student Ben Hudson, in his unpublished essay, "A 'Paradigm' Shift: Getting Pragmatic about Greek Voice," Moore Theological College, Sydney, 2010.

4.5 Ways Forward

If deponency is to be removed from the way we understand, describe, and teach the Greek voice system, it will be necessary to begin thinking through the various ways forward. A few preliminary thoughts follow in anticipation of more robust discussions over future years.

4.5.1 Understanding the Middle Voice

Neva Miller has provided a good starting point for improving our capacity with the middle voice. Her work ought to be studied carefully and perhaps even reproduced in a more accessible form, independent of Friberg's lexicon. Future grammars would do well to incorporate her analysis of the various uses of the middle voice.

For deeper reflection and research, Rutger Allan's dissertation provides substantial grounds for understanding the middle voice in the absence of deponency. Future dissertations on the topic will necessarily engage his work as the most important treatment of the Greek middle voice we have seen for some time.

4.5.2 Developing Voice–Lexeme Sophistication

The relation between voice and lexeme is not as easily addressed, and I fear this will take a great deal of time and effort. In the meantime, a useful suggestion has been posed by my former student, Ben Hudson. He views voice as a pragmatic outworking of the combination of morphology, lexeme, and context. In this way, voice may be seen in parallel to *Aktionsart*, which is a pragmatic outworking of the combination of aspect, lexeme, and context.[50]

4.5.3 Teaching and Learning

Perhaps most significant is the need to develop ways to teach Greek without the category of deponency. Incorporating Allan's and Miller's work on the middle voice will be useful here. It will also be necessary to acknowledge that some "passives" will actually be middle in meaning, even if it is not yet possible to explain with certainty why this is so.

It is welcome news that there are now at least two Greek grammars that

---

50. Ibid.

do not use deponency in their teaching of voice. Porter, Reed, and O'Donnell's *Fundamentals of New Testament Greek* teaches the middle voice with only the following brief note on deponency:

> Some verbs do not have all three voice forms in every tense, and some older grammars label such verbs **deponents**. **Deponency** is understood to mean that the middle voice form (or sometimes the passive voice form) performs the function of the active voice. Some grammarians, however, have questioned the category of deponency, as do we. In our view, every verb expresses the meaning of its voice form, even when other forms — such as the active voice — may not exist. That is, in interpreting the meaning of a verb form, we should try to understand its voice.[51]

Rodney Decker's *Reading Koine Greek* follows suit.[52] Both grammars are notably sophisticated in their treatment of advances in Greek linguistics, including voice and the rejection of deponency. They have set a new standard for modern grammars of New Testament Greek.

4.6 Further Reading

Allan, Rutger J. "The Middle Voice in Ancient Greek: A Study in Polysemy," Dissertation presented to the University of Amsterdam, 2002. http://dare.uva.nl/record/108528.

Conrad, Carl. "New Observations on Voice in the Ancient Greek Verb." Unpublished paper, 2002. See www.artsci.wustl.edu/~cwconrad/docs/NewObsAncGrkVc.pdf.

Miller, Neva F. "A Theory of Deponent Verbs." Pages 423–30, Appendix 2, in *Analytical Lexicon of the Greek New Testament*. Edited by Barbara Friberg, Timothy Friberg, and Neva F. Miller. Grand Rapids: Baker, 2000.

Pennington, Jonathan T. "Deponency in Koine Greek: The Grammatical Question and the Lexicographical Dilemma." *TJ* 24 (2003): 55–76.

———. "Setting Aside 'Deponency': Rediscovering the Greek Middle Voice in New Testament Studies." Pages 181–203 in *The Linguist as Pedagogue: Trends in the Teaching and Linguistic Analysis of the Greek*

---

51. Stanley E. Porter, Jeffrey T. Reed, and Matthew Brook O'Donnell, *Fundamentals of New Testament Greek* (Grand Rapids: Eerdmans, 2010), 125 [emphases are original].

52. Rodney J. Decker, *Reading Koine Greek: An Introduction and Integrated Workbook* (Grand Rapids: Baker, 2014), xxvi, 252–53.

New Testament. Edited by Stanley E. Porter and Matthew Brook O'Donnell. New Testament Monographs 11. Sheffield: Sheffield Phoenix, 2009.

Taylor, Bernard A. "Deponency and Greek Lexicography." Pages 167–76 in *Biblical Greek Language and Lexicography: Essays in Honor of Frederick W. Danker.* Edited by Bernard A. Taylor et al. Grand Rapids: Eerdmans, 2004.

CHAPTER 5

VERBAL ASPECT AND *AKTIONSART*

We do not care for people messing with our paradigms.
— *George H. Guthrie*

5.1 Introduction

Verbal aspect has been the most controversial issue within Greek studies in the last twenty-five years. While aspect has been a topic of scholarly discussion since the nineteenth century, the last quarter century has seen the revitalization of the subject, some intense debates about the nature of the Greek verbal system, and many fruitful insights that are of importance for exegesis and translation. Among aspect scholars there is a good level of consensus about a number of significant issues. There are, however, some areas of discussion that remain controversial.

Some of this chapter will overlap with my textbook introduction to the subject, *Basics of Verbal Aspect in Biblical Greek*.[1] It is not possible here to cover material to the same degree as that book (since the book you're reading now introduces several other topics as well). Furthermore, the previous book allocates a significant portion of its space to exegetical application, which is not a main purpose here. Careful study of *Basics of Verbal Aspect* is recommended for the student who wishes to understand and apply the insights gleaned from aspect studies.

---

1. Constantine R. Campbell, *Basics of Verbal Aspect in Biblical Greek* (Grand Rapids: Zondervan, 2008).

Furthermore, that book is intended to equip the reader to engage the more serious literature on the subject, such as the monographs by Porter, Fanning, and others. It is hoped that this chapter will lead students to my *Basics* book, which will in turn lead to the more fulsome literature on the subject. A distinct contribution of this chapter—alongside a brief introduction to the topic—is to canvas some key developments in the discussion that have taken place since the publication of *Basics of Verbal Aspect* in 2008.[2]

5.2 What Is Verbal Aspect?

While some other terminology will be introduced in the next section, it is important to define verbal aspect here. There are different ways in which the term *aspect* is used within linguistics, but the standard meaning—and that adopted most widely within Greek linguistics—is that aspect refers to *viewpoint*. The viewpoint is the way in which a verb is used to view an action, either from *outside* the action or from *inside* it. Buist Fanning describes aspect thus:

> The action can be viewed from a reference-point *within* the action, without reference to the beginning or end-point of the action, but with a focus instead on its internal structure or make-up. Or the action can be viewed from a vantage-point *outside* the action, with focus on the whole action from beginning to end, but without reference to its internal structure.[3]

The external viewpoint (outside the action) is known as *perfective* aspect; the internal viewpoint (inside the action) is known as *imperfective* aspect. Perfective aspect views an action "from a distance," as a whole, and is often used to present an action in summary form—*this happened, that happened*—without reference to how it happened and without viewing it

---

2. Greek verbal aspect is the chief area in which my own research in Greek has been focused, with two monographs alongside the textbook introduction. Therefore, my perspectives and conclusions will naturally feature in this chapter in a way that is more prominent than in other chapters of this book. It is not my intention, however, simply to "push my own barrow," but to introduce the reader to the important scholars, advances within the field, and issues of controversy. Regarding the latter, the reader will forgive me if my evaluations of certain controversies are self-endorsing! This is because I happen to believe they are correct—I wouldn't hold such views otherwise—but my intention nevertheless is to present a fair depiction of the state of affairs, and the reader is of course free to form their own conclusions.
3. Fanning, *Verbal Aspect*, 27.

as though happen*ing*. Imperfective aspect views an action "up close," from within it, and is often used to present an action as unfolding or in progress—*this was happening, that happens*—without reference to the whole action.

A standard illustration used for describing verbal aspect involves a reporter who is to report on a street parade.[4] If the reporter views the street parade from a helicopter, he sees the whole parade from a distance. He can describe the parade in a general way because he sees the whole thing, rather than seeing its details up close. This viewpoint represents *perfective aspect*. It is the view from the outside—the external viewpoint. If, however, that same reporter views the same street parade from the level of the street rather than from up in a helicopter, his view of the parade is different. This time the reporter is up close to the parade and watches as it unfolds before him. Rather than seeing the parade from a distance and as a whole, the parade is now seen from within. This viewpoint represents *imperfective aspect*. It is the view from the inside—the internal viewpoint.

Linguists agree that the Greek aorist is perfective in aspect—it is used to convey actions as a whole, and it frequently presents them in a summary fashion. Linguists also agree that the Greek present and imperfect are imperfective in aspect—they are used to convey an action as unfolding, frequently in progress or as a state. There is, however, lively debate about the aspect of the Greek perfect, pluperfect, and future tense-forms.

5.2.1 Distinctions between Tense, Aktionsart, and Aspect[5]

Verbal aspect is often discussed in relation to two other terms: tense and *Aktionsart*. It is important that careful delineation is made between the three terms.

5.2.1.1 Tense. In Greek, the verbs have traditionally been labeled as tenses. The aorist is a past tense, the present is a present tense, the future is a future tense, and so on. While there are more technical ways of defining tense, it normally refers to grammatical temporal reference. That is, referring to a particular time-frame is the built-in meaning of a tense. It doesn't

---

4.   The illustration originates with Isačenko and is adopted by Porter. See A. V. Isačenko, *Grammatičeskij stroj russkogo jazyka v sopostavlenii s slovatskim: Morfologija* (Bratislava: The Slovak Academy of Sciences Press, 1960); Porter, *Verbal Aspect*, 91.

5.   This section is taken from my *Basics of Verbal Aspect*, 21–22.

take long when beginning to read the Greek New Testament, however, to discover that tense is not the whole story. We quickly discover verbs in the present tense that refer to the past. There are also past tenses that refer to the present. There are even future-referring past tenses. Furthermore, what's the difference between two past tenses in Greek? Tense cannot be the whole story with Greek verbs, since there is a difference in meaning between the aorist and imperfect—both past tenses. The nineteenth century answer to this question—the difference between two past tenses in Greek—was not expressed in aspectual terms (perfective versus imperfective). Rather, they tried to define the difference in terms of the type of action, or *Aktionsart*.

5.2.1.2 *Aktionsart*. This word literally means "type of action." There are various types of action. There are punctiliar actions, iterative actions, ingressive actions, and so on. The category of *Aktionsart* describes the kind of action that took place. If it happened as a once-off, instantaneous event, it is called punctiliar. If the action was repeated over and over, it is called iterative. If the action is seen as beginning, it is called ingressive.

Early on in the academic discussion about such things, there was much confusion between *Aktionsart* and aspect. These days there is a general consensus as to the difference, and it is vital that we properly understand the distinction. *Aktionsart* refers to how an action actually takes place—what sort of action it is. Aspect refers to viewpoint—how the action is viewed. They are two different categories.

Take Romans 5:14 as an example. In that verse we are told that "death reigned from the time of Adam to the time of Moses." The verb "reigned" expresses perfective aspect. This is the view from the helicopter. We are presented with a summary of what happened; we are told simply that it happened. This is the external viewpoint. But when we consider *Aktionsart* and ask what *actually* happened, we are able to say a range of other things. For starters, this action took a long time! There were many years between Adam and Moses. Death's reign between Adam and Moses was an ongoing, expansive event. This was not a once-off, instantaneous type of action. With this example, we can appreciate that there is a clear difference between aspect and *Aktionsart*. Aspect refers to how the action is viewed: it is viewed externally as a whole. *Aktionsart* refers to what actually happened: it was an ongoing event that spanned many years.

5.2.2 A Tense-Aspect Confusion

One of the best-known debates within Greek verbal aspect studies is whether or not *tense* actually exists as a grammatical (semantic) category within the indicative mood. Remember that Greek scholars used to think that tense existed through the whole verbal system, due to the incorrect assumption that Greek was like Latin in this regard. Georg Curtius broke this consensus in the nineteenth century, and from that point on, the consensus has been that tense is restricted to the indicative mood (see §1.2.4).

Porter and others have argued, in effect, that that reassessment did not go far enough, and Greek does not encode tense at the grammatical level at all. While some of the contours of that particular discussion will be outlined in the following sections, it is worth dispelling one common misconception. Often students, and even New Testament professors, will pit aspect against tense as though they are competing categories. They are not. In many languages, including English, aspect and tense happily coexist. While Porter and others claim that tense does not exist in Greek, those who oppose that position do not therefore claim that aspect does not exist. Fanning, for example, affirms the grammatical category of tense in Greek, but also strongly endorses verbal aspect; it's not one or the other.

Thus the reader should take note that even if one does not agree with the "non-tense" position, you still need to grapple with aspect. No serious scholar doubts its existence in Greek (or any language, for that matter). Whether or not aspect is a legitimate category for Greek is not a debated point, even within the most esoteric treatments of the subject.[6]

5.3 A Brief History

As with the matter of deponency addressed in the previous chapter, it is useful to outline the history of scholarly discussion about Greek verbal aspect in order to understand the trajectory of its development and the significance of certain issues today.[7]

---

6. To this end, the common term *verbal aspect theory* should be amended simply to *verbal aspect*. The use of the word *theory* in this instance does not mean *unproven* (as in the sentence, "Well, it's just a theory"), but rather refers to theoretical discussions about aspect. Nevertheless, people often assume the former meaning of the word *theory*, and therefore regard the whole discussion as an unproven hypothesis. This is not the case, and for that reason I endorse abandoning the (potentially) misleading expression altogether.

7. This section represents a summary of my *Basics of Verbal Aspect*, 26–32.

5.3.1 Georg Curtius

Curtius was a nineteenth-century comparative philologist (see §1.2.4) who differentiated between different types of meaning expressed by the present and aorist verbal stems, describing the former as a durative action and the latter as a "quickly-passing" action (symbolized as a "line" versus a "point"). His term for this distinction was *Zeitart* (lit., "type of time").

He also argued that, in contrast to Latin, temporal meaning in the Greek verbal system was limited to the indicative mood. It is taken for granted now that there is no tense outside the indicative mood in Greek, but this was not formally acknowledged prior to Curtius.

Curtius's insights were largely accepted in the late nineteenth century, though his term *Zeitart* was later replaced by the term *Aktionsart*, since "type of action" was regarded as being a more precise label than "type of time."

5.3.2 Early Twentieth Century

Curtius sparked a period of productive investigation into the nature of the Greek verbal system, from 1890 to 1910. The range of aspect-values that occur in Greek and Indo-European languages was explored, resulting in the creation of a multiplicity of categories and conflicting terminology. Confusion occurred through the interchangeable usage of the terms *Zeitart*, *Aktionsart*, and aspect.[8]

In the mid-1920s the following definitions were crystallized: *Aktionsart* refers to how the action actually occurs and is primarily lexically determined; aspect refers to a way of viewing an action (*Zeitart* was dropped). This distinction is widely held today.

5.3.3 K. L. McKay

While there were several important contributions made through the middle of the twentieth century, such as those of Holt[9] and Ruipérez,[10] none would have quite the same impact on the modern discussion as the work

---

8. See Fanning, *Verbal Aspect*, 9–33, for more on this period.
9. Jens Holt, *Études d'aspect* (Acta Jutlandica Aarsskrift for Aarhus Universitet 15.2; Copenhagen: Munksgaard, 1943).
10. Martín S. Ruipérez, *Estructura del Sistema de Aspectos y Tiempos del Verbo Griego Antiguo: Análisis Funcional Sincrónico* (Theses et Studia Philologica Salmanticensia 7; Salamanca: Colegio Trilingüe de la Universidad, 1954).

of K. L. McKay. McKay posited that there were three or four aspects, depending on whether the future was regarded as a proper aspect. The present and imperfect tense-forms are imperfective in aspect, while the aorist is perfective (using our terminology). The future is not really an aspect, but McKay labels it a quasi-fourth aspect anyway. The perfect and pluperfect tense-forms are stative in aspect.

McKay wrote about aspect for the following thirty years and became progressively stronger in his assertions. In fact, he ended up saying that aspect is not just more important than time in the Greek verb, but that time is not there at all, except by implication from the verb's relationship to its context.[11]

5.3.4 Stanley E. Porter

It was the contributions of Stanley E. Porter[12] and Buist M. Fanning[13] that put verbal aspect firmly on the map again. Porter analyzed Greek verbal aspect through the prism of *Systemic Functional Linguistics*. This includes a strong adherence to the distinction between semantics and pragmatics. Semantics refers to values that cannot be canceled; pragmatics vary according to lexeme and context (see §2.6.1).

Like McKay, Porter concludes that Greek is aspectual and not tense-based at all. Since temporal reference is not always expressed by the verb, it therefore cannot be a semantic value. Temporal reference must be pragmatic. Porter also acknowledges three aspects in the Greek verbal system: perfective, imperfective, and stative. He views the future as nonaspectual.

Porter's contribution has caused the fiercest debate. The "tenseless" position is still in the minority, being rejected by most grammarians.

5.3.5 Buist M. Fanning

Fanning's analysis is more traditional than Porter's in that tense is still a legitimate category, though aspect is dominant. According to Fanning, there are only two aspects (perfective and imperfective), not three, since stativity is properly regarded as an *Aktionsart* category, rather than an aspect.

Fanning provides a detailed analysis of how aspect interacts with

---

11. McKay, *A New Syntax*, 39.
12. Porter, *Verbal Aspect*.
13. Fanning, *Verbal Aspect*.

Aktionsart, indicating how each aspect interacts with certain lexical types to produce predictable *Aktionsart* outcomes.

5.3.6 Mari Broman Olsen

Olsen is the first major contributor to follow Porter and Fanning, and her work reflects the enormous debt that the modern discussion owes them.[14] Like Fanning, Olsen advocates only two aspects, again affirming that stativity is an *Aktionsart* value rather than being aspectual.

Olsen utilizes the semantic/pragmatic distinction to argue that some Greek verb forms are tenses and others are not. Those that are consistent in their temporal reference encode it at the semantic level and those that are not consistent do not encode temporal reference at the semantic level.

5.3.7 Rodney J. Decker

The burden of Decker's work is to test Porter's nontense position in the Gospel of Mark.[15] While initially skeptical toward Porter's approach, he later accepted its validity. Decker isolated one particular issue — the existence or otherwise of semantic temporal reference — and investigated that question thoroughly with reference to the Gospel of Mark.

5.3.8 Trevor V. Evans

Evans's work focuses on the verbal syntax of the Greek Pentateuch and how it matches the underlying Hebrew verb usage.[16] On the temporality issue, Evans argues that tense is indeed expressed by the verbal system. On the question of aspects, he also affirms the existence of two aspects, rejecting the category of stative aspect. He suggests that the Greek perfect is *imperfective* in aspect.

5.3.9 Constantine R. Campbell

In my two monographs on Greek verbal aspect (the first being on aspect in narrative, in particular), I follow McKay, Porter, and Decker on the issue of tense: it is not regarded as a semantic value of verbs in the indicative

---

14. Mari Broman Olsen, *A Semantic and Pragmatic Model of Lexical and Grammatical Aspect* (Outstanding Dissertations in Linguistics; New York: Garland, 1997).

15. Rodney J. Decker, *Temporal Deixis of the Greek Verb in the Gospel of Mark with Reference to Verbal Aspect* (SBG 10; New York: Peter Lang, 2001).

16. T. V. Evans, *Verbal Syntax in the Greek Pentateuch: Natural Greek Usage and Hebrew Interference* (Oxford: Oxford University Press, 2001).

mood (except for the future indicative), even though each tense-form has a characteristic temporal reference on the pragmatic level.[17] I argue that there are only two aspects, rejecting the category of stative aspect. Following Evans, I argue that the perfect and pluperfect tense-forms are imperfective in aspect.

5.3.10 David L. Mathewson

Mathewson focuses on the function of verbal aspect in the book of Revelation.[18] Addressing the phenomenon of shifting tenses in Revelation's visionary segments, Mathewson accounts for such behavior through verbal aspect. His understanding of aspect and its attendant issues follows Porter, and he provides a helpful genre-specific study.

5.3.11 Wally V. Cirafesi

Cirafesi offers an interesting study that applies verbal aspect to the Synoptic Problem.[19] It is an example of how verbal aspect can interact with long-standing problems within New Testament studies. Whereas traditional approaches to Synoptic parallels have assumed *Zeitart* or *Aktionsart* values for the verbal system, Cirafesi demonstrates that verbal aspect has stronger explanatory power in accounting for Synoptic tense-form differences.[20] As with Mathewson, Cirafesi follows Porter on theoretical issues.

5.3.12 Douglas S. Huffman

Huffman applies verbal aspect to prohibitions in the Greek New Testament.[21] He argues that verbal aspect provides better explanatory power than *Aktionsart* in understanding prohibitions. From a theoretical point of view, Huffman primarily follows Porter, though he follows my work in some key respects, including the interaction between pragmatics and semantics in the imperatival mood.[22]

---

17. Constantine R. Campbell, *Verbal Aspect (Indicative Mood)*; idem, *Verbal Aspect and Non-Indicative Verbs: Further Soundings in the Greek of the New Testament* (SBG 15; New York: Peter Lang, 2008).
18. David L. Mathewson, *Verbal Aspect in the Book of Revelation: The Function of Greek Verb Tenses in John's Apocalypse* (LBS 4; Leiden: Brill, 2010).
19. Wally V. Cirafesi, *Verbal Aspect in Synoptic Parallels: On the Method and Meaning of Divergent Tense-Form Usage in the Synoptic Passion Narratives* (LBS 7; Leiden: Brill, 2013).
20. Ibid., 166.
21. Huffman, *Verbal Aspect Theory and the Prohibitions*.
22. E.g., ibid., 100–103, 511.

5.4 Verbal Aspect and Temporal Reference

As mentioned above, one of the best-known debates regarding verbal aspect has been whether Greek tense-forms semantically encode temporal reference alongside aspect. While this debate is not resolved, a growing number of aspect scholars have indicated that they do not believe temporal reference to be a core constituent feature of verbs in the indicative mood. Included in this camp are McKay, Porter, Decker, Olsen (for some tense-forms), Campbell (except for the future tense form), Mathewson, Cirafesi, and Huffman. Fanning, Evans, and most Ancient Greek scholars outside New Testament Greek circles remain convinced that tense is a legitimate feature of the indicative verbal system.

As anticipated in §2.6.1, this issue is primarily decided on theoretical grounds. While all contributors affirm the linguistic distinction between semantics and pragmatics, there are differing levels of adherence to it. For those who do not regard temporal reference to be a semantic value of the verb, this is due to a strict adherence to the semantic–pragmatic distinction. The fact that the default temporal reference of all tense-forms (except the future) can be canceled means that it cannot be described as a semantic feature, since "semantic meanings are uniform and uncancelable, whereas pragmatic meanings are variable and cancelable (Grice 1975)."[23]

For those who are willing to endorse tense, the semantic–pragmatic distinction is not regarded as determinative for this issue. The instances in which tense-forms do not behave "according to the rules" are regarded as exceptions that prove the rule, allowing for language to be rather messy, not always compliant to our neat distinctions. Or, it is thought that tense can be "overruled" by aspect, so that the latter semantic category can render the former undone in certain instances. To my mind, these latter approaches, while common, are not linguistically robust enough. This, then, is an issue in which one's commitment to linguistic theory makes all the difference.

This is not to say, however, that tense-forms do not have *default* temporal functions; for example, aorist indicatives normally refer to the past (about 85 percent of instances), and present indicatives normally refer to the present (about 70 percent of instances). Those who adhere to the traditional position may claim that default temporal reference of such

---

23. Olsen, *Aspect*, 219.

forms speaks against the "aspect only" argument. If only aspect exists at the semantic level, how do we account for the clear patterns of temporal reference for indicative verb usage? Something can be said for the way that aspect typically functions, especially within narratives. Since aorists, for example, normally convey the narrative mainline within narrative texts, due to their perfective aspect, they will naturally be past-referring because they occur within past-referring contexts (narrative relates a story in the past). But this is only a partial solution; what about all the aorists that do *not* occur in narrative and yet so commonly refer to the past?

I have suggested a solution that analyzes the indicative tense-form system from the perspective of aspect in combination with spatial values.[24] I argue that Greek verbs semantically encode aspect along with the spatial value of remoteness or proximity (with the exception of the future tense-form, which encodes aspect and future temporal reference). The difference between this description of the semantics of verbs and that of traditional analyses is that semantic temporal reference ("tense") has been replaced by semantic spatial categories. In other words, while traditional analyses might regard verbs as encoding aspect and tense, I regard verbs as encoding aspect and remoteness, or aspect and proximity.

Following this, I claim that these spatial values of remoteness and proximity, which are semantic, normally express temporal reference on the pragmatic level. This means that remoteness, for example, will most often be pragmatically expressed as temporal remoteness—the action is past-referring. The spatial value of proximity will most often express temporal proximity—present time.[25]

While my theories about such spatial metaphors have been somewhat controversial—though they resonate in part with the work of Porter and his followers—they offer, I believe, good power of explanation for the usage

---

24. The following paragraphs are based on *Basics of Verbal Aspect*, 129–30.

25. "It should be understood that the terms 'remoteness' and 'proximity' are best understood as metaphors. When an aorist is used, it does not mean that the action occurred far away in a geographical sense, just because it encodes the spatial value of remoteness. For example, if I were to describe an action that occurred on my street, I am not forced to employ a proximate tense-form simply because it happened close to me physically. By the same token, if the action occurred in Cuba, I would not be forced to use a remote tense-form simply because Cuba is on the other side of the planet from Australia. To conclude that an action must have occurred at a physical distance because remoteness is encoded by the verb is to take remoteness literally—or concretely—rather than metaphorically" (ibid., 129–30).

of indicative verbs.[26] The default temporal expression of various forms is accounted for, since a pragmatic function of remoteness is the expression of past temporal reference, and a pragmatic function of proximity is the expression of present temporal reference. The uses of tense-forms that do not, however, conform to their default temporal references may also be accounted for by these spatial metaphors. There are other pragmatic functions that spatial metaphors can implicate beyond temporal reference, such that all usage of the aorist tense-form is explained, whether past-referring or not; all present tense-form usage is explained, whether present-referring or not.

No doubt the issue will remain controversial, as will my proposed solution to it, but one final note will conclude this section. While intense debate has occurred about tense and temporal reference in the Greek indicative mood, it is worth recognizing that it is not the most important issue within verbal aspect studies. This is because the temporal reference of most verbs is already fixed by context, whether one adopts a tenseless view or not. For example, it is simply not possible to regard most aorists in narrative as anything other than past-referring, because of the past-referring (narrative) contexts in which they are found. Such is the case for most instances of indicative mood verbs in Greek.

At the end of the day, whichever theory one accepts, the results of exegesis and translation will not end up very different. Having said that however, there are *some* instances in which one's understanding of "tense" does make a difference. This is especially relevant for cases for which traditional approaches to the verb have struggled to account, or have proposed somewhat fanciful explanations for the use of one tense-form when another would be expected.

An example is found in Romans 8:30, with its string of aorist indicatives:

οὓς δὲ **προώρισεν**, τούτους καὶ **ἐκάλεσεν·** καὶ οὓς **ἐκάλεσεν**, τούτους καὶ **ἐδικαίωσεν·** οὓς δὲ **ἐδικαίωσεν**, τούτους καὶ **ἐδόξασεν.**

---

26. It is worth noting that spatial theories of language are not "weird"; "The connection between space and time is arguably part of any language. Languages that encode time through their verbal system (i.e., languages that have tenses) did not necessarily always do this. All languages change over time, and one of the major changes that can be observed in the history of a number of languages is that the verbal system tends to begin as a spatial system, and later develops into a temporal one. In other words, the idea that verbs should primarily convey actions in a spatial, rather than temporal, way is not unusual in the history of language, and several languages began in such a way" (ibid., 131).

*And those he **predestined**, he also **called**; those he **called**, he also **justified**; those he **justified**, he also **glorified**.*

There is no real problem here for the first five aorists (προώρισεν, ἐκάλεσεν, ἐκάλεσεν, ἐδικαίωσεν, and ἐδικαίωσεν), since they naturally make sense as past-referring verbs.[27] But ἐδόξασεν causes some trouble for interpreters, since it is not clear in what sense believers have already been *glorified*. Moo's commentary is representative of the kinds of comments made about this aorist:

> Most interpreters conclude, probably rightly, that Paul is looking at the believer's glorification from the standpoint of God, who has already decreed that it should take place. While not yet experienced, the divine decision to glorify those who have been justified has already been made; the issue has been settled.[28]

While the theological sentiment here may be correct, is this really what Paul means by the use of this aorist? It is much more likely that Paul uses all six aorists for a different purpose, which is simply to present these truths in summary form. It may well be a summary "from God's perspective," but the point is that these actions are presented as a whole, not necessarily as already completed in the past. The most likely analysis, then, is that all of these aorists are gnomic in *Aktionsart* (see §5.6.1) and are therefore universal and timeless.[29]

5.5 Debate over the Greek Perfect

As mentioned above, the most controversial issue in the modern aspect discussion has been whether or not the Greek indicative mood semantically encodes tense. At the SBL Conference in Baltimore in 2013, however, the focus shifted to the issue of the perfect tense-form. The Greek Language and Linguistics Unit hosted a session entitled "The Perfect Storm," at which Porter, Fanning, and I presented three differing positions on the Greek perfect.

---

27. But only if Paul is referring to those who have *already* been called and justified. If he has in mind *all* those whom God has predestined, then four of these five aorists become problematic, since not all those predestined have yet been called and justified.
28. Douglas J. Moo, *The Epistle to the Romans* (NICNT; Grand Rapids: Eerdmans, 1996), 536.
29. See Campbell, *Basics of Verbal Aspect*, 88–89, 147.

While the perfect had not been the focus of controversy to this point, it is arguably a much more significant issue than temporality and tense. The reality is that even with a tenseless position, the temporal reference of most Greek indicatives in the New Testament is relatively fixed by context. There are a few instances here or there in which one's position on tense can make a significant exegetical difference in reading the text, but the situation is much more volatile for the Greek perfect. How one understands the semantic nature of the perfect indicative will affect each of its 836 instances in the New Testament. And while the temporality of tense-forms is relatively well controlled by context, many instances of the Greek perfect can be read quite differently depending on the semantic nature that is assumed.

Fanning holds to an aspectually-modified version of the traditional understanding of the perfect. That is, he claims that the Greek perfect indicates a past action with present consequences. Fanning's reformulation of this description, which was built on *Aktionsart* categories rather than aspect, attempts to recast the traditional notions of past action and present consequences through aspectual categories. Fanning critiqued Porter for claiming that the Greek perfect is stative in aspect, since stativity is an *Aktionsart*, not an aspect. He critiqued my view of the perfect by offering Greek examples that in his opinion are not well accommodated by imperfective aspect.

Porter regards the Greek perfect as stative in aspect and thus holds to a three-aspect schema for the verbal system. He defends this through the claim that Greek's three verbal stems indicate three aspects. Porter critiqued Fanning's approach as yielding too many exceptions (as with the traditional view). Porter critiqued my approach by repeating arguments made in his written critique, published in the 2011 Festschrift for D. A. Carson.[30] This was largely concerned with methodology, taking particular issue with my attempted inductive approach to solving the problem of the perfect.

I regard the perfect as imperfective in aspect. It is clear that many perfects are stative in *Aktionsart*, and in general linguistics imperfective aspect is regarded as the standard aspect through which to convey stativity. I repeated some of my previous critiques of Fanning and Porter's positions on the perfect and responded at some length to Porter's written

---

30. Stanley E. Porter, "Greek Linguistics and Lexicography," in *Understanding the Times: New Testament Studies in the 21st Century* (ed. Andreas J. Köstenberger and Robert W. Yarbrough; Wheaton: Crossway, 2011), 46–54.

critique of my views (mentioned above). I defended the claim that there are two aspects in Greek, not three, and that stativity is an *Aktionsart*, not an aspect.

In Porter's critique he cited half a dozen general linguists who "endorse the notion of stative aspect," but I demonstrated that Porter had misrepresented the views of each scholar. In fact, each linguist endorsed the fact that stativity is an *Aktionsart* and is conveyed by imperfective aspect. I also argued that there are, in fact, *four* verbal stems in Greek, not three—a fact that presents a major challenge to Porter's methodology, which assumes that three stems indicates three aspects.

The three papers and responses to each are being published in a collected volume in the Peter Lang series, Studies in Biblical Greek 17, with an introduction by D. A. Carson. For more information about "The Perfect Storm" and our responses to each other's arguments about the Greek perfect, *The Perfect Volume: Critical Discussion of the Semantics of the Greek Perfect Tense under Aspect Theory.*

It is most likely going to be up to others to decide who is right about the Greek perfect (if any of us are right). Porter, Fanning, and I will continue to present our best arguments and defenses. In addition to our ongoing interactions, Robert Crellin has recently completed a doctorate on the perfect at the University of Cambridge, so we will no doubt see more discussion from other contributors in future years.

5.6 Verbal Aspect and Exegesis

We turn now to consider some of the uses of verbal aspect in exegesis of the Greek text. After all, complex theoretical discussions are one thing, but how it affects the way we read the Greek New Testament is the ultimate question that we are all interested in. There are several obvious ways in which an understanding of verbal aspect will positively enhance exegesis. Approaching verbs in context through an aspectual understanding will enable the interpreter to engage with the viewpoint conveyed through aspect. Perfective aspect conveys actions through an external viewpoint and often indicates that such actions are to be read as summaries of what happened. Imperfective aspect provides an inside look at actions that occur, whether they be unfolding (=progressing) or stative.

Negatively, an understanding of verbal aspect will help to eliminate common exegetical errors, such as we see with the following example.

Romans 5:6 Ἔτι γὰρ Χριστὸς ὄντων ἡμῶν ἀσθενῶν ἔτι κατὰ καιρὸν ὑπὲρ ἀσεβῶν **ἀπέθανεν**.

*For while we were still weak, at the right time Christ **died** for the ungodly.*

Some commentators write that because an aorist is used here, Romans 5:6 proves that Christ's death was a once-off, punctiliar event, never to be repeated, and therefore Christ could not be reoffered time and time again in the Roman mass. While not wanting to deny the once-for-all nature of Christ's death (cf. 1 Pet 3:18), the aorist in Romans 5:6 does not prove the point at all. Why not? Because that's not what an aorist means. People who argue such things about this verse base their argument on a faulty understanding of the aorist indicative. A proper understanding of verbal aspect would avoid such an error.[31] The aorist's perfective aspect simply presents Christ's death from an external perspective, and in this case as a summary of what happened. It is not a punctiliar event just because an aorist is used.[32]

5.6.1 Aspect and Aktionsart Interactions

Another way in which verbal aspect aids exegesis is through its cooperation with *Aktionsart*, or, to put it another way, through its partnership with the various other factors in a text that help to construe the nature of an action.

In my textbook introduction, *Basics of Verbal Aspect in Biblical Greek*, I present a simplified method for understanding aspect and *Aktionsart* interactions in Greek text. Drawing particularly on Fanning at this point, I acknowledge the usefulness of observing predictable patterns that emerge from the combinations of aspects with lexical types. The combination of aspect, lexeme, and context work together to create pragmatic *Aktionsart* expressions, or implicatures.

In older grammars and commentaries, various claims are made about the *Aktionsarten* of verb tenses as though the forms themselves denote categories such as punctiliar, ingressive, constative, and the like. This is simply not the case. There is nothing about an aorist, for example, that

---

31. Carson helpfully lists a catalogue of exegetical errors made by scholars with reference to the aorist indicative. See Carson, *Exegetical Fallacies*, 68–73.

32. See Campbell, *Basics of Verbal Aspect*, 13–16, for other examples of exegetical issues that aspect addresses.

is punctiliar in nature. Nevertheless, an aorist is capable of a punctiliar expression when used with a punctiliar lexeme in a context that allows it. In other words, punctiliarity is a pragmatic *function*, or *implicature*, of the aorist under certain conditions; it is not what the aorist itself means at the semantic level.

Thus, it is important to recognize that verbal aspect is encoded in verbal forms at the semantic level: it is an uncancelable value that exists in every occurrence of the verb—the aorist is always perfective in aspect; the present is always imperfective in aspect. How these forms then *function* in context takes into account the semantic value of aspect and its interaction with lexical type and context. The resultant function is called *Aktionsart.*[33]

In *Basics of Verbal Aspect*, I present a four-step process that identifies the key elements in exegeting the function of a verb in context. First, the semantic values of the verb are to be identified (e.g., perfective aspect). Second, the type of lexeme must be taken into account (e.g., punctiliar). Third, relevant elements of the context are considered (e.g., a repeated action is implied). Finally, the *Aktionsart* is determined based on predictable patterns of the combinations of the previous three elements (e.g., iterative *Aktionsart*). These steps are represented by various versions of the following diagram:

When semantic features (box 1) combine with pragmatic elements

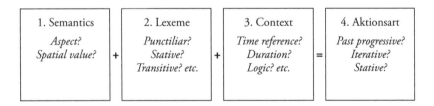

(boxes 2 and 3), the verb creates a specific *Aktionsart* implicature (box 4). The linguistic term *implicature* refers to the specific function of a form when in combination with certain pragmatic features. Every verbal form is capable of expressing a variety of implicatures, depending on the combination of pragmatic features at work in any given text. In *Basics of Verbal Aspect*, the main implicatures of each verb form are explained, together with the factors

---

33. This paragraph and the preceding one are taken from my *Colossians and Philemon: A Handbook on the Greek Text* (Baylor Handbook on the Greek New Testament; Waco, TX: Baylor University Press, 2013), xxii.

that can create them. By way of example, the simplified "equations" for the key implicatures of the aorist indicative are summarized below.[34]

Aorist indicative

Summary *Aktionsart*

Perfective aspect with a non-punctiliar, non-stative lexeme can implicate a summary *Aktionsart*. This is the default function of the aorist indicative and simply expresses that something happened, without further specification.

Punctiliar *Aktionsart*

Perfective aspect with a punctiliar lexeme can implicate a punctiliar *Aktionsart*. This expresses an action that is once-occurring and instantaneous.

Ingressive *Aktionsart*

Perfective aspect with a stative lexeme, in a context that indicates entrance into a state or sets a new direction, can implicate an ingressive *Aktionsart*. This expresses the entrance into a state or the beginning of a new action.

Gnomic *Aktionsart*

Perfective aspect with any lexeme in a context of "general reality" can implicate a gnomic *Aktionsart*. This expresses a universal and timeless action.

Present Aorist

Perfective aspect with any lexeme in a present referring context can implicate present temporal reference. Strictly speaking, this is not an *Aktionsart*, but is a special function of the aorist nonetheless.

Future Aorist

Perfective aspect with any lexeme in a future referring context can implicate a future aorist. More common than the present aorist, this is another special function of the aorist.

Some examples illustrate how this all works out in various texts.

> John 19:34 ἀλλ᾽ εἷς τῶν στρατιωτῶν **λόγχῃ** αὐτοῦ τὴν πλευρὰν ἔνυξεν, καὶ ἐξῆλθεν εὐθὺς αἷμα καὶ ὕδωρ.

> *But one of the soldiers **pierced** his side with a spear, and at once blood and water came out.*

---

34. These summaries are taken from Campbell, *Colossians and Philemon*, xxiv. See xxiv–xxvii for the full range of implicatures across tense-forms. The descriptions in that volume summarize information developed throughout *Basics of Verbal Aspect*.

1. Semantic meaning of the verb. The aorist indicative semantically encodes perfective aspect and the spatial value of remoteness.
2. Contribution of the lexeme. The lexeme is punctiliar; it is an instantaneous action.
3. Function in context. The context allows punctiliarity.

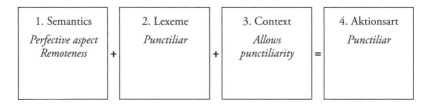

Romans 3:23 πάντες γὰρ **ἥμαρτον** καὶ ὑστεροῦνται τῆς δόξης τοῦ θεοῦ

*For all **have sinned** and fall short of the glory of God.*

1. Semantic meaning of the verb. The aorist indicative semantically encodes perfective aspect and the spatial value of remoteness.
2. Contribution of the lexeme. The lexeme is not punctiliar or stative.
3. Function in context. The context allows summary. Could perhaps provide a gnomic context: "For all sin...," but this is tentative at best.

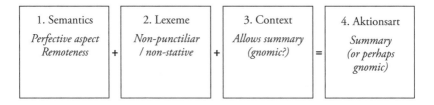

John 1:10 ἐν τῷ κόσμῳ ἦν, καὶ ὁ κόσμος δι᾽ αὐτοῦ ἐγένετο, καὶ ὁ κόσμος αὐτὸν **οὐκ ἔγνω**.

*He was in the world, and the world was created through him, yet the world **did not recognize** him.*

1. Semantic meaning of the verb. The aorist indicative semantically encodes perfective aspect and the spatial value of remoteness.
2. Contribution of the lexeme. The lexeme is stative.
3. Function in context. The context allows the entrance into a state.

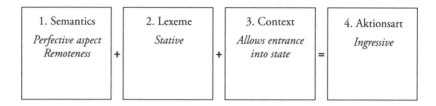

By careful consideration of verbal aspect, the lexeme of the verb in question, and the context, the student can discern the function of a verb in its context. While there is admittedly some subjectivity involved (especially in evaluating the context), this four-step process is a more reliable guide than the (sometimes questionable) intuition of interpreters of yesteryear. It is comparatively objective, and at the very least it allows for scrutiny of the process and results it produces.

5.6.2 Aspect and Narrative Structure

Another area of exegetical import is the way in which verbal aspect functions to structure narrative texts. These observations about verbal aspect within narrative were developed in my monograph, *Verbal Aspect, the Indicative Mood, and Narrative,* and the following summarizes some its main conclusions.

First, let us consider the structure of narrative texts.[35] Several strands of discourse may be delineated within the narrative text type. The most basic distinction within narrative is that between narrative proper and discourse proper; that is, those parts of the narrative that are communicated through event-based story, and those parts that are communicated through the reporting of speech, thought, and so on (reported discourse).[36]

Within this basic distinction, further distinctions are possible. Narrative proper may be understood as the combination of mainline and offline strands. Mainline communicates the sequential events that form the skeletal structure of the entire narrative text, while offline material provides supplemental information that comments on, explains, and fills out the mainline action.[37]

---

35. The remainder of this section is based on Campbell, *Verbal Aspect (Indicative Mood),* 239–47.

36. As Dooley and Levinsohn say, "the contents of reported speeches ... are embedded in the overall structure of the narrative." Robert Dooley and Stephen H. Levinsohn, *Analyzing Discourse: A Manual of Basic Concepts* (Dallas: SIL International, 2001), 128.

37. See Stanley E. Porter, "Prominence: An Overview," in *The Linguist as Pedagogue: Trends in the*

Discourse proper consists of direct discourse, which reports speech as though it is unfolding in real time; indirect discourse, which reports the content of speech or thought; and authorial discourse, which consists of the direct communication of the author to the reader by way of appeal or explanation.

It is argued, in agreement with previous research, that these various strands of discourse not only shape narrative texts, but they provide the macrostructure in which verbal aspect functions.[38] The various aspects are typically aligned with these strands of discourse, such that predictable patterns are formed whereby each aspect in the indicative mood has a default association with a particular strand of discourse. These patterns may be summarized as following.

Discourse Strands and Indicative Tense-Form Patterns	
Mainline material	Aorist indicative
Offline material	Imperfect and pluperfect indicatives
Direct discourse	Present, perfect, and future indicatives
Indirect discourse	Present and perfect indicatives
Authorial discourse	Present and perfect indicatives

These patterns of indicative verbal distribution are created through the functionality of verbal aspect. Perfective aspect is inherently suited to the reporting of events on the narrative mainline (aorist indicative); imperfective aspect inherently suits the provision of offline material (imperfect and pluperfect indicatives), as well as the various types of reported discourse found in narrative (present and perfect indicatives).

Having developed an aspectual model for the Greek verbal system on the basis of verbal patterns and their relationships to the various strands of discourse within narrative texts, we are able to pick out the structure of Greek narrative texts by identifying the locations of indicative verbal forms. In the following example, indicative verbs are double-underlined,

Teaching and Linguistic Analysis of the Greek New Testament (ed. Stanley E. Porter and Matthew Brook O'Donnell; Sheffield: Sheffield Phoenix, 2009), 57–58.

38. See, e.g., Paul J. Hopper, "Aspect and Foregrounding in Discourse," in *Discourse and Syntax* (ed. Talmy Givón; Syntax and Semantics 12; New York: Academic Press, 1979), 213–41; Robert E. Longacre, "Mark 5.1–43: Generating the Complexity of a Narrative from Its Most Basic Elements," in *Discourse Analysis and the New Testament: Approaches and Results* (eds. Stanley E. Porter and Jeffrey T. Reed; JSNTSup 170; Sheffield: Sheffield Academic, 1999), 169–96.

and beside each Greek excerpt is a simple structural outline depicting only the indicative verbs. The outline portrays mainline material on the left with a dot point next to the relevant verb, offline material indented with a dash next to the relevant verb, and reported discourse further indented and within square brackets. The outline is spaced so as to correspond approximately to the position of the verbs within the excerpt.

John 7:28–32

28 ἔκραξεν οὖν ἐν τῷ ἱερῷ διδάσκων ὁ Ἰησοῦς καὶ λέγων· κἀμὲ **οἴδατε** καὶ **οἴδατε** πόθεν **εἰμί**· καὶ ἀπ᾽ ἐμαυτοῦ οὐκ **ἐλήλυθα**, ἀλλ᾽ **ἔστιν** ἀληθινὸς ὁ πέμψας με, ὃν ὑμεῖς οὐκ **οἴδατε**· 29 ἐγὼ **οἶδα** αὐτόν, ὅτι παρ᾽ αὐτοῦ **εἰμι** κἀκεῖνός με **ἀπέστειλεν**. 30 **Ἐζήτουν** οὖν αὐτὸν πιάσαι, καὶ οὐδεὶς **ἐπέβαλεν** ἐπ᾽ αὐτὸν τὴν χεῖρα, ὅτι οὔπω **ἐληλύθει** ἡ ὥρα αὐτοῦ. 31 Ἐκ τοῦ ὄχλου δὲ πολλοὶ **ἐπίστευσαν** εἰς αὐτὸν καὶ **ἔλεγον**· ὁ χριστὸς ὅταν ἔλθῃ μὴ πλείονα σημεῖα **ποιήσει** ὧν οὗτος **ἐποίησεν**; 32 **ἤκουσαν** οἱ Φαρισαῖοι τοῦ ὄχλου γογγύζοντος περὶ αὐτοῦ ταῦτα, καὶ **ἀπέστειλαν** οἱ ἀρχιερεῖς καὶ οἱ Φαρισαῖοι ὑπηρέτας ἵνα πιάσωσιν αὐτόν.

- ἔκραξεν
  - [οἴδατε οἴδατε
  - εἰμί ἐλήλυθα
  - ἔστιν
  - οἴδατε οἶδα
  - εἰμι ἀπέστειλεν]
  — Ἐζήτουν
- ἐπέβαλεν
  — ἐληλύθει
- ἐπίστευσαν
  — ἔλεγον
  - [ποιήσει ἐποίησεν]
- ἤκουσαν
- ἀπέστειλαν

This example demonstrates the way in which the verbal outline accurately reflects the shape of the narrative. Mainline is carried by the aorist indicatives on the left of the outline, while offline material is carried by imperfects and one pluperfect. The reported discourse is carried by presents, perfects, two aorists, and a future indicative.[39]

The value of producing a chart of narrative text in such a way is to trace the structuring role that aspect plays in all narratives. It becomes a useful way to delineate the flow and development of narrative texts, and in this way the study of verbal aspect serves the process of exegesis.

---

39. It is to be stressed that this function of indicative verbs in narrative is *pragmatic* only; the functions can be cancelled. For instance, it is possible to find imperfect indicatives carrying the narrative mainline, alongside aorists, as in Luke 2:7; 24:30; and John 4:30. The point here, however, is that aspect in the indicative mood displays predictable patterns within narrative, even if these patterns are not absolute. See Campbell, *Verbal Aspect (Indicative Mood)*, 96–98.

5.6.3 Aspect and Planes of Discourse

One area of contention regarding the exegetical implications of verbal aspect concerns Porter's *planes of discourse*.[40] Porter argues that the aspects contribute to planes of discourse in text, in which three planes may be discerned: background, foreground, and frontground. Porter's model accordingly attributes least significance to perfective aspect (aorist tense-form), which provides *background* information; greater significance to imperfective aspect (present and imperfect), which provides *foreground* information; and greatest significance to stative aspect (perfect and pluperfect), which provides *frontground* information.[41] The pluperfect is thus well suited to evaluate Porter's planes of discourse model, since according to him it should display high prominence within frontground information.

Furthermore, Porter regards the pluperfect and perfect tense-forms as the most heavily marked, meaning that they carry the greatest significance when used in opposition to the perfective and imperfective aspects.[42] Two of the factors that Porter envisages as contributing to this markedness are the relatively infrequent use of the perfect and pluperfect and their comparative morphological bulk: "The Perfect has the most morphological bulk of all the tenses, because of its unthematic root, endings and reduplication."[43] "Morphologically the Pluperfect form is particular unwieldy ... often with an augment besides Perfect reduplication ... and primary endings with ει (or η) thematic vowels attached to the Perfect stem."[44] It is this markedness that underpins Porter's planes of discourse theory.

Hatina tests Porter's theory by examining the perfect tense-forms in Galatians[45] and Colossians.[46] He concludes that "the hypothesis is plausible in some cases at this preliminary stage.... It is generally not the case that

---

40. This section is based on ibid., 233–37.
41. Stanley E. Porter, *Idioms of the Greek New Testament* (2nd ed.; Biblical Languages: Greek 2; Sheffield: Sheffield Academic, 1994), 23; "In Defence of Verbal Aspect," in *Biblical Greek Language and Linguistics: Open Questions in Current Research* (ed. Stanley E. Porter and D. A. Carson; JSNTSup 80; Sheffield: Sheffield Academic, 1993), 35. Reed and Reese recategorize these as BACKGROUND, THEME and FOCUS; see Jeffrey T. Reed and Ruth A. Reese, "Verbal Aspect, Discourse Prominence, and the Letter of Jude," *Filologia Neotestamentaria* 18.9 (1996): 187–88.
42. Porter, *Idioms*, 22.
43. Porter, *Verbal Aspect*, 246.
44. Ibid., 289.
45. Thomas R. Hatina, "The Perfect Tense-Form in Recent Debate: Galatians as a Case Study," *Filologia Neotestamentaria* 15/8 (1995): 3–22.
46. Thomas R. Hatina, "The Perfect Tense-Form in Colossians: Verbal Aspect, Temporality and the Challenge of Translation," in *Translating the Bible: Problems and Prospects* (ed. Stanley E. Porter and Richard S. Hess; JSNTSup 173; Sheffield: Sheffield Academic Press, 1999).

the perfect is found in a comparatively insignificant position."[47] Reed and Reese are not quite so satisfied: though they regard stative aspect to be the most accentuated aspect, they admit that "in the event that the aspectual function conflicts with its value of prominence, verbal aspect takes precedence."[48] This admission has important implications in that prominence is not seen to be grammaticalized in the verb. They state that "the use of verbal aspect . . . to indicate prominence is a secondary role—a pragmatic function of grammar—and, thus, a *discourse function* not a morphological function of Greek grammar."[49] Reed and Reese conclude that it cannot be claimed that every time a particular tense-form occurs, it should always be interpreted in terms of prominence.[50] Prominence is therefore a matter of pragmatics, not semantics.

Silva is more skeptical yet, claiming that

> no reasonable writer would seek to express a major point by leaning on a subtle grammatical distinction—especially if it is a point not otherwise clear from the whole context (and if it *is* clear from the context, then the grammatical subtlety plays at best a secondary role in exegesis).[51]

Rather, Silva argues that the choice of aspect is largely determined by the circumstances, rather than to accentuate the point,[52] and thus "an interpreter is unwise to emphasize an idea that allegedly comes from the use of a tense (or some other subtle grammatical distinction) unless the context as a whole clearly sets forth that idea."[53]

Indeed, while the perfect generally may be found in comparatively significant positions, the same cannot easily be said of the pluperfect, and despite some occurrences of the pluperfect that may be regarded as prominent in their contexts, several others may not. Admittedly, there is no objective test as to the prominence or otherwise of these verbs; subjective appreciation of context must be our guide. These examples demonstrate nonprominent usages of the pluperfect.

---

47. Ibid., 249–50.
48. Reed and Reese, 'Discourse Prominence', 190.
49. Ibid., 190 [italics are original].
50. Ibid. 190.
51. Silva, *God, Language, and Scripture*, 115 [italics are original].
52. Ibid. 118.
53. Ibid. 118. See also Moisés Silva, "Discourse Analysis and Philippians," in *Discourse Analysis and Other Topics in Biblical Greek* (ed. Stanley E. Porter and D. A. Carson; JSNTSup 113; Sheffield: Sheffield Academic, 1995), 105.

Matthew 13:2

καὶ συνήχθησαν πρὸς αὐτὸν ὄχλοι πολλοί, ὥστε αὐτὸν εἰς πλοῖον ἐμβάντα καθῆσθαι, καὶ πᾶς ὁ ὄχλος ἐπὶ τὸν αἰγιαλὸν **εἱστήκει.**

*Such great crowds gathered to him, that he got into a boat and sat down; and the whole crowd **was standing** on the beach.*

Luke 4:29

καὶ ἀναστάντες ἐξέβαλον αὐτὸν ἔξω τῆς πόλεως καὶ ἤγαγον αὐτὸν ἕως ὀφρύος τοῦ ὄρους ἐφ᾽ οὗ ἡ πόλις **ᾠκοδόμητο** αὐτῶν ὥστε κατακρημνίσαι αὐτόν·

*They got up and cast him out of the city and took him to the brow of the hill on which their city **was built**, so that they could throw him down the cliff.*

John 18:18

εἱστήκεισαν δὲ οἱ δοῦλοι καὶ οἱ ὑπηρέται ἀνθρακιὰν πεποιηκότες, ὅτι ψῦχος ἦν, καὶ ἐθερμαίνοντο· ἦν δὲ καὶ ὁ Πέτρος μετ᾽ αὐτῶν ἑστὼς καὶ θερμαινόμενος.

*Now the slaves and officers had made a charcoal fire, because it was cold, and **they were standing** and warming themselves; Peter also was with them, standing and warming himself.*

Clearly these pluperfects are not prominent; only by improbable explanations could they be understood as such. Indeed, approximately one third of pluperfects in the New Testament are not easily regarded as being prominent.[54]

Moreover, Porter's conception of morphological bulk, and its role in indicating prominence, seems somewhat contrived. While the pluperfect perhaps should theoretically carry greatest morphological bulk, the reality is that many pluperfects are not comparatively large, as the forms ᾔδει ἐγεγόνει, εἱστήκει, and εἰώθει demonstrate. Another of Porter's indicators of markedness, however, is the low frequency of the pluperfect, and since there is no question as to the form's low frequency, this indicator of markedness is not invalid. It is reasonable to conclude, therefore, that any use of the pluperfect does represent a significant choice. This markedness, however, as seen above, does not necessarily result in the prominence of the pluperfect.

---

54. See also Mark 10:1; 14:40; 16:9; Luke 8:2, 29, 38; 19:15; 22:13; 23:35, 49; John 1:31; 7:37; 11:30, 44; 18:2, 16; 20:11; Acts 4:22; 7:44; 8:27; 9:7; 12:9; 20:16; Rev 7:11.

The demonstrable lack of prominence of at least one third of pluperfects in the New Testament suggests that Porter's planes of discourse model does not adequately accommodate pluperfect usage. For the pluperfect at least, prominence is best determined according to context, and is not grammatically marked according to verbal forms. As such, it seems prudent to call into question the planes of discourse model in general: if it does not accommodate the pluperfect, how accurate is the model?

It is far more secure to recognize the usage of the pluperfect in terms of providing supplemental, descriptive, and explicatory material, which together is designated by Hopper as background information. The provision of such information is the normal pragmatic expression of the aspect of the pluperfect.

5.7 Other Unresolved Issues

There is a great deal of agreement about various significant issues within Greek verbal aspect studies, such as how to define aspect, the distinction between semantics and pragmatics, the importance of aspect in the verbal system, and the awareness that exegesis of the Greek New Testament desperately needs to be well-informed regarding these insights. While debate about the perfect is probably the most important issue of contention among aspect scholars, it is not the only one. Other issues require further research, debate, and, hopefully, resolution.

The issue of whether Greek verbs are tenses remains unresolved. Do Greek verbs encode temporal reference at the semantic level, or is temporal reference a pragmatic category created through the combination of semantic features and context? How many aspects are there? Everyone agrees that there are at least two (perfective and imperfective), but what about a third (stative) aspect? There is also disagreement about the aspectual nature of the Greek future tense-form. Does it convey aspect? If so, which aspect? Following "The Perfect Storm," the aspectual nature of the future indicative is probably the next area that requires focused attention from scholarship. Two doctoral students have recently completed dissertations on the Greek future—Francis Pang at McMaster Divinity College, and Craig Long at Trinity Evangelical Divinity School. We look forward to their contributions.

5.8 The Ways Forward

While verbal aspect remains the most controversial and volatile area of research in Greek studies today, much has been gained from the discussion. As further research is conducted and methodological issues are carefully considered, I am hopeful that more will be achieved in terms of clarity and consensus. The worst thing that could happen, however, is that other students of the Greek New Testament decide to remain disengaged from verbal aspect, citing that "the scholarship is unresolved." In fact, in the wider world, many areas of scholarship face such debates, but this does not mean that they are not studied, taught, and applied. Students of Greek simply must become conversant with what is going on in aspect studies.

Even just employing the insights about which there is agreement has potential to yield significant advances in exegesis and translation. The most obvious way in which to begin to incorporate the insights of verbal aspect studies into Greek exegesis is to adopt the four-step method outlined in *Basics of the Verbal Aspect* (see §5.6.1). While the approach is oversimplified at certain points (especially regarding lexical analysis, which is enormously complex on its own), it provides a method for approaching aspect and *Aktionsart* interactions in the text. No doubt more research is needed here, and *Basics of Verbal Aspect* is only a starting point. But a starting point is what's needed for those who have not yet started.

Another important area for future research is the interaction of verbal aspect in different text-types, or genres. My monograph, *Verbal Aspect, the Indicative Mood, and Narrative: Soundings in the Greek of the New Testament*,[55] explores the function of aspect in narrative texts (see §5.6.2). David Mathewson's *Verbal Aspect in the Book of Revelation* explores aspect in the apocalyptic genre. While other studies have of course included consideration of epistolary material, there is scope for more work to be done on aspect's function in how epistles operate at the discourse level.

Related to genre is the issue of idiolect—an individual's "dialect." The relationship between idiolect and verbal aspect is an interesting one, especially with respect to frequency and patterns of usage. An obvious problem

---

55. Rodney Decker's monograph also deals with aspect in narrative (Mark's gospel), but his focus is not on the function of aspect in the narrative genre per se; he is primarily interested in the question of temporal reference.

that this relationship has potential to address is the so-called Synoptic Problem, so far as idiolect is able to explain certain changes from, say, Markan to Lukan usage. This issue has begun to be explored in Cirafesi's work (see §5.3.11), and idiolect is explored further in the next chapter of this book.

Furthermore, there is scope for additional research on the function of aspect in the nonindicative verb forms. Another monograph of mine, *Verbal Aspect and Non-Indicative Verbs: Further Soundings in the Greek of the New Testament* addresses this area directly, but there is more to be done, perhaps by way of focused research on individual moods, such as the subjunctive. In light of this need, it is encouraging to see Huffman's recently released volume on prohibitions (including the imperative and subjunctive moods).

5.9 Further Reading

Campbell, Constantine R. *Verbal Aspect, the Indicative Mood, and Narrative: Soundings in the Greek of the New Testament.* SBG 13. New York: Peter Lang, 2007.

———. *Verbal Aspect and Non-Indicative Verbs: Further Soundings in the Greek of the New Testament.* SBG 15. New York: Peter Lang, 2008.

———. *Basics of Verbal Aspect in Biblical Greek.* Grand Rapids: Zondervan, 2008.

Cirafesi, Wally V. *Verbal Aspect in Synoptic Parallels: On the Method and Meaning of Divergent Tense-Form Usage in the Synoptic Passion Narratives.* LBS 7. Leiden: Brill, 2013.

Decker, Rodney J. *Temporal Deixis of the Greek Verb in the Gospel of Mark with Reference to Verbal Aspect.* SBG 10. New York: Peter Lang, 2001.

Evans, T. V. *Verbal Syntax in the Greek Pentateuch: Natural Greek Usage and Hebrew Interference.* Oxford: Oxford University Press, 2001.

Fanning, Buist M. *Verbal Aspect in New Testament Greek.* Oxford Theological Monographs; Oxford: Clarendon, 1990.

Huffman, Douglas S. *Verbal Aspect Theory and the Prohibitions in the Greek New Testament.* SBG 16. New York: Peter Lang, 2014.

Mathewson, David L. *Verbal Aspect in the Book of Revelation: The Function of Greek Verb Tenses in John's Apocalypse.* LBS 4. Leiden: Brill, 2010.

McKay, K. L. *A New Syntax of the Verb in New Testament Greek: An Aspectual Approach.* SBG 5. New York: Peter Lang, 1994.

Olsen, Mari Broman. *A Semantic and Pragmatic Model of Lexical and Grammatical Aspect.* Outstanding Dissertations in Linguistics. New York: Garland, 1997.

Porter, Stanley E. *Verbal Aspect in the Greek of the New Testament with Reference to Tense and Mood.* SBG 1. New York: Peter Lang, 1989.

Porter, Stanley E., Buist M. Fanning, and Constantine R. Campbell. *The Perfect Volume: Critical Discussion of the Semantics of the Greek Perfect Tense under Aspect Theory.* Introduction by D. A. Carson. SBG 17. New York: Peter Lang, 2015.

CHAPTER 6

IDIOLECT, GENRE, AND REGISTER

Idiolect is not the opposite of intellect.   —*Anonymous*

6.1 Introduction

This chapter introduces recent advances in the areas of idiolect, genre, and register. Two of these three terms are poorly understood (if at all), yet all three have significant impact for our understanding of the Greek of the New Testament. The chapter will explore the exegetical implications of individual authors' Greek style (idiolect) and the type of literature contained in the New Testament (register). The way in which Greek differs according to genre and text type also has bearing on exegesis.

These categories are relevant for the study of all texts, but in the New Testament they are especially interesting for understanding the Gospels. Synoptic criticism has long focused on differences and similarities between Matthew, Mark, and Luke, but much of that research (especially that from earlier periods) has not availed itself of the best thinking about idiolect, genre, and register. An obvious factor for this is that much Synoptic criticism was conducted before such thinking had developed into its modern form. As such, we will take note of the implications of idiolect, genre, and register with particular reference to the Gospels. The inclusion of John—alongside the Synoptics—actually helps us to understand the Synoptics better. To focus the issue further, we will concentrate on aspectual patterns across the

Gospels, understood through the lenses of idiolect, genre, and register. This will also help to demonstrate how interrelated the three concerns are.

It should be noted, however, that all parts of speech are relevant for the study of idiolect, genre, and register. We could examine noun usage, use of the article, connectives, vocabulary, and so forth. The focus here on aspect is for the purpose of illustration, and it also demonstrates some of the wider applications of aspect studies.

6.2 Idiolect

When defining "idiolect" to students, I sometimes joke that it is not the opposite of *intellect*. Rather, idiolect is to an individual what *dialect* is to a group. As Crystal observes, idiolect refers to "to the linguistic system of an individual speaker—one person's dialect. A dialect can be seen as an abstraction deriving from the analysis of a large number of idiolects."[1] To study idiolect, then, is to observe the ways in which an author (or speaker) uses language according to a personalized style. "Style" is a term that older grammarians may have used, understandably, to convey a similar notion, but idiolect is a more useful term. For instance, as with dialect, idiolect implies that the language user operates within the accepted bounds of the language in question, but puts an indelible stamp on how it "sounds."

This is not simply the cultivation of a "writing style" that can be adopted to suit certain occasions, then is dropped when deemed inappropriate. In that sense, most writers are capable of executing different styles as they see fit (so too speakers). Idiolect, rather, is more of a permanent pattern of language use, regardless of occasion or, indeed, regardless of style. Idiolect is not "dropped" according to occasion—the writer cannot help but sound like herself in a broad sense. In fact, as Crystal claims, "idiolectal features are particularly noticeable in literary writing, as stylistic markers of authorship."[2] While an author's style, or tone, might vary from one document to another, there will be relatively stable features that reveal an author's hand—though it is also true that differing genres can greatly complicate the issue (see below, on genre).

Plenty of examples of idiolect abound in various types of literature.

---

1. Crystal, *Linguistics and Phonetics*, 235.
2. Ibid.

Avid theology readers will likely not have much trouble picking the writing of, say, N. T. Wright, Karl Barth, or John Calvin. Fiction readers might find it easy to pick out a few lines of Jane Austen, Tom Clancy, or Fyodor Dostoyevsky. We can discern their authorship through certain linguistic features that characterize their writing.

Applying such a concept to the Gospels, Wifstrand is able to conclude that Luke employs standard Hellenistic prose, which was more "Attic" in style than everyday spoken Hellenistic language.[3] Nevertheless, while Luke demonstrates a more cultivated style than Mark, this does not make Luke an "Atticist."[4] Mark, however, is more representative of popular everyday language.[5]

Some of the points of interest in observing idiolect are vocabulary, syntactical constructions, patterns of verbal usage, and more macro features, such as those observed through discourse analysis (see chapter 7). Older analyses of style were primarily focused on vocabulary usage, which of course is a significant indicator of idiolect.

But there is much more to it than vocabulary. Syntactical constructions, for instance, can yield important results. The ways in which authors like to construct a sentence, with differing levels of clausal complexity and a variety of preferences for coordination and subordination within clause structure, are but a few examples of syntactical elements that are relevant to idiolect. These, however, are harder to observe than simple vocabulary usage, since they require careful consideration of clausal analysis (perhaps through syntax diagramming) and are not easily measured. Levels of clausal complexity are discerned through widespread patterns that leave an impression of authorial preference. This kind of thing becomes evident if one moves from, say, examining the syntax of Paul to the syntax of Peter. While Paul's clausal syntax is far from simple, Peter's syntax represents an unmistakable step up in complexity. This is most obviously appreciated through comparison of syntax diagrams. A syntax diagram of 1 Peter instantly reveals multiple layers of subordination and long and complex clauses. This feature alone—even apart from vocabulary usage—reveals a hand distinct from Paul's.

3. Albert Wifstrand, "Luke and Greek Classicism," in *Epochs and Styles: Selected Writings on the New Testament, Greek Language and Greek Culture in the Post-Classical Era* (ed. Lars Rydbeck and Stanley E. Porter; trans. Denis Searby; WUNT 179; Tübingen: Mohr Siebeck, 2005), 19.
4. Ibid.
5. Ibid.

6.2.1. Aspectual Patterns of the Gospels

Another important element of idiolect is the ways in which verbs are used. Analysis of verbal usage is more sophisticated than vocabulary usage, but it is easier to measure than clausal syntax. In terms of macro-patterns, how does Mark's use of verbal aspect differ from that of Matthew and Luke? In what ways do their respective macro-patterns align? Some of the comparisons presented below will be intra-Synoptic, observing, for example, how Lukan usage differs from Markan. Other comparisons will be extra-Synoptic, such as how the Synoptics together differ from Johannine usage. The three focal points for this exploration into convergent and divergent patterns will be the use of the perfect indicative, pluperfect indicative, and historical present.

Let us first consider the use of the perfect indicative within the Gospels. Matthew employs 52 perfect indicatives, which represents 2.3 percent of the 2,245 indicatives in his gospel. Of these 52 perfects, 50 are found within direct discourse (96 percent). Mark employs 47 perfects, representing 3 percent of his 1,520 total indicatives. Of these, 44 are found in reported discourse (94 percent). Luke uses 60 perfect indicatives, representing 2.5 percent of 2,444 indicatives. In strong contrast to the Synoptics, however, John uses 205 perfects, representing 8 percent of his 2,556 total indicatives. Of these, 199 are within reported discourse (97 percent).[6]

Immediately noticeable is the fact that the Synoptics employ the perfect in frequencies ranging from 2 to 3 percent, while John's frequency is 8 percent—more than triple that of Matthew and Luke (and nearly triple that of Mark). Nevertheless, there is also a convergent pattern to be observed between Synoptic and Johannine uses of the perfect indicative; this relates to distribution. Across all four Gospels, between 94 and 97 percent of perfect indicatives are found within reported discourse.

Let us turn now to consider the use of the pluperfect. Matthew employs 8 pluperfect indicatives, which represent 0.35 percent of his 2,245 total indicative verbs. All of these function to provide supplemental or explanatory material in offline narrative contexts. Likewise, Mark uses 8 pluperfects, which represent 0.5 percent of his 1,520 total indicative verbs. As with Matthew, all of these provide supplemental or explanatory material. Luke employs 16 pluperfect indicatives, representing 0.65 percent of

---

6. These statistics are gathered from the NA28-T module of the *Accordance* Bible Software.

2,444 indicative verb forms. Of these, 15 pluperfects provide supplemental or explanatory material. Of 2,556 indicative verb forms, John employs 34 pluperfects, representing 1.3 percent of total indicative usage. All of these function to provide supplemental, explanatory, or descriptive material in offline narrative contexts.

Once again, Synoptic frequencies for the use of the pluperfect diverge from that of John. While the Synoptics exhibit pluperfect usage at a rate between 0.35 to 0.65 percent of total indicative verbs, John's frequency of usage represents 1.3 percent of indicatives. Thus, John uses more than double the number of pluperfects relative to the Synoptic Gospels, and again the question is raised as to why this is so. As with the perfect, however, there is also a convergent pattern to be observed between Synoptic and Johannine uses of the pluperfect indicative, which is related to function. Virtually all pluperfects across all four Gospels provide supplemental, explanatory, or descriptive material, each being found within offline narrative contexts.

Let us turn now to consider the use of the historical present. Matthew's gospel employs 89 historical presents, which represent 12 percent of the 753 present indicatives in the book. Of these historical presents, 70 function to introduce reported discourse, while 17 are verbs of propulsion, which are related to coming and going, moving from one place to another, giving and receiving, and so forth.[7]

Mark has 151 historical presents, representing 29 percent of his total 514 present indicatives. Of these, 90 historical presents introduce reported discourse, while 61 are verbs of propulsion. Mark also tends to use historical presents in paragraph-initial positions, to introduce new characters, and for scene changes. There are also some instances of clustering with 8 historical presents within 11 verses in 15:17–27.

Luke has only 12 historical presents, which constitutes 1.9 percent of his 623 present indicatives. Of these 12 historical presents, 11 are used to introduce reported discourse, and 1 is the verb of propulsion, ἔρχομαι. Luke does not appear to use these historical presents in paragraph-initial positions or to introduce new characters or scenes. Apart from introducing reported discourse, therefore, Lukan usage of the historical present does not have an obvious role in shaping the structure of units.

---

7. For more on verbs of propulsion, see Campbell, *Verbal Aspect (Indicative Mood)*, 46–47.

John employs 167 historical presents, representing 16 percent of 1,027 present indicatives in total. Of these, 144 historical presents are used to introduce reported discourse, while 23 are verbs of propulsion. There are also several clusters of historical presents, in chapters 1, 4, 13, 20, 21 — all being units of heightened significance.

Casting the net a little wider, the Koine fictional biography of Aesop, *Vita Aesopi G*, contains 769 present indicatives, 253 of which are historical presents representing 33 percent of present indicatives. In *Vita Aesopi G* reported discourse is more frequently introduced by historical presents than by aorists, with 230 historical presents performing this function compared to 208 aorists. Of these historical presents, 12 are verbs of propulsion, while 1 is found at the beginning of a pericope. There are no clusters of historical presents in the book.

The first book of Chariton's Koine novel *The Story of Callirhoe* contains 20 historical presents, which constitutes 16 percent of the 123 present indicatives therein. Of these, 19 function to introduce reported discourse, while 1 is a verb of propulsion. There are no clusters of historical presents, and none are to be found at the beginning of pericopae.

Moving outside Koine literature altogether, a sample of 41 chapters from Thucydides contains 39 historical presents, representing 46 percent of 84 present indicatives.[8] Of these, 11 historical presents introduce reported discourse, while 28 are verbs of propulsion. Four historical presents are found in pericope-initial positions, but there are no clusters of historical presents.

This brief overview of several documents reveals at least two divergent patterns in the use of the historical present. First, there are different frequencies of usage. Luke displays a low frequency of usage with historical presents, forming only 1.9 percent of present indicatives. Matthew, John, and Chariton each exhibit a midrange frequency of historical present usage at 12 percent, 16 percent, and 16 percent of total present indicatives respectively. Mark, *Vita Aesopi G*, and Thucydides each display a high frequency of historical present usage with 29 percent, 33 percent, and 46 percent of present indicatives respectively.

Second, there are divergent patterns of historical present usage with

---

8. *The Peloponnesian War*, 1.89–118, 128–38.

respect to discourse functions. Mark uses historical presents in pericopae-initial positions or to signal a change of speaker or scene. Mark also exhibits some clusters of historical presents, as does John. On the other hand, Matthew, Luke, *Vita Aesopi G*, Chariton, and Thucydides do not clearly follow such patterns. In spite of these strongly divergent patterns, there are two convergent patterns of usage that pervade all the documents surveyed. Virtually all historical presents are used either to introduce reported discourse or as verbs of propulsion. This holds true regardless of frequency of usage and perceived discourse patterns.

By examining verbal use alone—and only three tense-forms at that—it is already clear that authors display distinct patterns of frequency that mark them out. Their use of verbs partially reveals their idiolect.

6.3 Genre

There is some looseness in the literature as to what constitutes genre and how it is to be defined. Porter and Pearson distinguish between literary *genres*—which are used to describe whole works—and literary *forms*, such as parables, embedded narratives, and so forth.[9] This distinction between genre and form is useful and is adopted here. Furthermore, while Halliday regards genre to be identical to register, this is not the position held here, since it is useful to maintain a distinction between these things.

With respect to literary genre, the Pauline epistles adhere to Hellenistic letterform, while the Gospels align with Greco-Roman biography, as Richard Burridge has identified.[10]

While literary genre is usefully distinguished from literary form, there is an obvious relationship between the two. Ancient biographies are normally narrative in form as they are today, and so the Gospels, while being biographical in genre, are also narrative in form. Their form is narrative; their genre is biography. As we investigate the function of verbal aspect within the Gospels, we are therefore looking at its function in narrative forms, since biographical genre implies narrative form.

In narratives, there are many pragmatic similarities that may be

---

9. Brook W. R. Pearson and Stanley E. Porter, "The Genres of the New Testament," in *Handbook to Exegesis of the New Testament* (ed. Stanley E. Porter; Leiden: Brill, 2002), 134.

10. Richard A. Burridge, *What Are the Gospels? A Comparison with Graeco-Roman Biography* (SNTSMS 70; Cambridge: Cambridge University Press, 1992).

accounted by genre, since the narrative form employs predictable aspectual patterns.[11] Aorist indicatives, which are perfective in aspect, normally carry the mainline of narrative proper, marking out its skeletal structure. Imperfect indicatives, which are imperfective in aspect, are normally used for offline material. Likewise, pluperfect indicatives, which I regard as imperfective in aspect,[12] are also used for offline material that supplements, describes, and explains other events, characters, or situations. Present indicatives, which are also imperfective in aspect, find their default usage in direct and indirect discourse. They also function as historical presents in the narrative mainline. Perfect indicatives, which I regard as imperfective in aspect,[13] are nearly exclusively found in reported discourse. In the Synoptics, the convergent patterns of aspectual usage are determined by their shared genre and form.

Indeed, aspectual usage within the narrative genre/form contrasts with the usage within the epistolary genre. Epistles generally do not contain narrative structures such as mainline,[14] offline, and reported discourse, though embedded narratives can be found in which such structures do exist. Thus, while the semantics of the verbal forms are the same in any genre, the change in genre and form produces different aspectual functions.

6.4 Register

According to Halliday, in differing situations individuals select particular configurations of the semantic options available to them, which are in turn realized in the lexicogrammatical system.[15] This definition of register is synonymous with genre for Halliday. Reed, however, more simply defines register as referring to language according to use.[16] It corresponds to linguistic expressions occasioned by common, social activities, such

---

11. Campbell, *Verbal Aspect (Indicative Mood)*, 239–41.
12. Ibid., 228–29.
13. Ibid., 184–89.
14. Though Levinsohn does discern *theme line* in epistles, which normally consists of hortatory material. See Stephen H. Levinsohn, "Self-Instruction Materials on Non-Narrative Discourse Analysis" (www.sil.org/-levinsohns/, 14–16).
15. M. A. K. Halliday, *Language as Social Semiotic: The Social Interpretation of Language and Meaning* (London: Edward Arnold, 1978), 141.
16. Jeffrey T. Reed, "Discourse Analysis," in *Handbook to Exegesis of the New Testament* (ed. Stanley E. Porter; Leiden: Brill, 2002), 198.

as telephone conversations, teacher–pupil interchanges, doctor–patient appointments, or ancient letters.[17] Register may be defined as *a configuration of meanings that is associated with a particular situation.*[18]

Take blogs, for example. Blogs have become their own online genre, offering discussion or information published on the Internet, consisting of individual entries called posts, which can be single or multi-authored. The *genre* of a blog is understood. But different blogs can exhibit an array of different *registers*. Some blogs are personal "journals" shared online for friends and family. Others are high-end, official publications of corporations such as *The New York Times*. Most blogs are somewhere on a spectrum between the two. They are all blogs, but they can have radically different social functions. And the point is that the language of each blog will be shaped according to its social function. This is what is meant by register.

As O'Donnell observes, language serves as a social tool through which individuals manipulate and communicate with the environment: "Thus two significantly different varieties of language may be produced by the same speaker in close temporal succession on account of the differing goals for which language is being utilized."[19] The relationship between register, so described, and genre may be illustrated with reference to Paul's epistles. While these share the same genre — being all letters — they nevertheless exhibit a certain amount of register variation as a result of their being written at different times in the apostle's life, for different purposes, and to different audiences.[20] Letters written to individuals, for instance, clearly differ from congregational correspondence. Just compare Philemon to Romans to appreciate how the differing purposes and recipients of each epistle affect their content. And yet they are both letters.

Ferguson distinguishes between "high" and "low" forms of language, in which "high" forms are used for public, formal, and official situations, while "low" forms are spoken and not normally written down. Religious texts tend to pertain to the first category, while the second category captures the language

---

17. Ibid.
18. M. A. K. Halliday and R. Hasan, *Language, Context, and Text: Aspects of Language in a Social-Semiotic Perspective* (Oxford: Oxford University Press, 1989), 38–39. See also Dooley and Levinsohn, *Analyzing Discourse*, ch.3.
19. Matthew Brook O'Donnell, "Designing and Compiling a Register-Balanced Corpus of Hellenistic Greek for the Purpose of Linguistic Description and Investigation," in *Diglossia and Other Topics in New Testament Linguistics* (JSNTSup 193; Sheffield: Sheffield Academic Press, 2000), 255.
20. Ibid., 280.

of the collective soul.[21] Porter, however, prefers not to make rigid distinctions between "high" and "low" codes, in order to allow for multivariate analyses of individual registers as they are used in various communicative settings.[22]

The relationship between register and the New Testament is not straightforward. Against popular consensus, Rydbeck does not regard the New Testament, or the papyri for that matter, as "vulgar." The various collections of papyri range from extremely carefully written official documents, through business letters, to vulgar private letters.[23] Contra Deissmann and Moulton, Rydbeck argues that the New Testament does not exhibit any really vulgar characteristics.[24]

With respect to Luke's gospel, Wifstrand argues that Luke has to a great extent consciously patterned his style on the Septuagint's manner of expression.

> The sum of it all is that Luke, in contrast to the other synoptics, sought to give his narrative a more elevated and dignified style by consciously and deliberately associating it with the peculiar style of Greek prevalent in the LXX which ... had acquired a sacred status in the eyes of Hellenized Jews and proselytes as well as of the first Christians.[25]

Thus, according to Wifstrand, it would be appropriate to describe Lukan register as prestige language, deliberately emulating the Septuagint. It might be speculated that this is in order to present his work as "Scripture," alongside the Greek Old Testament.

With respect to Mark's gospel, Porter observes that it appears to be written in a literate culture, and the context of situation seems to be one in which the recipient community was already convinced of who Jesus was.[26] Though this is certainly debatable, if Porter is correct it might be concluded that Mark is not persuasive in register, but is intended to teach believers.

---

21. C. A. Ferguson, "Diglossia Revisited," *Southwest Journal of Linguistics* 10 (1991): 227–29.
22. Stanley E. Porter, "The Functional Distribution of Koine Greek," in *Diglossia and Other Topics in New Testament Linguistics* (JSNTSup 193; Sheffield: Sheffield Academic Press, 2000), 62.
23. L. Rydbeck, "On the Question of Linguistic Levels and the Place of the New Testament in the Contemporary Language Milieu," in *The Language of the New Testament: Classic Essays* (JSNTS 60; Sheffield: Sheffield Academic, 1991), 200.
24. Ibid., 200–203.
25. Albert Wifstrand, "Luke and the Septuagint," in *Epochs and Styles: Selected Writings on the New Testament, Greek Language and Greek Culture in the Post-Classical Era* (ed. Lars Rydbeck and Stanley E. Porter; trans. Denis Searby; WUNT 179; Tübingen: Mohr Siebeck, 2005), 41.
26. Stanley E. Porter, "Verbal Aspect and Discourse Function in Mark 16:1–8: Three Significant Instances," in *Studies in the Greek Bible: Essays in Honor of Francis T. Gignac, S.J.* (ed. Jeremy Corley and Vincent Skemp; CBQMS 44; Washington: Catholic Biblical Association of America, 2008), 123–37.

With respect to John's gospel, it is important to take heed of the direct appeals that the author makes to his readers, such as is found in 20:31. In this connection, the book exhibits relatively frequent instances of "authorial discourse," in which the author effectively "speaks" to the reader.[27] O'Donnell points to John's much higher frequency of so-called "private" verbs, such as πιστεύω and γινώσκω.[28] John is also comparatively low on features that are normally associated with informational production.[29] Thus Johannine register appears to be more explicitly persuasive and personal, which accords with the stated purpose of the book.

6.5 Divergent Aspectual Patterns: Pragmatics, Idiolect, and Register

The differences in the usage of aspect across the Synoptics occur within the realm of pragmatics. For example, the use of the historical present to introduce paragraphs is apparently a cancelable feature, since not all authors use the historical present this way. While the semantic constituency of the historical present remains constant, there are different pragmatic uses for which it may be employed.

Some of the differences in aspectual usage are shaped by idiolect. The frequency of the historical present is probably idiolectal. Perhaps the high frequency of historical present usage in Mark and John indicates a more "flamboyant" style, while Luke is much more reserved. Luke's restraint might also be shaped by register in that his apparent "prestige" language, emulating the sacred Septuagint, might have led to a reserved usage of "flamboyant" devices.

However, it is here that Thucydides provides an important comparison since his is also regarded as "prestige" language, written in Attic historical prose—Attic itself being a prestige dialect. Thucydides has been dubbed the father of "scientific history" because of his strict standards of evidence-gathering. And yet, Thucydides displays a high frequency of historical presents. It is not likely, therefore, that historical presents were repugnant to the more elevated registers. As such, Luke's restraint is tenta-

---

27. Campbell, *Verbal Aspect (Indicative Mood)*, 42–43.
28. Brook O'Donnell, "Register–Balanced Corpus," 282–83.
29. Ibid., 283.

tively regarded as idiolect rather than register-specific. It was simply part of Luke's style to use the historical present sparingly.

Some differences in aspectual usage are shaped by register. John's high frequency of the perfect indicative may be idiolectal, especially since the Johannine Epistles also demonstrate a high frequency of perfect usage. However, this phenomenon may also be related to register, since John's gospel has been described as persuasive and personal in function. With respect to historical present frequency, John parallels Mark, and both authors demonstrate free use of it as a highlighting device. Mark's use of the perfect, however, parallels the other Synoptics, with the perfect accounting for only 2–3 percent of all indicatives, while John demonstrates perfect usage at 8 percent of total indicatives. If the perfect functions to express prominence—as many scholars have argued[30]—this highlighting device is favored by John, but not by Mark (nor the other Synopticists).

If John's register is regarded as persuasive and personal—and therefore less informational—this could in part account for the high frequency of perfects. Such frequency is no doubt related to idiolect, but the point here is that it may also be influenced by the register of the document. Conversely, this conclusion also fits with Markan register, which (as suggested above by Porter) is nonpersuasive and more informational. Mark's ordinary use of the perfect therefore fits such a profile.

6.6 Conclusion

What may be concluded from all this? Four things may be suggested. First, semantics are semantics. That is, regardless of genre, form of literature, idiolect, or register, the semantic values of verbs remain constant.

Second, genre and form account for the convergent aspectual patterns observed. The patterns of narrative structure are predictable and verbal aspect usage fits within such patterns. Furthermore, aspectual usage in the epistles is markedly different from that in narratives.

Third, idiolect and register account for the divergent aspectual patterns detected throughout the documents in view. Certain authors demonstrate a preference for certain verbal phenomena, while other authors have a preference against such. It is sometimes difficult to determine if divergent patterns

---

30. Campbell, *Verbal Aspect (Indicative Mood)*, 195–210.

are due to either idiolect or register, though these may often go hand in hand. Indeed, the extant samples of each author's writing are probably too small to make definitive statements one way or the other. This process would be easier if multiple examples of each author's writing across varying registers were available to us. Then we could discern which patterns belong to idiolect alone and which relate to register. There is some potential for progress, however, in comparing different authors writing within similar registers.

Fourth, further research into idiolect and register with respect to the Greek New Testament will no doubt yield greater understanding of aspectual usage, as determined by each author's style and the social context and purpose of each document.

As mentioned in this chapter's introduction, verbal aspect is but one area of investigation when it comes to idiolect, genre, and register. By increasing the parts of speech under consideration, we will exponentially increase the amount of data that may be processed through these lenses. This will aid our appreciation of the nature of New Testament literature as well as enhance our understanding of the Greek language.

6.7 Further Reading

Burridge, R. A. *What Are the Gospels? A Comparison with Graeco-Roman Biography.* SNTSMS 70. Cambridge: Cambridge University Press, 1992.

Halliday, M. A. K. *Language as Social Semiotic: The Social Interpretation of Language and Meaning.* London: Edward Arnold, 1978.

Halliday, M. A. K., and R. Hasan. *Language, Context, and Text: Aspects of Language in a Social-Semiotic Perspective.* Oxford: Oxford University Press, 1989.

O'Donnell, Matthew Brook. "Designing and Compiling a Register-Balanced Corpus of Hellenistic Greek for the Purpose of Linguistic Description and Investigation." Pages 255–97 in *Diglossia and Other Topics in New Testament Linguistics.* Edited by Stanley E. Porter. JSNTSup 193. Sheffield: Sheffield Academic, 2000.

Pearson, Brook W. R., and Stanley E. Porter. "The Genres of the New Testament." Pages 131–65 in *Handbook to Exegesis of the New Testament.* Edited by Stanley E. Porter. Leiden: Brill, 2002.

Porter, Stanley E. "The Functional Distribution of Koine Greek." Pages 53–75 in *Diglossia and Other Topics in New Testament Linguistics.* JSNTSup 193. Sheffield: Sheffield Academic, 2000.

Rydbeck, L. "On the Question of Linguistic Levels and the Place of the New Testament in the Contemporary Language Milieu." Pages 191–204 in *The Language of the New Testament: Classic Essays.* JSNTSup 60. Sheffield: Sheffield Academic, 1991.

Wifstrand, Albert. "Language and Style of the New Testament." Pages 71–77 in *Epochs and Styles: Selected Writings on the New Testament, Greek Language and Greek Culture in the Post-Classical Era.* Edited by Lars Rydbeck and Stanley E. Porter. Translated by Denis Searby. WUNT 179. Tübingen: Mohr Siebeck, 2005.

———. "Luke and Greek Classicism." Pages 17–27 in *Epochs and Styles: Selected Writings on the New Testament, Greek Language and Greek Culture in the Post-Classical Era.*

———. "Luke and the Septuagint." Pages 28–45 in *Epochs and Styles: Selected Writings on the New Testament, Greek Language and Greek Culture in the Post-Classical Era.*

CHAPTER 7

DISCOURSE ANALYSIS I: HALLIDAYAN APPROACHES

Since I welcome every available opportunity to pontificate on sub-jects that I know nothing about, a colloquium on discourse analysis provides a singularly apt occasion to display this rare skill.

—Moisés Silva

7.1 Introduction

Discourse analysis is a burgeoning field and is one of the most exciting new areas of research related to Greek exegesis. While it has been a topic of discussion for decades within the wider world of linguistics (sometimes referred to as *text linguistics*),[1] it is relatively new to New Testament studies and Greek linguistics. Discourse analysis is an interdisciplinary approach to understanding how units of text relate to one another in order to create the theme, message,

---

1. Some early contributions (other than those by members of SIL — see §7.2.1) include Wolfgang Dressler, *Einführung in die Textlinguistik* (Tübingen: Niemeyer, 1972); Joseph E. Grimes, *The Thread of Discourse* (The Hague: Mouton, 1975); Teun A. van Dijk, *Text and Context: Explorations in the Semantics and Pragmatics of Discourse* (London: Longman, 1977); Gillian Brown and George Yule, *Discourse Analysis* (Cambridge: Cambridge University Press, 1983); M. Coulthard, *An Introduction to Discourse Analysis* (2nd ed.; London: Longman, 1985); Timothy W. Crusius, *Discourse: A Critique and Synthesis of Major Theories* (New York: Modern Language Association, 1989).

and structure of a text. It is concerned to discover linguistic patterns in text, using grammatical and semantic criteria, such as cohesion, anaphora, and inter-sentence connectivity.[2] Discourse analysts are often interested in "discourse markers," which are elements of language that demarcate units of text.

The simplest way to think of discourse analysis is that it deals with text beyond the level of the sentence—the pericope, paragraph, wider units, and the text as a whole. In this way, it has obvious overlap with the interests of literary analysis (such as theme and structure) and also with the interests of rhetorical analysis (such as the way in which ideas are communicated). Discourse analysis does not attempt to replace these more traditional modes of exegesis, but is complementary to them. The most distinctive contribution that discourse analysis brings alongside literary and rhetorical analysis is its robustly linguistic nature. It generally moves from the grammar and syntax of a text out to these larger textual concerns, rather than starting with the big picture.

As we will see, discourse analysis will often yield results that are similar to traditional methods of Greek exegesis, and yet it will sometimes provide quite different outcomes. Nevertheless, even when the results of discourse analysis seem similar to traditional exegetical outcomes, the methods set out by such analysis provide a firmer foundation for results. Discourse analysis operates with a linguistically robust methodology that provides somewhat objective criteria by which to adjudicate exegetical issues. By contrast, traditional exegetical approaches often rely on the intuitive insights of the interpreter. While the intuitive conclusions of gifted interpreters will often be correct, it is difficult to assess such conclusions without a linguistic methodology in place. Discourse analysis provides a method (or, in fact, a variety of methods) by which to assess various conclusions about the text.

Because of the importance of discourse analysis and because of the variety of approaches within the field, we are dedicating two chapters to this topic. Each chapter will focus on one major "school" of discourse analysis, though there are many others. This chapter focuses on approaches to discourse analysis developed by M. A. K. Halliday, which have been applied by several scholars to the Greek New Testament. The following chapter focuses on the work of Stephen H. Levinsohn and Steven E. Runge. To put

---

2. Crystal, *Linguistics and Phonetics*, 148.

both of these chapters in context, we will begin by exploring four major schools of discourse analysis that are relevant to New Testament studies.

7.2 Four Major Schools of Discourse Analysis

Writing twenty years ago, Stanley E. Porter sketched out four major schools of discourse analysis in an essay belonging to the important volume, *Discourse Analysis and Other Topics in Biblical Greek*.[3] Even then, the four schools that Porter addressed did not exhaust the various approaches to discourse analysis that existed in 1995, and today that is all the more the case. Nevertheless, Porter's essay remains a useful introduction to the types of concerns found in discourse analysis, how methodologies differ across schools, and who some of the key exponents working in the field are — at least those who impact New Testament studies. It also offers mild critique of these schools. The following is summarized from Porter's essay, with some argumentations.

7.2.1 Summer Institute of Linguistics (SIL)

Influenced by linguists such as Nida, Pike, and Lamb,[4] SIL has predominantly been occupied with issues relating to Bible translation.[5] Initially, the SIL school demonstrated interest in layers of language, proceeding from the smallest elements of language to increasingly larger structures (see §1.4.11).[6] Kathleen Callow, for example, contributed a discussion of elements beyond the sentence level in her book, *Discourse Considerations in Translating the Word of God*.[7] After Callow, however, Porter observes a return to sentence-level interest, citing works by Stephen H. Levinsohn (to be discussed in the next chapter) and David A. Black, who devote significant space to the sentence. While Porter applauds the contribution of

---

3. Stanley E. Porter and D. A. Carson, eds., *Discourse Analysis and Other Topics in Biblical Greek* (JSNTSup 113; Sheffield: Sheffield Academic Press, 1995). Porter's essay in the volume is "Discourse Analysis and New Testament Studies: An Introductory Survey" (14–35).
4. E. A. Nida, *Toward a Science of Translating: With Special Reference to Principles and Procedures Involved in Bible Translating* (Leiden: Brill, 1964); Pike, *Unified Theory*; S. M. Lamb, *Outline of Stratificational Grammar* (Washington: Georgetown University Press, 1966).
5. It is possible to discern two distinct strands within SIL. American members such as Pike and Longacre put emphasis on extending the grammatical hierarchy to include paragraph and discourse levels. Kathleen Callow, John Callow, and John Beekman are more European (Firthian) in their approach, which is known as "Semantic Structure Analysis."
6. Porter, "Discourse Analysis," 25.
7. Kathleen Callow, *Discourse Considerations in Translating the Word of God* (Grand Rapids: Zondervan, 1974).

SIL to Bible translation, he critiques the movement for not extending far beyond sentence-level analysis.[8]

7.2.2 Halliday and Hasan

According to Porter, M. A. K. Halliday and R. Hasan offer the most integrative approach of the four schools discussed.[9] Rather than treating discourse as the extension of the sentence, Halliday and Hasan begin with discourse at the broad level, discussing the ideational, interpersonal, and textual features of text (see §§2.4.1–2).[10] Since Halliday's approach to discourse analysis is the topic of this chapter, more will be said later. For now, however, it is worth noting that this school of discourse analysis has not been "mapped" into Ancient Greek yet (having been developed in English), meaning that its correlation to the language of the New Testament must be considered by the practitioner. While there is much theoretical merit to the approach of this school, it requires a high level of commitment to be of use to New Testament studies. Fortunately, some scholars have already attempted to bridge the gap, such as Porter, Reed, Guthrie, and Westfall.[11]

7.2.3 Continental Europe

This school is the least cohesive, demonstrating a number of influences and a focus on rhetoric. While there is a helpful concern with the macrostructure of texts in the work of scholars such as Hellholm, Schenk, and Johanson,[12] Porter thinks the wide-ranging and interdisciplinary features of the Continental European school is so diverse that it becomes its own liability.[13]

---

8. Porter, "Discourse Analysis," 25–26. Porter overstates this criticism, since several of Levinsohn's publications deal with issues well beyond the level of the sentence. See, e.g., Stephen H. Levinsohn, *Textual Connections in Acts* (Atlanta: SBL, 1987); "The Groupings and Classification of Events in Mark 14," *Notes on Translation* 66 (1977): 19–28; "Preliminary Observations on the Use of the Historic Present in Mark," *Notes on Translation* 65 (1977): 13–28.

9. Halliday and Matthiessen, *Functional Grammar*; Halliday and Hasan, *Cohesion*; idem, *Language, Context, and Text*.

10. Porter, "Discourse Analysis," 28.

11. Stanley E. Porter, *Idioms of the Greek New Testament* (2nd ed.; Sheffield: Sheffield Academic Press, 1994), 298–307; J. T. Reed, "Cohesive Ties in 1 Timothy: In Defense of the Epistle's Unity," *Neot* 26 (1992): 131–47; George H. Guthrie, *The Structure of Hebrews: A Text-Linguistic Analysis* (NovT-Sup 73; Leiden: Brill, 1994), 45–75; Cynthia Long Westfall, *A Discourse Analysis of the Letter to the Hebrews: The Relationship between Form and Meaning* (JSNTSup 297; New York: T&T Clark, 2005).

12. D. Hellholm, *Das Visionenbuch des Hermas als Apokalypse: Formgeschichtliche und texttheoretische Studien zu einer literarischen Gattung*. I. *Methodologische Vorüberlegungen und makrostrukturelle Textanalyse* (ConBNT 13.1; Lund: Gleerup, 1980); W. Schenk, *Der Philipperbrief des Paulus* (Stuttgart: Kohlhammer, 1984); B. C. Johanson, *To All the Brethren: A Text-Linguistic and Rhetorical Approach to 1 Thessalonians* (ConBNT 16; Stockholm: Almqvist & Wiksell, 1987).

13. Porter, "Discourse Analysis," 31.

7.2.4 J. P. Louw

J. P. Louw's essay "Discourse Analysis and the Greek New Testament" first introduced discourse analysis to the wider New Testament world,[14] and his later *Semantics of New Testament Greek* and *A Semantic Discourse Analysis of Romans* have been important influences on the field.[15] Louw developed a method of colon analysis in which the text is analysed through its constituent cola. These cola are units formed around a nominative and predicate structure.[16] The interconnectedness of the cola is diagrammed, demonstrating the relationships between the smallest units of meaning (the cola) and larger semantic units. While Porter regards Louw's South African school of discourse analysis to be the best-coordinated school, having widespread influence, he identifies some weaknesses. The diagrammed structure of cola relationships is somewhat subjective in its creation, and in fact multiple structures may be offered. The question is how to judge which possible structure is best, and there is no clear methodology to address this problem.[17] There are also questions raised about the nature of the colon itself and how syntax may affect analysis of cola.

As acknowledged above, the foregoing sketch of these four schools of discourse analysis does not include recent developments and is no doubt an oversimplification. Nevertheless, it remains useful insofar as it introduces the seminal currents of New Testament discourse analysis, and it helps us to understand contemporary developments in the context of the discussion. We turn now to look more closely at Halliday's approaches to discourse analysis.

7.3 Cohesion

For Halliday, the central concern of discourse analysis is cohesion. His conception of cohesion was developed with Hasan in the seminal volume *Cohesion in English*,[18] with a more recent expression found in Halliday and Matthiessen's *Halliday's Introduction to Functional Grammar*.[19] Cohesion

---

14. J. P. Louw, "Discourse Analysis and the Greek New Testament," *BT* 24 (1973): 101–18.
15. J. P. Louw, *Semantics of New Testament Greek* (Philadelphia: Fortress, 1982); idem, *A Semantic Discourse Analysis of Romans* (Pretoria: University of Pretoria, 1987).
16. Porter, "Discourse Analysis," 33.
17. Ibid., 34.
18. Halliday and Hasan, *Cohesion*.
19. Halliday and Matthiessen, *Functional Grammar*, chapter 9.

refers to the way in which a text hangs together: "it refers to relations of meaning that exist within the text, and that define it as a text."[20] According to Halliday and Matthiessen, language has "resources for managing the flow of discourse: for creating semantic links across sentences—or rather, semantic links which work equally well either within or across sentences."[21]

The study of cohesion asks how speakers form texts into complete units. What makes a text a text rather than a collection of unrelated utterances? In fact, any text or speech will fit somewhere on a spectrum of cohesiveness that ranges from highly coherent through to incoherent. So, why are some texts more coherent than others? As Labov says, "The fundamental problem of discourse analysis is to show how one utterance follows another in a rational, rule-governed manner—in other words, how we understand coherent discourse."[22] Reed further elaborates:

> At a very basic level, *linguistic cohesiveness* refers to the means by which an immediate linguistic context meaningfully relates to a preceding context and/or a context of situation (i.e. meaningful relationships between text, co-text and context). Linguistic cohesiveness provides speakers with the means to produce a "message" (i.e. theme) from individual and sometimes unrelated words and phrases.[23]

In answer to the question of what makes a text coherent or incoherent (or somewhere in between), Halliday and Hasan refer to two types of context. The first is the relationship between the text and its inner world—its co-text (what is normally called "context" or "literary context").[24] The second is the relationship between the text and its external world—its context of situation and culture (usually referred to as "historical context" or "background" within New Testament studies).[25]

The second type of context "refers to all those extra-linguistic factors which have some bearing on the text itself."[26] It aids cohesion in that the reader mentally links the text to a concept in the culture to which the

---

20. Halliday and Hasan, *Cohesion*, 4.
21. Halliday and Matthiessen, *Functional Grammar*, 114.
22. William Labov, *Sociolinguistic Patterns* (Philadelphia: University of Philadelphia Press, 1972), 252.
23. Jeffrey T. Reed, "The Cohesiveness of Discourse: Towards a Model of Linguistic Criteria for Analyzing New Testament Discourse," in *Discourse Analysis and the New Testament*, 29.
24. Halliday and Hasan, *Cohesion*, 6–19.
25. Ibid., 19–21.
26. Ibid., 21.

text belongs.[27] If a text's cultural context is totally alien to the reader, its effective coherence would be significantly compromised. In this way, the coherence of a text is somewhat subjectively determined, depending on the reader's ability to understand its external references.

The context of situation relates closely to register (see §6.4), since "the more specifically we can characterize the context of situation, the more specifically we can predict the properties of a text in that situation."[28] Cohesion and register work together to define a text: "A text is a passage of discourse which is coherent in these two regards: it is coherent with respect to the context of situation, and therefore consistent in register; and it is coherent with respect to itself, and therefore cohesive."[29]

The first type of context does not depend on the world outside the text (external references), but is entirely internally focused. Halliday and Hasan refer to the interpretation of some element in the discourse that is dependent on that of another.[30] The elements of a text are mutually defining and cannot be understood apart from each other. Cohesive relationships will be observed between words, phrases, sentences, and pericopes.

Both types of context are, of course, important for understanding any text. Our primary interest here, however, is the first. What are the ways in which a text creates cohesion within itself? It is to this topic we now turn.

7.4 Resources of Cohesion

Halliday and Matthiessen identify four ways in which cohesion is created in English: through conjunction, reference, ellipsis, and lexical cohesion.[31] These four resources for cohesion are sketched out below.

7.4.1 Conjunction

Conjunction refers to markers that indicate that a clause relates to a previous one, thus creating continuity in a text. Words such as "but,"

---

27. Reed, "Cohesiveness of Discourse," 32.
28. Halliday and Hasan, *Cohesion*, 22.
29. Ibid., 23.
30. Ibid., 4.
31. Halliday and Matthiessen, *Functional Grammar*, 603. Their treatment summarizes the major discussions of these categories in Halliday and Hasan, *Cohesion*: conjunction is the burden of ch. 5 (pp. 226–73); reference, ch. 2 (pp. 31–87); ellipsis, ch. 4 (pp. 142–225; see also substitution in ch. 3); and lexical cohesion, ch. 6 (pp. 274–92).

"meanwhile," and "so" are obvious conjunctions in English.[32] Subtypes of conjunction include elaboration, extension, and enhancement. Elaboration refers to the relationship between clauses in which one clause elaborates on another, either by way of apposition or clarification (epexegesis).[33] Extension involves addition to a clause or a variation from it.[34] Enhancement types include spatio-temporal (place, time), manner (how, why), causal-conditional (result, contingency), and matter (topic).[35]

Obviously, Greek conjunctions such as καί, ἀλλά, and ἵνα, and other connectives such as τότε and διὰ τοῦτο, may be understood as cohesive devices in the ways that Halliday and Hasan elucidate.

7.4.2 Reference

Reference creates cohesion by creating links between elements in a text. Reference can be exophoric, meaning a text points to things outside the text, or endophoric, meaning it points to something within the text itself.[36] Repeated reference to the same things creates referential chains; such chains are natural bonds of cohesion. Repeated reference need not involve the same word, but there are a variety of means with which to refer to the same item: the ball... which he threw... it was red. Here the item (the ball) is referenced by means of the word "ball," but also "which" and "it." These three references to the same thing create a referential chain. Types of reference include personal (reference to the same person), demonstrative (reference using "this" or "that"), and comparative reference (relations of contrast, using words such as "different," "bigger").[37] For Greek, we should pay special attention to the personal, reflexive, and relative pronouns ἐγώ, ἐμαυτοῦ, and ὅς, as well as the demonstratives οὗτος and ἐκεῖνος.

7.4.3 Ellipsis

Whereas reference refers to explicit markers that point to a common item (the referent), ellipsis leaves things out when they can be presumed from the context.[38] The fact that the reader can supply the missing element/s from

---

32. Halliday and Matthiessen, *Functional Grammar*, 605.
33. Ibid., 615–16.
34. Ibid., 616–17.
35. Ibid., 617–20.
36. Ibid., 623–25.
37. Ibid., 626–34.
38. Ibid., 606.

the wider context creates cohesion since the ellipsis itself depends on the text being read as a whole. Romans 3:27 provides a good example of this:[39]

> Where then is boasting? It is excluded. By what kind of law? Of works? No, but a law of faith. (NASB)

The nonelliptical form would read:

> Where then is boasting? It is excluded. By what kind of law [is boasting excluded]? [Is boasting excluded by a law] Of works? No [boasting is not excluded by a law of works], but [boasting is excluded by] a law of faith.

7.4.4 Lexical Cohesion

This kind of cohesion relies on the relationships between lexical items. Some types of lexical relationships include repetition, synonymy, hyponymy, meronymy, and collocation.[40] Repetition refers, obviously, to the repetition of the same lexeme.[41] An example of this is found in Romans 3, through the repetition of the word *faith*:

> This righteousness is given through faith.... God presented Christ as a sacrifice of atonement, through the shedding of his blood — to be received by faith ... he did it to demonstrate his righteousness at the present time, so as to be just and the one who justifies those who have faith in Jesus.... [Boasting is excluded] because of the law that requires faith. For we maintain that a person is justified by faith. (Romans 3:22, 25, 26, 27, 28, NIV)

Synonymy, however, creates lexical cohesion by using multiple words that overlap in meaning (they do not need to be perfectly overlapping to be described as synonymous).[42] Hyponymy is about classification, so that one lexical item represents a class of thing and the second represents a (subordinate) subclass within the first (superordinate) class.[43] Meronymy refers to lexical items that are each a part of something else, like *flowers* and *fountains*, which are meronyms of *garden*.[44] Collocation recognizes a particular association between words that tend to occur together, such as *flesh and blood, day and age, fish and chips*.[45]

---

39. The biblical examples in this section were developed by Daniel Waldschmidt for an Advanced Greek class at Trinity Evangelical Divinity School, Spring 2014.
40. Halliday and Matthiessen, *Functional Grammar*, 644–50.
41. Ibid., 644–45.
42. Ibid., 645–46.
43. Ibid., 646–47.
44. Ibid., 647–48.
45. Ibid., 648–50.

7.5 The Analysis of Cohesion

In the final chapter of Halliday and Hasan's *Cohesion in English*, they suggest a method for the analysis of cohesion in a text. Key to the general principles of analysis of cohesion is the concept of the "tie," which is a cohesive element that connects parts of a text together.[46] In order to analyze any sentence, we should determine how many cohesive ties it contains, and "how many instances of a cohesive element that are not resolved by presupposition within the sentence. This shows the total extent of the demands it makes on the preceding (or rather the surrounding) text."[47] Next, it is important to specify what type of cohesion is involved (e.g., reference, substitution, et al.).[48]

Other pertinent questions relate to genre (differing genres "may exhibit a general tendency towards the use of certain features or modes rather than others"),[49] idiolect (do particular individuals favor one type of cohesion over others?), variation of the density of cohesive ties at various points in a text,[50] and the relation between cohesion and the division of a text into paragraphs.[51]

In order to explore further Halliday and Hasan's notion of cohesive ties, we will draw on Jeffrey Reed's summary of them since he relates them to the Greek of the New Testament.[52]

7.5.1 Organic Ties

Organic ties are elements built into a language for connective purposes, such as markers of transition (e.g., γάρ, ἀλλά, δέ, καί), grammatical structures (e.g., genitive absolute using γίνομαι), and certain lexical items (e.g., λοιπόν).[53] Organic ties consist of two functional systems, parataxis and hypotaxis. The former involves the relation between items of equal status, while the latter involves the relation between an independent item and an item that is dependent on it.[54] Organic ties also set boundaries within a

---

46. Halliday and Hasan, *Cohesion*, 329.
47. Ibid., 332.
48. Ibid.
49. Ibid.
50. Ibid.
51. Ibid., 333.
52. Reed, "Cohesiveness of Discourse," 28–46.
53. Ibid., 32–33.
54. Ibid., 33.

discourse; "they provide a means of organizing groups of componential ties [see below] into thematic sections/paragraphs."[55]

7.5.2 Componential Ties

Componential ties concern "the meaningful relationships between *individual linguistic components* in the discourse (e.g., repetition of words)."[56] In other words, these are ties between words or phrases. There are three types of componential ties: co-reference, co-classification, and co-extension.

7.5.2.1 Co-reference. Co-reference refers to cohesive ties between items of the same identity (see §7.4.2). This might involve "person deixis," which is the encoding of various participants into a discourse using pronouns, proper nouns, and verbal suffixes.[57] Temporal deixis can create cohesion through references to the same temporal frame, indicated by adverbs such as τότε, νῦν, and μέχρι.[58] Place deixis is closely related, tying a section together by the fact that events are unfolding in a single location.[59]

7.5.2.2 Co-classification. This second type of componential tie involves cohesive ties between linguistic items of the same class or genus. By substituting one item for another in the same class, this type of tie is created. Reed offers the following example: "I want the children to draw with crayons, and I want the teenagers to draw with pencils." He says, "By substituting 'teenagers' for 'children' and 'with pencils' for 'with crayons,' the two sentences form a cohesive tie of co-classification with respect to who should do the drawing and how it should be done."[60]

7.5.2.3 Co-extension. The third type of componential tie "refers to cohesive ties between linguistic items of the same semantic field, but not necessarily of the same class."[61] Reed elaborates:

> In the sentences "John ate the pizza" and "Susie gobbled down the cake" the linguistic pairs "John" / "Susie," "ate" / "gobbled down" and "pizza" / "cake" do not refer to the same entities nor do they refer to the same class

---

55. Ibid., 36.
56. Ibid.
57. Ibid., 38.
58. Ibid., 39.
59. Ibid., 40.
60. Ibid., 40–41.
61. Ibid., 41.

(e.g. pizza is not a kind of cake).... By using words with similar senses speakers talk about similar things in similar ways.[62]

When cohesive ties are used throughout a text, they create different kinds of referential chains (see §7.4.2). "Identity chains" are expressed by co-classificational ties, while "similarity chains" are expressed by co-classificational and co-extensional ties.[63] While the discernment of such referential chains form only a part of how a text achieves cohesion, they are nevertheless objectively and explicitly determined. That is, the discourse analyst can point to these explicit markers with a degree of ease in describing how a particular text hangs together.

7.6 Evaluation

The foregoing represents a summary of Halliday and Hasan's theory of cohesion. Their approach has several strengths and useful applications for study of the Greek New Testament, some of which ought to be self-evident. Nevertheless, there are a few drawbacks, including criticisms of the theory and the lack of direct application to the language of Greek (having been developed in English).

Some of the critique of Halliday and Hasan is summarized by Annemieke Drummen:

> Halliday and Hasan's description of cohesion has been criticized (e.g. Car-rell 1982, Sanders et al. 1992, Sanders and Pander Maat 2006) for treating the concept as a necessary condition for the connectedness of a discourse. In Carrell's view (1982:486), cohesion is not the cause, but the effect of coherence. Similarly, Sanders et al. (1992:2–3) point out that cohesive elements are "important though not necessary features of discourse; they are linguistic markers, expressing the underlying conceptual relations that are of a cognitive nature." These authors present coherence and cohesion as alternative approaches, but in fact (the students of) both concepts look at different phenomena, and can therefore also be seen as complementary.
>
> Investigating cohesion means focusing on the linguistic reflections of coherence. Tanskanen (2006:7), for instance, adopts this milder view, assuming that cohesion contributes to coherence.[64]

---

62. Ibid.
63. Ibid., 43.
64. Annemieke Drummen, "Cohesion," in *Encyclopedia of Ancient Greek Language and Linguistics* (ed. Georgios K. Giannakis et al.; Brill Online, 2014).

Clearly there is some disagreement as to whether cohesion *effects* the coherence of a text or is itself the *effect* of its inherent coherence. Either way, students of the Greek New Testament will benefit from tracing the coherence of a text through the markers of cohesion elucidated by Halliday and Hasan.

An obvious drawback for the application of Halliday and Hasan's theory of cohesion to the Greek of the New Testament, however, is that it is developed with respect to English and has not been "translated" into Greek, so to speak. There have been various attempts to use Hallidayan approaches for the study of the New Testament, and these offer helpful models for others who might wish to do likewise.[65] That is not the same, however, as a comprehensive account of how Halliday "maps" onto Greek.

Perhaps the work that most closely approximates this goal is found outside New Testament Greek scholarship: *Discourse Cohesion in Ancient Greek*, edited by Stephanie Bakker and Gerry Wakker.[66] This volume consists of papers presented at the Sixth International Colloquium on Ancient Greek Linguistics in June 2007 and acknowledges the foundational role that Halliday and Hasan occupy in discussions about cohesion. The two editors state:

> there is no consensus on what exactly discourse cohesion is (nor on the question whether it really exists ...). Most scholars working on discourse cohesion, however, will more or less accept the ideas of Halliday and Hasan (1976), the fathers [*sic*] of the concept of cohesion.[67]

The essays in this volume explore the cohesion functions of various parts of speech, such as third person pronouns,[68] various particles and conjunctions,[69]

---

65. See Jeffrey T. Reed, *Discourse Analysis of Philippians: Method and Rhetoric in the Debate over Literary Integrity* (JSNTSup 136; Sheffield: Sheffield Academic, 1997); idem, "To Timothy or Not: A Discourse Analysis of 1 Timothy," in *Biblical Greek Language and Linguistics: Open Questions in Current Research* (ed. Stanley E. Porter and D. A. Carson; JSNTSup 80; Sheffield: Sheffield Academic, 1993), 90–118; Guthrie, *Hebrews*; Westfall, *Hebrews*. There are also various points of confluence between Halliday and Levinsohn (cf., e.g., 7.5.1 and 8.4.1–2; 8.8).
66. Stephanie Bakker and Gerry Wakker, eds., *Discourse Cohesion in Ancient Greek* (Amsterdam Studies in Classical Philology 16; Leiden: Brill, 2009).
67. Ibid., xii.
68. Anna Bonifazi, "Discourse Cohesion through Third Person Pronouns: The Case of κεῖνος and αὐτός in Homer," in ibid., 1–20.
69. Stéphanie J. Bakker, "On the Curious Combination of the Particles γάρ and οὖν," in ibid., 41–62; Gerry C. Wakker, "Well I Will Now Present My Arguments": Discourse Cohesion Marked by οὖν and τοίνυν in Lysias," in ibid., 63–82; Antonio R. Revuelta Puigdollers, "The Particles αὖ and αὖτε in Ancient Greek as Topicalizing Devices," in ibid., 83–110; A. Maria van Erp Taalman Kip, "Καὶ μήν, καὶ δή and ἤδη in Tragedy and Comedy," in ibid., 111–34; Annemieke Drummen, "Discourse Cohesion in Dialogue. Turn-Initial ἀλλά in Greek Drama," in ibid., 135–54; Coulter H. George, "Greek Particles: Just a Literary Phenomenon?," in ibid., 155–70.

differing text types,[70] and some verbs.[71] The scope of literature discussed ranges through Homer, Lysias, Euripides, Hesiod, Greek tragedy, comedy, drama, and Classical and Ancient Greek in general.

This volume represents a significant addition to the literature that explores cohesion in Ancient Greek. Nevertheless, it is not the comprehensive "translation" of Halliday and Hasan into Greek that remains desirable. In fact, the volume exhibits a concentration on Greek particles, leaving much else of the language uncovered. This observation is not intended to be critical, since the volume is a collection of conference papers rather than a comprehensive treatment of the topic. But the fact remains that it is *not* a comprehensive treatment of the topic. Moreover, it obviously does not offer an application of Halliday and Hasan to the Greek of the New Testament.

7.7 Further Reading

Bakker, Stephanie and Gerry Wakker, eds. *Discourse Cohesion in Ancient Greek*. Amsterdam Studies in Classical Philology 16. Leiden: Brill, 2009.

Guthrie, George H. *The Structure of Hebrews: A Text-Linguistic Analysis*. NovTSup 73. Leiden: Brill, 1994.

Halliday, M. A. K., and R. Hasan. *Cohesion in English*. London: Routledge, 1976.

Halliday, M. A. K., and Christian M. I. M. Matthiessen. *Halliday's Introduction to Functional Grammar*. Fourth revised edition. London: Routledge, 2014.

Porter, Stanley E. "Discourse Analysis and New Testament Studies: An Introductory Survey." Pages 14–35 in *Discourse Analysis and Other Topics in Biblical Greek*. Edited by Stanley E. Porter and D. A. Carson. JSNTSup 133. Sheffield: Sheffield Academic, 1995.

Reed, Jeffrey T. "The Cohesiveness of Discourse: Towards a Model of

---

70. Rutger J. Allan, "Towards a Typology of the Narrative Modes in Ancient Greek. Text Type and Narrative Structure in Euripidean Messenger Speeches," in ibid., 171–204; Albert Rijksbaron, "Discourse Cohesion in the Proem of Hesiod's *Theogony*," in ibid., 241–66.

71. Louis Basset, "The Use of the Imperfect to Express Completed States of Affairs. The Imperfect as a Marker of Narrative Cohesion," in ibid., 205–20; Sander Orriens, "Involving the Past in the Present: The Classical Greek Perfect as a Situating Cohesion Device," in ibid., 221–40.

Linguistic Criteria for Analyzing New Testament Discourse." Pages 28–46 in *Discourse Analysis and the New Testament: Approaches and Results*. JSNTSup 170. Edited by Stanley E. Porter and Jeffrey T. Reed. Sheffield: Sheffield Academic, 1999.

Westfall, Cynthia Long. *A Discourse Analysis of the Letter to the Hebrews: The Relationship between Form and Meaning*. JSNTSup 297. New York: T&T Clark, 2005.

CHAPTER 8

DISCOURSE ANALYSIS II: LEVINSOHN AND RUNGE

Discourse without prominence would be like pointing to a piece of black cardboard and insisting that it was a picture of black camels crossing black sands at midnight.　　　—*Robert E. Longacre*

8.1 Introduction

In the previous chapter, the Summer Institute of Linguistics (SIL) was introduced as one of the four major schools of discourse analysis. Perhaps the most important SIL linguist for the study of Greek is Stephen Levinsohn. While Levinsohn is not "Hallidayan" in the sense that his approach is an application of the work of Prague School linguists Jan Firbas and E. Beneš,[1] rather than of Halliday himself, there is some overlap in certain areas, so that we see that the two approaches are not mutually exclusive. An important distinction of Levinsohn's work, however, is that it is explicitly applied to the Greek of the New Testament, though he does not claim to

---

1. Jan Firbas, "Thoughts on the Communicative Function of the Verb in English, German and Czech," *BRNO Studies in English* 1 (1959): 39–63; Jan Firbas and K. Pala, "Review of Ö. Dahl, *Topic and Comment: A Study in Russian and General Transformational Grammar*," *Journal of Linguistics* 7 (1971): 91–101; E. Beneš, "Die Verbstellung im Deutschen, von der Mitteilungsperspektive her betrachtet," *Philologica Pragensia* 5 (1962): 6–19.

do so comprehensively.[2] This chapter will offer an outline and evaluation of Levinsohn's approach to discourse analysis as recorded in his volume *Discourse Features of New Testament Greek*,[3] as well as that of Levinsohn's most significant disciple—Steven Runge.

Stephen H. Levinsohn

8.2 Basic Theory

According to Levinsohn, the value of discourse analysis is that it "draws its explanations, not from within the sentence or word (i.e., the factors involved are not syntactic or morphological), but *extrasententially* (from the linguistic and wider context)."[4] In view of Porter's criticism that he does not go far beyond the level of the sentence (see §7.2.1), Levinsohn acknowledges that this is necessarily true for some units of study, but not for others that involve extrasentential factors.[5]

8.2.1 Eclecticism

Levinsohn begins by describing his approach to discourse analysis as *eclectic*, "making use of the insights of different linguists and different linguistic theories to the extent that I feel they are helpful."[6] Levinsohn is even prepared to admit that he will take a "seed idea" from another linguist and "develop it in another direction." He finds, for example, the ideas of Givón valuable but often arrives at opposite conclusions in their application.[7]

8.2.2 Functional Approach

Levinsohn's linguistic approach is functional in the sense that he is interested in what functions linguistic structures serve, rather just being interested in the structure of a language for its own sake.[8] One implication of

---

2. "This book in no sense claims to offer a comprehensive coverage of the multitude of discourse features found in the Greek New Testament. Rather, it is an attempt to describe a limited number of features." Stephen H. Levinsohn, *Discourse Features of New Testament Greek: A Coursebook on the Information Structure of New Testament Greek* (2nd ed.; Dallas: SIL International, 2000), vii.

3. See also Stephen H. Levinsohn, "The Relevance of Greek Discourse Studies to Exegesis," *Journal of Translation* 2.2 (2006): 11–21. Footnotes make reference to more recent publications that supplement or even correct assertions in Levinsohn's *Discourse Features*.

4. Ibid., viii.

5. Ibid., ix.

6. Ibid., vii.

7. Ibid.

8. Ibid.

a functional approach is the principle that *choice implies meaning*. When an author has a choice of expressing something in more than one way, the choice of one expression over another is significant. This is not simply a question of style; there is a linguistic reason for the choices that are made.[9]

8.2.3 Idiolect

While Levinsohn does not use the term *idiolect* (at least not in the book of interest here),[10] he acknowledges the significance of the concept nonetheless. He assumes that an individual author will use discourse features in a consistent way and that there is potential for variation of such usage between authors. Levinsohn also admits that this means his own presentation contains a weakness, namely, that he has not studied every biblical author in depth. The elucidation of certain discourse features only applies with reference to the biblical author under discussion.[11]

8.2.4 Markedness

According to the concept of markedness, "when a certain marker is present, the feature implied by the marker is present."[12] The reverse, however, is not necessarily true: the absence of the marker does not mean that the feature is absent. Levinsohn illustrates the importance of markedness with respect to the Greek article. One of the uses of the article is that its substantive refers to a particular item, but its absence does not indicate non-particularity; the referent of the substantive might well be particular and known (as is the case with proper nouns).[13]

8.2.5 Semantic Meaning and Pragmatic Effects

Levinsohn regards the distinction between semantics and pragmatics as essential to his approach. A particular construction will have an inherent semantic meaning but differing pragmatic uses according to context.[14]

Levinsohn's volume contains six parts: constituent order, sentence

---

9. Ibid., viii.
10. Instead, Dooley and Levinsohn (*Analyzing Discourse*, 11) follow John Lyons (*Semantics* [vol 2; Cambridge: Cambridge University Press, 1977], 614) in using "the term individual style to refer to 'those features of a text ... which identify it as being the product of a particular author.'"
11. Ibid.
12. Ibid., ix.
13. Ibid.
14. Ibid.

conjunctions, patterns of reference, backgrounding and highlighting, reported conversation, and recognizing subunits and boundaries. The following is a brief sketch of Levinsohn's presentation of these topics.

8.3 Constituent Order

The term "constituent order" is used rather than "word order," acknowledging that "the elements that are ordered are often phrases and clauses, not single words."[15]

8.3.1 Coherence and Discontinuities

In the first chapter in this section, Levinsohn discusses the ways in which sections, subsections, and paragraphs are demarcated through four dimensions of continuity and discontinuity, operating with the assumption that New Testament books are coherent.[16] In narrative, these dimensions are time, place, action, and participants; for other discourse genres, the dimensions are generalized as situation, reference, and action. Paragraph and section breaks become fairly obvious through discerning significant shifts in one or more of these four dimensions in the text.[17]

8.3.2 Points of Departure

The second chapter discusses a device called a "point of departure" (or topicalization), which designates an element placed at the beginning of a clause with the double function of providing a starting point for communication and anchoring the following clause(s) to something already in the context.[18] Points of departure signal discontinuities of situation, reference, and sometimes of action.[19] In this chapter, Levinsohn also endorses the claim that Greek is a verb-subject-object (VSO) language.[20] While acknowledging that this cannot be proved without thorough statistical confirmation, he draws on the implications of this claim to say that varia-

---

15. Ibid., 1, n. 1.
16. Ibid., 2.
17. Ibid., 3.
18. Ibid., 8.
19. Ibid., 7.
20. In later publications, Levinsohn follows Matthew S. Dryer ("On the Six-Way Word Order Typology," *Studies in Language* 21.1 1997. : 69–103) in referring to Greek as a VS/VO language. See, e.g., Stephen H. Levinsohn, "Self-Instruction Materials on Narrative Discourse Analysis" (www.sil.org/~levinsohns/, 6).

tions of the VSO constituent ordering creates an emphasis on the fronted constituent.[21]

8.3.3 Constituent Order

Chapters 3 and 4 in Levinsohn deal with the order of constituents in the remainder of the sentence, whereas the previous chapter was concerned with fronted items. Chapter 3 discusses four default ordering principles: the placement of pronominal constituents immediately following the verb, the placement of core constituents before peripheral ones, the placement of an overtly expressed propositional topic before the comment about that topic, and the placement toward the end of a clause or sentence of the most important or focal constituent of the comment.[22] Chapter 4 includes further discussion of constituent order, dealing with issues such as negated sentences, information questions, focus switching, and discontinuous constituents.[23]

8.4 Sentence Conjunctions

Levinsohn's second major part addresses the most common nonsubordinating conjunctions in the New Testament. While traditional approaches to conjunctions identify their various "senses," Levinsohn follows the linguistic principle of semantic constraints. Each conjunction expresses a single constraint that it places on the way a sentence is to be understood with reference to its context.[24] The differing senses identified by traditional approaches are produced by the one constraint applied in different contexts. In other words, the *constraint* is the semantic value of the conjunction, while its various *senses* are pragmatic functions of the semantic value.

8.4.1 Καί and Δέ in Narrative

Levinsohn's fifth chapter addresses these common conjunctions in narrative, discerning their semantic content rather than focusing on the gloss translations that are so common in grammars. In the Gospels and Acts, καί

---

21. Ibid., 16–17.
22. Ibid., 29–47. According to Levinsohn's terminology, the "comment" is part of a *topic-comment* articulation, which contains the topic of a sentence (usually the subject) and a comment giving information about the topic; see Ibid., 7.
23. Ibid., 48–67.
24. Ibid., 69.

is the default form for linking sentences (in John, asyndeton is default). The most common conjunction when καί is not used is δέ. The distinct semantic element that δέ expresses is that it signals a new step or development in the author's story or argument.[25]

8.4.2 Τότε, Nonconjunctive Καί, and Τέ Solitarium

Τότε is an adverb that may function as a conjunction, especially in Matthew and Acts. When it is not functioning as a conjunction, it retains its temporal expression ("then"), but when in conjunctive use, it functions as a cohesive device "indicating continuity of time *and of other factors* between the subsections."[26] When τότε functions adverbially rather than as a conjunction, it is used at subsections of an ongoing story and to highlight a conclusion—especially in Matthew and Acts.[27]

Levinsohn addresses nonconjunctive καί as a means of "indicating that a sentence or proposition is to be related to its context by *addition*."[28] Rather than functioning as a conjunction to link sentences (see §8.4.1), nonconjunctive καί indicates "*parallelism* between the proposition concerned and an earlier one," and also "backwards confirmation," which refers to a proposition "added to confirm an earlier one."[29]

Τέ Solitarium refers to the use of τέ by itself without any corresponding καί or τέ. Almost all of such occurrences are found in Acts, and they add "distinct propositions that are characterized by *sameness*, in the sense that they refer to different aspects of the same event, the same occasion, or the same pragmatic unit."[30]

The final chapter in this section addresses thematic development in non-narrative text. It "concentrates on the four most common ways in which sentences in non-narrative text are formally related: by means of δέ; simple juxtaposition, i.e., asyndeton; conjunctive καί; and οὖν."[31]

---

25. Ibid., 72. Later publications (e.g., Stephen H. Levinsohn, "'Therefore' or 'Wherefore': What's the Difference?," in *Reflections on Lexicography* [ed. Richard A. Taylor and Craig E. Morrison; Perspectives on Linguistics and Ancient Languages 4; Piscataway, NJ: Gorgias, 2013], 340) express the constraint on interpretation conveyed by δέ as "+Distinctive."
26. Ibid., 95.
27. Ibid., 95–97.
28. Ibid., 99.
29. Ibid.
30. Ibid., 106–7.
31. Ibid., 112. For discussion of ten inferential connectives used in the Pauline epistles, see Levinsohn, "'Therefore' or 'Wherefore,'" 325–43.

In non-narrative text (as with narrative text), δέ "is used to mark new developments, in the sense that the information it introduces builds on what has gone before and makes a distinct contribution to the argument."[32]

Asyndeton is often used "when the relation of the following material to the context is not logical or chronological," yielding two opposite functions in non-narrative text: to indicate a *close* connection between the information concerned, and to indicate that there is *no* direct connection between the information concerned. In other words, asyndeton can indicate that certain information belongs together in the same unit, or that information belongs to different units.[33]

In non-narrative text, conjunctive καί "constrains the material it introduces to be processed as being added to and associated with previous material," but this material does not represent a new development in the context.[34]

As with its use in John's gospel, οὖν is used inferentially and as a resumptive in non-narrative material.[35] The inferential use introduces inferences drawn from a previous statement. The resumptive use of οὖν follows digressional material in order to return to the point of a preceding assertion.[36]

8.5 Patterns of Reference

Levinsohn's third major section deals with some elements "that determine how an entity is referred to."[37] Reference may be created through use of a noun, an article plus a noun, a pronoun, or an articular pronoun, or through implicit information conveyed by a verb (the person and number of the subject).[38] Of particular interest is the identification of default patterns of reference, so that marked forms of reference may also be

---

32. Ibid.
33. Ibid., 118.
34. Ibid., 124.
35. Ibid., 126.
36. Ibid., 126–27.
37. Ibid., 133.
38. The role of οὗτος and ἐκεῖνος in participant reference is discussed in Stephen H. Levinsohn, "Towards a Unified Linguistic Description of οὗτος and ἐκεῖνος," in *The Linguist as Pedagogue: Trends in the Teaching and Linguistic Analysis of the Greek New Testament* (ed. Stanley E. Porter and Matthew Brook O'Donnell; Sheffield: Sheffield Phoenix, 2009), 206–19.

recognized, informing the reader "that a new section is beginning or that a particular event or speech is being highlighted."[39]

The first chapter in this section addresses participant reference. The most fundamental distinction regarding participant reference is that between major and minor participants. There is a variety of ways in which participants may be introduced in texts, including presentational articulations (e.g., "Now a certain man in Caesarea named Cornelius"), through a verb of arrival (e.g., "A Samaritan woman came to draw water"), through a verb of perception (e.g., "and he saw a tax collector named Levi"), or through association with another participant.[40]

The chapter continues with a discussion of further references to activated participants. That is, characters who have already been introduced in a story may reappear through a variety of means.[41]

This chapter also includes the issue of references to VIPs. A VIP is a Very Important Participant, who is distinguished from all other participants. The VIP can be identified on the global level, meaning for a whole book, or on a local level, meaning a section of a book or a single episode. Levinsohn states that each gospel treats Jesus as the global VIP, whereas Acts focuses on different apostolic leaders as VIPs at different sections.[42] Interestingly, the most common way for the Gospels to indicate that Jesus is the global VIP is to make no overt reference to him at the beginning of new narrative units, thus establishing him as the "given" subject of the entire discourse. According to Levinsohn, this also means that when Jesus is referenced overtly, it is a marked reference. This may be used to introduce a major break in the story or a key speech or action.[43]

The second chapter in this section addresses the article with substantives. Levinsohn makes the following claim: "if the referent of an *anarthrous* noun phrase is known and particular ... this gives it *prominence*. It is marked as prominent because it is of particular importance."[44] The default rule is that a participant is introduced for the first time by name without the article. Subsequent references to him or her within the same episode

---

39. Ibid.
40. Levinsohn, *Discourse Features*, 134–35. The examples offered here are cited by Levinsohn.
41. Ibid., 135–36.
42. Ibid., 142–43.
43. Ibid., 143.
44. Ibid., 148.

use the article.[45] Instances in which subsequent references do not use the article are therefore prominent.[46]

When a character is reintroduced in a story, the norm is for that character to be "reactivated" with an anarthrous reference, with exception to the VIP. Reactivations of the global VIP are articular, while other participants' reactivations are anarthrous.[47]

8.6 Backgrounding and Highlighting Devices

Levinsohn begins this section by differentiating between the distinction of background and foreground material and that of background*ed* and foreground*ed* material. That is, the latter distinction is concerned with the relative relationship between elements — some elements will be backgrounded with reference to their context, and others foregrounded with reference to their context. This distinction is his concern, rather than trying to establish criteria for the fixed categories of background and foreground.[48]

Levinsohn follows Callow's relating of foreground to thematic prominence: "this is what I'm talking about." It carries the discourse forward, contributing to the progression of the narrative or argument.[49] He adds that features that may be used for highlighting in one genre may be used for backgrounding in another, and vice-versa. Thus, highlighting and backgrounding features are not universal; they are genre-specific.[50]

In the first chapter in this section, Levinsohn discusses three devices that indicate that a sentence has been backgrounded: prospective μέν, verbal aspect, and the use of ἐγένετο. (1) The prospective μέν is its use that anticipates a corresponding sentence containing δέ. Levinsohn claims that this function downgrades the importance of the sentence containing μέν, in comparison with what is introduced with δέ.[51]

(2) With respect to verbal aspect, Levinsohn claims that it is natural for imperfective aspect to convey information of less importance than that

---

45. Ibid., 150.
46. Ibid., 155–56.
47. Ibid., 152.
48. Ibid., 169.
49. Ibid., citing Callow, *Discourse Considerations*, 52–53.
50. Levinsohn, *Discourse Features*, 169.
51. Ibid., 170.

conveyed by perfective aspect.[52] This pattern, however, does not always hold. For example, imperfects that do not convey an incomplete action (its default meaning) are marked, since it would be normal to expect an aorist to be used to convey completed events.[53] All of this pertains to narrative in particular.

(3) Levinsohn also addresses the combination of ἐγένετο and a temporal expression, such as ἐγένετο δὲ ἐν ταῖς ἡμέραις ἐκείναις in Acts 9:37a. This device, found in the LXX, is used by Luke "to background information with respect to the following foreground events."[54]

The second chapter in this section is concerned with backgrounding *within* sentences, rather than the backgrounding of entire sentences. The features discussed here are anarthrous participial clauses and a particular type of relative clause. Anarthrous participial clauses that precede the main clause to which they are dependent (Levinsohn calls these "prenuclear" clauses) are always backgrounded with respect to their nuclear clause,[55] whereas "no such claim can be made about postnuclear participial clauses."[56]

Regarding relative clauses, Levinsohn focuses on continuative relative clauses, which "describe an event that involves the referent of the relative pronoun and occurs subsequent to the previous event or situation in which the referent featured."[57] Normally, the information preceding the relative pronoun is backgrounded with respect to what follows. An example of this is seen in Acts 28:23c, which occurs subsequent to 23b: (b) ἦλθον πρὸς αὐτὸν εἰς τὴν ξενίαν πλείονες (c) οἷς ἐξετίθετο διαμαρτυρόμενος τὴν βασιλείαν τοῦ θεοῦ.

The third chapter of this section deals with the highlighting function of the historical present. Levinsohn states that the "presence of a *historical present* most often has the effect of highlighting what follows."[58] The historical present highlights the event(s) that follow, especially in Mark

52. Ibid., 172–74.

53. Ibid., 174–75. See also Stephen H. Levinsohn, "Aspect and Prominence in the Synoptic Accounts of Jesus' Entry into Jerusalem," *Filología Neotestamentaria* 23 (2010): 161–74, which challenges the approaches to aspect and prominence of both Robert E. Longacre and Stanley E. Porter.

54. Ibid., 177.

55. For exceptions to this assertion, see Stephen H. Levinsohn, "Adverbial Participial Clauses in Koiné Greek: Grounding and Information Structure" (paper presented at the International Conference on Discourse and Grammar, Universeit Ghent, Belgium, May 2008 [www.sil.org/levinsohns/papers]).

56. Ibid., 181.

57. Ibid., 191.

58. Ibid., 197 [italics are original].

and John.[59] It indicates prominence and has different patterns of usage in Matthew, Luke-Acts, and John.[60]

8.7 The Reporting of Conversation

In this section, Levinsohn addresses the fact that reported conversations are not structured like ordinary narrative events.[61] The first chapter in this section explains the default strategy for reporting conversations, considering the way in which the speech is introduced in order to indicate whether the speech is an end in itself or is an intermediate step to the actions that result from the conversation.[62]

The second chapter offers more on reported conversations in the Synoptic Gospels and Acts, addressing such topics as asyndeton in reported conversations in Matthew's gospel[63] and speech verbs in the historical present in Matthew.[64]

The third chapter in this section discusses reported conversations in John's gospel, primarily dealing with historical presents in speech orienters in John.[65]

The fourth chapter details three ways of reporting speech, which are the indirect reporting of speech,[66] direct reporting of speech with ὅτι *recitativum*,[67] and ὅτι following λέγω σοι/ὑμῖν.[68]

8.8 Boundary Features

The final section of Levinsohn's book concerns "the criteria that enable the reader to recognize boundaries between paragraphs and larger semantic or pragmatic units, such as 'sections' of a book."[69] The chief characterization of a major unit of text is the coherence of a single theme within it. Levin-

---

59. Ibid., 200.
60. Ibid., 202–11.
61. Ibid., 215.
62. Ibid., 218.
63. Ibid., 235–38.
64. Ibid., 240–44.
65. Ibid., 248–60.
66. Ibid., 261–64.
67. Ibid., 264–66. See also Stephen H. Levinsohn, "Is ὅτι an Interpretive Use Marker?" in *The Linguist as Pedagogue: Trends in the Teaching and Linguistic Analysis of the Greek New Testament* (ed. Stanley E. Porter and Matthew Brook O'Donnell; Sheffield: Sheffield Phoenix, 2009), 163–82.
68. Ibid., 266–68.
69. Ibid., 271.

sohn therefore acknowledges that the surface features explored earlier in the book can only provide supporting evidence for boundaries, which must be established on other grounds. The problem here "is that supporting evidence can be cited for conflicting boundaries, so a need exists to discern *which* evidence is valid."[70] He then suggests that "the presence or absence of a *point of departure* has a major part to play in determining the validity of potential evidence."[71]

A point of departure signals some sort of discontinuity, which "indicates the *primary basis* for relating what follows to the context."[72] In this way, a point of departure reveals which supporting evidence is valid. Levinsohn then spends the rest of the section detailing items that constitute supporting evidence for boundaries within text. These are briefly summarized below.

1. **Conjunctions and Asyndeton.** Levinsohn states that δέ and τότε and asyndeton often occur at paragraph and section boundaries, whereas καί and τέ are less frequently found at such boundaries.[73]

2. **Spatiotemporal Changes.** When the text indicates a temporal change at the beginning of a sentence, this is supporting evidence for a boundary. The temporal change is thus a point of departure. Changes of location may coincide with a boundary, but this is not determinative.[74]

3. **Summary Statements.** A summary statement unites the preceding material as a block, and in so doing terminates or begins units of text.[75]

4. **Chiastic Structures.** A chiasm is obviously a self-contained unit and thus creates its own boundaries.[76]

5. **Inclusio Structures.** Like a chiasm, an inclusio is a self-contained unit that creates its own boundaries.[77]

6. **Rhetorical Questions.** Sometimes rhetorical questions signal a new subject or some new aspect of same subject and can collaborate with a developmental conjunction to indicate a boundary.[78]

---

70. Ibid.
71. Ibid. [italics are original].
72. Ibid., 274 [italics are original].
73. Ibid., 275.
74. Ibid., 276–77.
75. Ibid., 277.
76. Ibid.
77. Ibid.
78. Ibid., 278.

7. **Participant Reference by Means of a Noun Phrase.** Sometimes a redundant noun phrase reference to a participant is used to mark the beginning of a unit.[79]

8. **Vocatives.** Likewise, use of a vocative can provide supporting evidence for a boundary, though they do not automatically indicate a boundary.[80]

9. **Changes of Cast and Role.** A change of cast in narrative that affects the global VIP supports a section break. Additionally, a significant change of role of the global VIP constitutes grounds for supporting a paragraph or section break.[81]

10. **Changes of Verb Tense-aspect, Mood, and/or Person.** Changes in aspect and mood may support the discernment of a boundary. A change of person parallels a change of cast. Nonspeech historical presents commonly occur at the beginnings of subsections.[82]

11. **Back-reference.** Reference to a preceding paragraph often occurs at the beginning of new paragraph; hence such back-reference provides an evidence for a boundary.[83]

8.9 Evaluation

Levinsohn has made a significant contribution to Greek discourse analysis, and one reason that I have provided a thoroughgoing summary of his *Discourse Features* is the hope that more students and teachers of Greek will become familiar with it. Clearly, there is much useful material that supplements traditional grammars, and it offers the opportunity to think more about how parts of the sentence relate to one another and how wider units of text are demarcated. Unlike Halliday, of course, Levinsohn has studied Greek parts of speech in depth and has married such investigation with several principles of the wider linguistic world. The volume is worthy of serious study by all Greek students.

There are, however, some areas of concern. Though Porter's critique was based on Levisohn's first edition, published in 1992, some of

---

79. Ibid.
80. Ibid.
81. Ibid., 278–79.
82. Ibid., 279–80.
83. Ibid., 280–84.

his comments remain potent. His chief criticism of Levinsohn is that it remains fairly well preoccupied with the level of the sentence,[84] and it is true that much of Levinsohn's material concerns sentential analysis, though there is much that moves beyond the sentence too. The sections on constituent order, sentence conjunctions, and backgrounding and foregrounding (at least in part) concern intra-sentential issues. Yet, these discussions hardly represent a "return to sentence grammar"; they are more linguistically robust than traditional grammar discussions about the Greek sentence and offer helpful insights not normally gleaned through traditional approaches. Moreover, there is much in Levinsohn that extends beyond the level of the sentence. The sections on patterns of reference, reported speech, and especially boundary features all explore wider units of text.

Porter adds that "there is a tendency to focus upon idiolect, or even the language of a single book" in Levinsohn's work.[85] This is certainly a fair observation, though it is not necessarily a negative aspect of *Discourse Features*. On the one hand, it might be a little frustrating to the reader to have so many approaches outlined, moving from discussion of a discourse feature in Matthew's gospel only to learn about a different pattern at work in John. On the other hand, it is good to be aware of idiolect and to avoid the mistake of illegitimately attributing a pattern found in one book to all other books. Then again, I would like to see the model move to a deeper analysis of semantics that is able to account for the pragmatic functions of discourse features across idiolects and genres. For example, in discussion of the historical present, a semantic analysis that explains all historical presents, and yet can also cope with the differing ways in which Mark and John employ the phenomenon, would be ideal.

My own concerns may be put alongside Porter's. Levinsohn self-consciously adopts an eclectic linguistic approach rather than adhering to an established linguistic school (see §8.2.1). Some linguists would object to this, while there is also a case to find it an acceptable approach. After all, every linguistic school builds on the work of others to some extent, usually adopting insights from a variety of sources. In that sense, they are all eclectic to some extent—at least initially. Certainly, Levinsohn is well schooled in

---

84. Porter, "Discourse Analysis," 26.
85. Ibid.

linguistics and he knows what he's doing.[86] Perhaps that fact alone should alleviate the concern, but a chief advantage of adopting a particular linguistic approach is that linguistic schools are rigorously tested and pushed for consistency. An ad hoc linguistic approach will not have had the same level of scrutiny and may fall short at the theoretical level. This is not to say that Levinsohn does fall short here, but it means that we need to stand back from the work and reflect on whether the whole system hangs together, or whether there are subtle linguistic contradictions or lapses in theory.

On this topic, I will offer one caution at the level of linguistic theory. Levinsohn will oftentimes make a claim about Greek by way of reference to similar features in other languages; his work as a Bible translator leads him to stress the importance of comparing the discourse features of Greek with those of other languages, using the methods of typology (see §1.4.9).[87] While there is no doubt much to be learned about Greek through typological comparison with other languages, this risks introducing similar problems that came through the methods of nineteenth-century comparative philology. In my opinion, the comparative approach has caused much trouble for Greek linguistics over the past century, since Greek was traditionally associated closely to Latin. Deponency is the obvious example (see §4.2.4), and the traditional understanding of the Greek perfect may be another. These are highly controversial and difficult issues, ones that arguably arose because of the comparative approach. Levinsohn's determinations about Greek based on what happens in other languages therefore gives me pause.

At the practical level, *Discourse Features* suffers from a presentation that is difficult to navigate. It is hard to find definitions (apart from the glossary), and it is probably a little bewildering to the student. Nevertheless, it remains a valuable resource that is worth the effort. We turn now to consider Levinsohn's most influential student, Steven Runge.

---

86. See, e.g., Dooley and Levinsohn on the methodology of their volume, *Analyzing Discourse*, iii: "First, we intend it to be practical, addressing issues commonly confronted by field linguists. Rather than attempting to apply a rigid theory or survey a variety of approaches, we provide a methodology that has been refined over years of use. Second, although we follow no rigid theory, we aim for more than a "grab-bag" of diverse methodologies by attempting to present the material within a coherent and productive framework. Specifically, we follow a functional and cognitive approach that seems to be a good approximation of how discourse is actually produced and understood."

87. See, e.g., Stephen H. Levinsohn, "Towards a Typology of Story Development Marking," in *Bantu Languages: Analyses, Description and Theory* (ed. Karsten Legère and Christina Thornell; Köln: Rudiger Köppe Verlag, 2010), 143–51.

Steven E. Runge

8.10 Introduction

In the short time in which Runge's *Discourse Grammar of the New Testament* has been available,[88] it has done more to bring discourse analysis to the attention of the wider New Testament studies world than any other work. A few distinctives set this work apart. The most obvious is its accessible nature, making *Discourse Grammar* the best entry-level work for Greek discourse analysis. It is popular among students and is easily teachable. Moreover, *Discourse Grammar* is part of a suite of resources that Runge and his team at Logos have developed, including *The Lexham Discourse Greek New Testament*,[89] which is an application of Runge's discourse-analytical approach to the entire New Testament.

The significance of the *Discourse Greek New Testament* is twofold. First, if the exegete is unsure as to how to apply Runge's approach to text, he or she can simply look up the New Testament text in question and discover how Runge himself sees it applied. Second, the preparation required to produce the *Discourse Greek New Testament* means that Runge has examined the entire New Testament in preparation for his *Discourse Grammar*. It is not ad hoc but comprehensive; it is not without application, but it has already been applied in full to the New Testament.

The book is arranged into four major sections: foundations, forward-pointing devices, information structuring devices, and thematic highlighting devices. We will survey the key points throughout.

8.11 Foundations

In his introductory chapter, Runge adopts a function-based and cross-linguistic approach,[90] presupposing three core principles: choice implies meaning; semantic meaning should be differentiated from pragmatic effect; and default patterns of usage should be distinguished from marked

---

88. Steven E. Runge, *Discourse Grammar of the Greek New Testament: A Practical Introduction for Teaching and Exegesis* (Bellingham: Lexham, 2010).
89. Steven E. Runge, ed., *The Lexham Discourse Greek New Testament* (Bellingham: Logos Research Systems, 2008) (available only as an electronic product as part of the Logos Bible Software system).
90. Runge, *Discourse Grammar*, 3.

ones.[91] The reader should be familiar now with the first two of these principles; the third may require some explanation. As Runge explains, "Markedness is fundamentally the study of 'markers,' those things that signal the presence of some quality or linguistic feature."[92] In sets of oppositions, one member of the set may be marked for a particular linguistic feature, while the other member may not be. The latter might be able to express the linguistic feature in question in certain contexts, but the former will always express it, since it is marked for that feature. This distinction leads to another:

> To summarize, markedness theory presupposes that one member of a set is the most basic or simple member, called the "default" member. All of the other members signal or "mark" the presence of some unique quality, one that would not have been marked if the default option were used. The marked options are described based on how they uniquely differ both from the default and from one another.[93]

Runge also presupposes the importance of prominence and contrast. A prominent feature is one that attracts extra attention within its context—anything that stands out is prominent.[94] One of the effects of prominence is to create contrast, since the prominent feature will stand out from others in the same context.[95]

8.11.1 Connectives

Runge's second chapter addresses connectives, a term to be preferred over conjunctions, since other (non-conjunction) parts of speech, such as adverbs, are also able to function to connect clauses. "Connectives" thus includes conjunctions and non-conjunctions that operate in a connective fashion.[96] Runge focuses on the *function* of each connective in "constraining" the discourse, rather than their English gloss translations.[97] He deals with asyndeton, καί, δέ, narrative τότε, οὖν, δία τοῦτο, γάρ, μέν, and ἀλλά.

---

91. Ibid., 5.
92. Ibid., 11.
93. Ibid.
94. Ibid., 13.
95. Ibid., 15.
96. Ibid., 17. See also Steven E. Runge, "Now and Then: Clarifying the Role of Temporal Adverbs as Discourse Markers," in *Reflections on Lexicography* (ed. Richard A. Taylor and Craig E. Morrison; Perspectives on Linguistics and Ancient Languages 4; Piscataway, NJ: Gorgias, 2013), 327–48.
97. Runge, *Discourse Grammar*, 18–19.

8.11.1.1 Asyndeton. Asyndeton is "the default means of connecting clauses in the Epistles and in speeches reported within narrative."[98] It is used at the beginning of a new thought or where the relation between clauses is clear.[99]

8.11.1.2 Καί. This is a coordinating conjunction used to connect words, phrases, clauses, or paragraphs,[100] linking items of equal status.[101]

8.11.1.3 Δέ. This is a coordinating conjunction with the constraint of signaling a new development.[102] "The use of δέ represents the writer's choice to explicitly signal that what follows is a new, distinct development in the story or argument, based on how the writer conceived of it."[103]

8.11.1.4 Narrative Τότε. In narrative, the temporal adverb τότε can be used as a connective when no conjunction is present. It is marked for development, like δέ, but has the additional constraint of temporal sequence.[104]

8.11.1.5 Οὖν. This is another development marker, but adds "the constraint of close continuity with what precedes."[105] This is why the English gloss "therefore" is often appropriately used to the translate οὖν: it is closely connected to a preceding statement, but also marks out a new development in thought or event.

8.11.1.6 Διὰ τοῦτο. This phrase is another example of another non-conjunction connective. It indicates a causal relation with the preceding discourse.[106] The function of διὰ τοῦτο overlaps with that of οὖν, but its constraint is narrower since it is marked for causality, which is not the case for οὖν.

8.11.1.7 Γάρ. The central constraint of the conjunction γάρ is its explanatory function, as it adds "background" information that strengthens or supports preceding material.[107]

8.11.1.8 Μέν. This connective correlates its own clause with an element that follows, which usually employs δέ. Unlike the connectives listed above, μέν is *forward* pointing, creating an expectation of something to follow.[108]

---

98. Ibid., 20.
99. Ibid., 21.
100. Ibid., 23.
101. Ibid., 24.
102. Ibid., 31.
103. Ibid.
104. Ibid., 37–38.
105. Ibid., 43.
106. Ibid., 48.
107. Ibid., 52.
108. Ibid., 54.

8.11.1.9 Ἀλλά. This conjunction is used to sharpen the contrast between two clauses. It is not marked for continuity or development, but is marked for the constraint of "correction."[109]

8.11.1.10 Function of Greek Connectives. Runge concludes the chapter on connectives with a useful table of their functions, which is worth reproducing here.[110]

	Continuity	Development	Correlation	Forward-pointing	Semantic constraint
Ø	-	-	-	-	-
καί	+	-	+	-	-
δέ	-	+	-	-	-
τότε	-	+	-	-	Temporal
οὖν	+	+	-	-	-
διὰ τοῦτο	+	+	-	-	Causal
γάρ	+	-	-	-	Support
μέν	+	-	+	+	Expectation
ἀλλά	-	-	+	-	Correction

8.12 Forward-Pointing Devices

The second major part of Runge's *Discourse Grammar* addresses forward-pointing devices, which are "used to attract attention to something significant in the discourse."[111] In the book's third chapter, Runge develops the notions of a forward-pointing reference and its target. In Greek, there are three ways of creating such a forward-pointing reference: through forward-pointing interrogatives, forward-pointing demonstratives, and substitutional forward-pointing adverbs.[112] Since such forms normally point backward, their use to point forward receives additional prominence.[113]

In chapter 4, Runge discusses point/counterpoint sets, which refers to

---

109. Ibid., 56.
110. Ibid., 57.
111. Ibid., 59.
112. Ibid., 64.
113. Ibid., 70.

"clauses or clause elements that have been related to one another through one or more grammatical means."[114] These means are as follows: the use of μέν to create anticipation of something to follow; the use of an interrogative or negated clause restricted by εἰ μή or πλήν; the use of ἀλλά to correct something in the previous context.[115] These devices constrain the relationship between two elements, such as two clauses or phrases.

Chapter 5 deals with metacomments, which occur when a speaker stops "saying what they are saying in order to comment on what is going to be said."[116] An English example would be "I want you to know that...." While metacomments do not come in a fixed form, there are some common devices associated with them, such as "attention-getters" like ἀμήν, and redundant forms of address, like ἀδελφοί, and redundant vocatives and nominatives of address.[117]

In chapter 6, Runge addresses the historical present. Key to his understanding is the fact that the use of the Greek present to refer to a past event in narrative creates prominence since it goes against the expected tense (past) and the expected aspect (perfective), since it is a present referring verb with imperfective aspect.[118] Historical presents are used "to make sure that the reader does not miss changes or transitions in the discourse."[119] Runge clarifies that the historical present does not *create* a discourse boundary, but can be used to draw attention to one.[120] The other significant function of the historical present is to highlight a significant speech or event that follows, so that the action of the verb is not itself prominent, but what follows it.[121]

Chapter 7 is concerned with redundant quotative frames. A quotative frame signals a transition from narrative proper to speech within the narrative. It is redundant when more than one verb is used to introduce the same speech-act, or when there is no need to use another quotative frame,

---

114. Ibid., 73.
115. Ibid., 74.
116. Ibid., 101.
117. Ibid., 117. Such devices can also occur by themselves without functioning as metacomments.
118. Ibid., 128–29. Runge has subsequently described the present as indicating "non-past" temporal reference: "The present tense-form often functions as an unmarked form for non-past reference" (Steven E. Runge, "The Verbal Aspect of the Historical Present Indicative in Narrative," in *Discourse Studies & Biblical Interpretation: A Festschrift in Honor of Stephen H. Levinsohn* [ed. Steven E. Runge; Bellingham: Logos, 2011], 218).
119. Runge, *Discourse Grammar*, 134.
120. Ibid.
121. Ibid., 137.

since the same speaker is simply continuing a speech that has already been introduced. "Both have the effect of attracting more attention to the speech or segment of speech that follows."[122]

In chapter 8, Runge describes "tail-head linkage," which is a type of repetition that involves an action from one clause being restated at the beginning of the next clause. "In other words, the 'tail' of one clause becomes the 'head' of the next."[123] Its effect is to slow down the discourse in anticipation of something surprising or significant.[124]

8.13 Information Structuring Devices

Part 3 of Runge's *Discourse Grammar* addresses information structuring devices. It describes "how variation in the ordering of propositions is used to pragmatically structure the flow of the discourse."[125]

Chapter 9 treats information structure, which is most often referred to as "word order" analysis.[126] Runge discusses the debate and confusion surrounding Greek word order and whether or not there is a default way of ordering Greek sentences.[127] As preliminary to dealing with information structure in Greek, Runge spends most of this chapter sorting through theoretical issues within the wider linguistic world and criticizing Halliday's systemical functional approach in particular.[128] Key to Runge's approach is the Prague School's *theme* and *rheme*, where "theme corresponds to the 'established' material of the clause, while the rheme corresponds to the newly asserted or focal information."[129] This leads to an interest in thematic frames of reference for the clause that follows the frame.

In chapter 10, Runge begins to explore framing devices found in the New Testament. The function of these frames is to establish an explicit

---

122. Ibid., 145.
123. Ibid., 163.
124. Ibid.
125. Ibid., 179.
126. Ibid., 181.
127. Ibid., 182–84.
128. "Most all of Halliday's theoretical work to develop his framework was conducted on rigidly ordered languages, particularly English. Halliday's definition of 'focus' is inextricably tied to stress and intonation, just as in English. His theory is well suited for English because prosody is the primary means of marking focus in rigidly ordered languages.... SFL postulates that the initial element in a clause, be it a conjunction, subject, or fronted focal constituent, is always the 'theme.' This idea works fairly well in a rigidly configurational language, but it proves inadequate for non-configurational languages" (ibid., 203).
129. Ibid., 201.

frame of reference for the clause that follows.[130] They are "fronted"—used at the beginning of a clause—which gives them a highlighting function. Topical frames highlight the introduction of a new participant or topic, or draw attention to a topic change.[131] Temporal frames are created when temporal information is placed at the beginning of a clause.[132] Spatial frames involve a fronted prepositional phrase that relates to a location.[133]

Chapter 11 continues with more framing devices. Conditional frames are simply the protases of conditional sentences.[134] Comparative frames "establish a basis against which something in the main clause is compared."[135] Reason/result frames "provide the reason for or the result of the main proposition that follows."[136]

Chapter 12 addresses circumstantial frames, focusing on adverbial participles and their functions within subordinate clauses. Circumstantial frames precede the main clause to which they are subordinated, and they "set the scene for the main action that follows, but the action is backgrounded with respect to the main action rather than made prominent."[137]

In chapter 13, Runge addresses the issue of emphasis, which he defines strictly "as taking what was already the most important part of a clause and placing it in a position of prominence in order to attract even more attention to it."[138] The most common way that emphasis is created in Greek is through the reordering of the default structure of the clause so that the item to be emphasized is found in a prominent position.[139]

Chapter 14 deals with left-dislocations, which are known elsewhere as cleft constructions, hanging nominatives, pendent nominatives, *casus pendens*, and independent nominatives.[140] The two basic functions of left-dislocations in Greek are to streamline the introduction of a complex entity into one clause instead of two, and to highlight the introduction of an entity.[141]

---

130. Ibid., 207.
131. Ibid., 210.
132. Ibid., 216.
133. Ibid., 220.
134. Ibid., 227.
135. Ibid., 233.
136. Ibid., 237.
137. Ibid., 250.
138. Ibid., 269.
139. Ibid., 284.
140. Ibid., 287.
141. Ibid., 291.

8.14 Thematic Highlighting Devices

In the fourth and final part of Runge's *Discourse Grammar*, the topic of thematic highlighting devices is addressed. These devices draw attention to redundant elements, which are promoted in order to shape what follows.[142]

Chapter 15 treats over-specification and right-dislocation. Rather than using the most succinct way in which to refer to a person or thing, instances of over-specification involve longer, overly specified references.[143] Right-dislocation refers to the practice of adding more information about an already mentioned person or thing at the end of a clause.[144] According to Runge, "both devices serve the common purpose of highlighting particular thematic information that the writer wants the reader to consider at that particular point in the discourse."[145]

In chapter 16, Runge explains thematic addition, which is the use of adverbial modifiers "to attract extra attention to parallel elements in the discourse."[146] The adverbial use of καί, the intensive use of αὐτός, and other features are additives that signal to the reader to look for a corresponding element in the context.[147]

Chapter 17 explains the significance of changed reference and thematic address. Changed reference occurs when a character is referred to in some way that is not the default way to refer to them, often with the effect of recharacterizing them or supplementing the mental representation of who they are. Thematic address refers to the use of a vocative or nominative of address with reference to a certain character and can have a similar effect in recharacterizing him or her.[148]

Runge's final chapter discusses the near/far distinction with reference to the demonstrative pronouns οὗτος and ἐκεῖνος. At the semantic level, the distinction between these demonstratives is spatial—the former "near," the latter "far." But in certain contexts these can be used for particular pragmatic effects.[149] Runge claims that "when there are other elements in the discourse that potentially compete with the default thematic element, the near and far

---

142. Ibid., 315.
143. Ibid., 317.
144. Ibid.
145. Ibid.
146. Ibid., 337.
147. Ibid., 339, 341.
148. Ibid., 363.
149. Ibid., 368.

demonstrative pronouns provide a means for the writer to disambiguate the role that these competing elements play."[150] The near demonstrative indicates thematic entities, while the far demonstrative indicate nonthematic entities.

At the end of the book, Runge includes a helpful summary of all the discourse devices discussed throughout, with an indication of their discourse distribution.[151]

8.15 Runge on Romans 6:1–6

A strength of Runge's material is that he has already provided an analysis of discourse features across the whole Greek New Testament in *The Lexham Discourse Greek New Testament*. Below is an extract of that work from Romans 6:1–6.[152] It is provided here to demonstrate the theory in action. A key is provided following the diagram.[153]

PRINCIPLE 6 ‹→Τί‹→› οὖν ἐροῦμεν
SENTENCE ‹⊙ ἐπιμένωμεν τῇ ἁμαρτίᾳ
  SUB-POINT ἵνα [TP] ἡ χάρις [TP] πλεονάσῃ⊙›
SENTENCE ² μὴ γένοιτο
SENTENCE [TP] οἵτινες ἀπεθάνομεν τῇ ἁμαρτίᾳ [TP] **πῶς ἔτι** ζήσομεν ἐν αὐτῇ
SENTENCE ³ ἢ ➧ ἀγνοεῖτε ➧ ὅτι [TP] ὅσοι ἐβαπτίσθημεν εἰς Χριστὸν Ἰησοῦν [TP] **εἰς τὸν θάνατον αὐτοῦ** ἐβαπτίσθημεν
PRINCIPLE ⁴ συνετάφημεν οὖν αὐτῷ διὰ τοῦ βαπτίσματος εἰς τὸν θάνατον
  SUB-POINT ἵνα [LD] ὥσπερ ἠγέρθη Χριστὸς ἐκ νεκρῶν διὰ τῆς δόξης τοῦ πατρός [LD] [CP] οὕτως [CP] [TP] ‹+ καὶ ἡμεῖς +› [TP] **ἐν καινότητι ζωῆς** περιπατήσωμεν
    SUPPORT ⁵ [CD] εἰ γὰρ **σύμφυτοι** γεγόναμεν τῷ ὁμοιώματι ✕ τοῦ θανάτου αὐτοῦ✕ [CD] ἀλλὰ ‹✓ ‹+ καὶ **τῆς ἀναστάσεως** +›✓› ἐσόμεθα
      ELABORATION ⁶ ‹→ **τοῦτο** ‹→› γινώσκοντες
        SUB-POINT ὅτι ‹⊙ [TP] ὁ **παλαιὸς** ἡμῶν ἄνθρωπος [TP] συνεσταυρώθη⊙›
          SUB-POINT ἵνα ‹⊙καταργηθῇ τὸ σῶμα τῆς ἁμαρτίας τοῦ **μηκέτι** δουλεύειν ἡμᾶς τῇ ἁμαρτίᾳ⊙›

---

150. Ibid., 369.
151. Ibid., 385–91.
152. Runge, *Lexham Discourse Greek New Testament*, Romans 6:1–6.
153. Definitions are taken from the glossary of the *Lexham Discourse Greek New Testament*.

Key

Principle A sentence that is marked as drawing an inference or assertion from the preceding discourse. Principles are normally signaled by οὖν, διά, διὰ τοῦτο or πλήν. Cf. Levinsohn (2000:128-133).

Sentence One or more clauses that have a coordinate relationship to the preceding discourse. Sentences which begin a speech reported within the discourse are labeled as "sentences," but are indented one level in the outline to reflect that they are technically dependent upon (i.e. subordinate to) the verb of speaking that introduces them. Sentences are coordinated to the preceding discourse using καί, δέ, or asyndeton (the absence of a conjunction).

Sub-point A clause that is grammatically dependent upon another one. In most cases, the clause upon which it depends *precedes* the sub-point. In "Complex" constructions, the sub-point may precede the clause upon which it depends. Sub-points are normally signaled in Greek by ὅτι, ἵνα, εἰ, ἐάν, καθώς, or by a relative pronoun. Sentences which build upon the sub-point are indented and labeled as sub-points.

Support A sentence that is marked as strengthening or supporting the preceding discourse. Support sentences do not extend or develop an argument, but serve instead to reinforce the preceding point. Cf. Heckert (1996:32–36); Levinsohn (2000:91–94).

Elaboration A participial clause that expands upon the action of the main clause on which it depends. Elaboration follows the clause it elaborates.

→ **Forward-pointing Reference**—The use of pronouns like "this," "those" or "it" to point *ahead* to some "target" that has not yet been introduced. The forward-pointing pronoun is the *reference*. The forward-pointing reference has the effect of attracting extra attention to the thing to which it refers.

⊙ **Forward-pointing Target**—The use of pronouns like "this," "those" or "it" to point *ahead* to some "target" that has not yet been mentioned or introduced. The thing to which it points is the *target*. The effect of using the forward-pointing reference is to attract extra attention to the thing to which it refers.

TP **Topical frame**—The fronting of some thematic element of the clause (often the grammatical subject) in order to establish a specific frame of reference regarding the theme of the clause that follows. Topical frames are used to:
  • introduce brand new participants or concepts
  • draw extra attention to changes in topic, sharpening comparisons or contrasts

🖢 **Metacomment**—When a speaker stops saying what they are saying in order to comment on what is *going* to be said, speaking abstractly about it, e.g. "*I want you to know that...*," "Don't you know that..."

^{LD} **Left-dislocation**—The introduction of information that is syntactically outside the main clause (i.e. it is "dislocated"), which is then reiterated somewhere in the main clause using a pronoun or other generic reference. Left-dislocations typically introduce something that is too complex to include in the main clause, one that might otherwise cause confusion. The resumptive element of the left-dislocation essentially summarizes the new content, allowing a comment about the new entity to be easily made.

^{CP} **Conditional frame**—The fronting of subordinate conditional clauses to create a specific frame of reference for the proposition that follows, making clear that the proposition is contingent upon the condition of the frame being met. The condition is not the most important information in the clause, the main predication is. Fronting the condition does not result in emphasis, but establishes an explicit frame of reference for what follows. Conditional frames are often used to establish hypothetical situations in one easy step. The conditional frame enables the writer to introduce the situation and to comment about it in a single complex clause, instead of using several clauses.

+ **Thematic Addition**—The use of καὶ as an adverb (instead of as a conjunction) to create a connection between two things, essentially "adding" the current element to some preceding parallel element. Thematic addition is generally translated in English using "also" or "too." Thematic addition can also be used to indicate confirmation of something, which is generally translated in English using "even." Cf. Levinsohn (2000:100).

✓ **Point (Clause Level)**—One part of a paired set of statements that usually replaces the counterpoint, and is the more important of the two. Point-counterpoint sets accomplish two primary purposes:

  - Explicitly linking two things together that otherwise might not have been connected.
  - Drawing more attention to the "point" that it would not otherwise have received.

8.16 Evaluation

It should be noted that Runge does not claim to present a comprehensive guide to discourse analysis. In fact, he does not claim that his *Discourse Grammar* is an account of discourse analysis at all. Strictly speaking, it is a book on discourse *grammar*, not discourse *analysis*. The goal is to present the building blocks of discourse; once these basic features are described, it is possible to move on to a formal analysis of larger discourses. Thus, it is

Runge's goal to produce a subsequent volume that moves from discourse grammar to discourse analysis.[154] Unfortunately, the distinction between his goals for the *Discourse Grammar* and a full discourse analysis is not laid out in the volume, which has led others to criticize Runge for not achieving a more comprehensive, extra-sentential analysis of discourse.

Nevertheless, there is no question that Runge's *Discourse Grammar* represents a significant step forward for the advancement of discourse analysis within New Testament studies, since a careful articulation of the building blocks of discourse is needed for discourse analysis. Runge's theoretical framework is well grounded in linguistic principles, having been constructed through rigorous study of an array of general linguists, discourse analysts, and Greek linguists and grammarians. Runge's work indeed complements conventional grammatical insights by going deeper into semantics, the use of markedness theory, and articulating Greek phenomena with the tools of linguistic analysis. Highly dependent on Levinsohn (though certainly not exclusively so), Runge alleviates some of the difficulties raised with reference to the former's work. Runge's evidence covers the entire New Testament, and his theories have been tested and applied across the board. Moreover, the book is clearly written, with excellent illustrations, applications, and definitions that nonspecialists will find accessible. Perhaps best of all for his target audience, Runge's methods are immediately applicable for exegesis of the Greek New Testament. The result is a practical and insightful tool that offers genuine advancement to students and teachers alike.

Nevertheless, there are some limitations due to the nature of the work. The most obvious is the fact that, like Levinsohn, there is a preoccupation with discourse at the level of the clause and sentence. In fact, Runge is even more focused at this level than Levinsohn, who includes a section on boundary markers of wider units of discourse. Runge offers little for studying wider units of text, boundary markers, or discourse-wide cohesion (cf. Halliday). But again, this is not the goal of the book; both Levinsohn and Runge analyse discourse *features*, rather than full-blown discourse analysis.

Moreover, while Runge provides a much clearer and linguistically robust account of prominence, highlighting, and emphasis than is common in Greek studies, one could be forgiven for thinking that feature analysis is

---

154. So Runge commented via personal correspondence.

the primary focus of discourse analysis. Rather, such analysis must serve as the necessary precursor to higher level analysis of the discourse. We must bear in mind that the discernment of prominence, highlighting, and emphasis is only a preliminary step of discourse analysis. Rather, Runge addresses those concepts he deems to be of most exegetical significance.[155]

Finally, at the theoretical level, Runge lays many of his conclusions on his assumptions about default strategies of expression. Markedness theory, of course, depends on knowing what is default in a language, but, as Runge points out, there is much scholarly unrest about default structures in Greek. Devices that depend on markedness theory can only be fully accepted as legitimate if one accepts Runge's claims about the default patterns. Some Greek scholars will be comfortable going in this direction; others will be less so.

8.17 Conclusion

These last two chapters have explored important models for discourse analysis, and the ways in which Halliday, Levinsohn, and Runge relate are worth exploring briefly. At the linguistic level, Halliday has his own linguistic school, Systemic Functional Linguistics, while Levinsohn and Runge are eclectic in their linguistic theory. There is much overlap, since all three are functional linguists and draw on much of the same research and many of the same linguistic principles that arise out of it. But Runge thinks that some features of Halliday's SFL are not well suited to the study of Greek since it was developed primarily for English, and in certain ways there are mismatches between English and Greek that render some of Halliday's approaches misleading for the latter. Yet others will be concerned about trusting an eclectic theoretical model.

Functionally, the biggest difference between Halliday and Levinsohn/ Runge is that the former seeks to develop a comprehensive model of language and communication, discussing coherence across the whole text, the development of theme, and the interrelatedness of units wider than the sentence. Levinsohn and Runge are, as noted, more focused on the level of the clause and sentence, since their work is concerned with discourse *features*—the building blocks necessary for discourse analysis. Nevertheless, also as noted, Levinsohn and Runge discuss *Greek* discourse features,

---

155. Ibid., xix.

which makes their work immediately more applicable for the average New Testament student and is no doubt more precise in such application.

Despite such differences, Halliday, Levinsohn, and Runge are not incompatible, since they are aiming to achieve different things through differing means. The student of the Greek New Testament could profitably embrace all three scholars in a complementary manner. For broad, discourse-level consideration of coherence, Halliday is the seminal authority. For gritty, Greek-based, clausal-level analysis, Levinsohn and Runge have no rivals.

Finally, it is encouraging to observe that discourse analytical concerns are now being taken up by some New Testament commentary series. Runge's own *High Definition Commentary* series has begun with volumes on Philippians and Romans. It seeks to incorporate the observation of Greek discourse features into widely accessible commentaries on the English text. The *Zondervan Exegetical Commentary on the New Testament* is a well-developed exegetical series that pays attention to clause and pericope structure, employing syntax diagrams in English. The *Baylor Handbook on the Greek New Testament* is a burgeoning series that engages with Greek discourse features in its focused analysis of Greek syntax.

8.18 Further Reading

Levinsohn, Stephen H. *Discourse Features of New Testament Greek: A Coursebook on the Information Structure of New Testament Greek.* Second edition. Dallas: SIL International, 2000.

———. "Some Constraints on Discourse Development in the Pastoral Epistles." Pages 316–33 in *Discourse Analysis and the New Testament: Approaches and Results.* Edited by Stanley E. Porter and Jeffrey T. Reed. JSNTSup 170. Sheffield: Sheffield Academic, 1999.

Porter, Stanley E. "Discourse Analysis and New Testament Studies: An Introductory Survey." Pages 14–35 in *Discourse Analysis and Other Topics in Biblical Greek.* Edited by Stanley E. Porter and D. A. Carson. JSNTSS 133. Sheffield: Sheffield Academic Press, 1995.

Runge, Steven E. *Discourse Grammar of the Greek New Testament: A Practical Introduction for Teaching and Exegesis.* Bellingham: Lexham, 2010.

———. *The Lexham Discourse Greek New Testament.* Bellingham: Logos Research Systems, 2008 (available only as an electronic product as part of Logos Bible Software system).

CHAPTER 9

PRONUNCIATION

Erasmus' error finally succeeded in ousting the Greek pronunciation of Greek.
　　　　　　　　　　　　　　　　　　　　— Chrys Caragounis

9.1 Introduction

A topic that has been gaining momentum in recent years is the pronunciation of Koine Greek. For some, the pronunciation of a "dead" language is basically irrelevant, since no one uses it in normal conversation, there are no native speakers to offend, and it doesn't affect our reading of the New Testament or other documents from the Koine period. For others, the response is the opposite. The way we choose to pronounce Koine Greek represents our respect for Greek as a real, living language. As people interested in history (after all, who reads Koine apart from *some kind* of interest in history?), we ought to take pronunciation seriously out of respect for historical accuracy—not to mention the fact that pronunciation *can* affect our understanding of text, especially in the area of textual criticism, but also in relation to the affective and aesthetic nature of Greek literature. Others remain in the middle between these two responses, perhaps somewhat unclear of the issues involved and why they really matter.

My view is that pronunciation matters. Accurate pronunciation is a sign of respect for the Greek language, its people, and its history. It also has implications for one's enjoyment and mastery of Greek. Nevertheless, it is not an issue of the same order as, say, lexicography or verbal aspect.

Those topics have potential to change our understanding of what the text *means*. Pronunciation does not have that potential (except perhaps in the area of textual criticism). Nevertheless, it is worth our attention, not least because it has obvious implications for the teaching and learning of Greek, but also because it is one of the areas of debate within current Greek scholarship.

The trajectory of the chapter is to demonstrate why the Erasmian pronunciation is now regarded to be incorrect, to explore the evidence for how Koine Greek was pronounced in its own time, to consider a defense of Erasmus, and to evaluate these issues and their implications. First, we turn to consider "Erasmus' error."

9.2 Erasmus' Error (?)

The Dutch humanist Desiderius Erasmus of Rotterdam (1466–1536) was a towering figure for the reintroduction of the Greek New Testament into western consciousness. His *Novum Instrumentum omne*, produced in 1516, was the first published Greek New Testament and was highly influential for the Protestant Reformation. Erasmus became a huge influence over all who studied the Greek New Testament during the Renaissance and Reformation.

Erasmus introduced a system for the pronunciation of Greek that remains the standard way in which Ancient Greek is pronounced to this day, but has (again) become highly controversial. There are at least three differing accounts of the way in which he produced this system of pronunciation, and two of these claim that Erasmus did *not* believe the system—which would henceforth be known as *Erasmian*—was accurate or useful.

The first account is recorded by Robertson, in which Erasmus promotes the new pronunciation as a joke:

> Jannaris quotes the story of Voss, a Dutch scholar (1577–1649), as to how Erasmus heard some learned Greeks pronounce Greek in a very different way from the Byzantine custom. Erasmus published a discussion between a lion and a bear entitled *De recta latini graecique sermonic pronuntiatione*, which made such an impression that those who accepted the ideas advanced in this book were called Erasmians and the rest Reuchlinians. As a matter of fact, however, Engel has shown that Erasmus merely

wrote a literary squib to "take off" the new non-Byzantine pronunciation, though he was taken seriously by many.[1]

The second account is more credible, since it is taken directly from Voss's Latin citation of the story,[2] as Caragounis expounds:

> In 1528, however, the humanist scholar Desiderius Erasmus of Rotterdam ... composed a dialogue in Latin between a bear and a lion, in which he set forth a novel way of pronouncing Greek, which has since come to be called the "Erasmian pronunciation of Greek," or "Etacism," and to be regarded by its proponents as *the scientific pronunciation of Greek*. The incentive to write this book came from a practical joke that was played on Erasmus by the Swiss scholar Henricus (Loritus of Glarus, hence) Glareanus. Glareanus, who had arrived from Paris, met Erasmus, who, being "inordinately fond of novelties and credulous" ... was eager to learn what was the latest news in the City of Lights; he told him that certain Greek scholars of stupendous erudition ... had arrived in Paris who pronounced Greek in a different fashion than the one received in Europe, and proceeded to give him an account of the new pronunciation.[3]

Having promoted this pronunciation system in his *De recta latini graecique sermonic pronuntiatione* (the dialogue between the lion and the bear), when Erasmus learned that he had been the victim of a trick, "he desisted from using the pronunciation he had concocted," but it was too late: "the 'news' spread like wildfire, and after centuries of struggle with the traditional pronunciation, Erasmus' error finally succeeded in ousting the Greek pronunciation of Greek and in establishing itself in all countries outside Greece."[4]

In both accounts, the Erasmian pronunciation is conceived as a joke, one that was either played *on* Erasmus, or of which he was the perpetrator. Either way, they portray an Erasmus who did not believe in the accuracy of his system of pronunciation.

There are, however, more positive accounts of Erasmus' contribution. Sidney Allen traces the prior contributions of two earlier figures, the Spanish humanist Antonio of Lebrixa (Antonius Nebrissensis), writing

---

1. Robertson, *Grammar*, 237.
2. The story is dated 27th October 1569 and is cited in Gerardi Ioannis Vossii, *Aristsarchus, sive de arte grammatica libri septem* etc., (Amstelædami: I. Blaev 1635, Editio secunda 1662), 106ff. See Caragounis for the Latin text cited in full; Caragounis, *Development of Greek*, 342, fn. 7.
3. Caragounis, *Development of Greek*, 341.
4. Ibid., 341–42.

in 1486 and 1503, and the Venetian Aldus Manutius, writing in 1508.[5] Their reforming movement culminated in the 1528 publication of Erasmus' dialogue. Thus, by Allen's account, Erasmus was not playing a joke, nor was one played on him; rather, he was influenced by Lebrixa and Manutius. It is not likely a coincidence that all three figures spent time together in Venice in 1508 in a group dedicated to reading and speaking Ancient Greek.[6]

Moreover, it seems that Erasmus was not wrong regarding *classical* Greek. Allen traces the evidence for the classical period, which demonstrates that it was pronounced differently from the Byzantine pronunciation (which is how Greeks pronounced their language in Erasmus' day), as even Byzantine scholars such as Constantine Laskaris and Ianos Laskaris apparently acknowledged.[7] Modern Greeks, such as Caragounis, reject Allen's evidence, but it seems largely legitimate.

What Erasmus got wrong was that he did not appreciate that Koine Greek and Classical Greek were different entities—but nor did anyone else at that time. The dramatic phonetic changes that took place between 400 B.C. and A.D. 100 had yet to be appreciated. Thus, what Erasmus advocated did *not* fit the New Testament period, but for the most part it *did* fit Classical Greek.

While the Erasmian system took hold in much of Continental Europe because of his towering influence, it remained controversial, initially being rejected in Britain. Robertson refers to this fascinating example of the seriousness of the issue in the sixteenth century:

> In 1542 Stephen Gardiner, Chancellor of the University of Cambridge, "issued an edict for his university, in which, e.g. it was categorically forbidden to distinguish αι from ε, ει and οι from ι in pronunciation, under penalty of expulsion from the Senate, exclusion from the attainment of a degree, rustication for students, and domestic chastisement for boys."[8]

In other words, Cambridge men were to adhere to the Byzantine pronunciation of Greek (on pain of expulsion), which was similar, if not

---

5. W. Sidney Allen, *Vox Graeca: A Guide to the Pronunciation of Classical Greek* (3rd ed.; Cambridge: Cambridge University Press, 1987), 141–42.
6. Matthew Dillon, "Erasmian Pronunciation," in *EAGLL*.
7. Ibid.
8. Robertson, *Grammar*, 237, citing F. Blass, *Pronunciation of Ancient Greek* (trans. W. J. Purton; Cambridge: Cambridge University Press, 1890), 3.

identical, to the way modern Greek is spoken today. The question remains, however, how was Greek pronounced in the first century? It is to this topic we now turn.

9.3 The Evidence

The immediate question to be asked is, "How would we know how Greek was pronounced two thousand years ago?" There are no recordings of the ancient Greeks speaking Greek—not even on vinyl! Do we simply take the position of some modern-day Greeks, who claim with exasperation, "*This* is how Greek is and always has been pronounced!"? That argument (if it is an argument) is not compelling since we know that languages often exhibit changes in their systems of pronunciation over time. If anything, it would be an exception to the rule if Greek really does sound the same today as it did two thousand years ago. Accordingly, as Caragounis acknowledges, "during its four-thousand-year-long history, Greek has not been pronounced uniformly."[9] So then, what evidence can be adduced to establish how Greek was pronounced in the period in which the New Testament was written?

It is not possible to determine the pronunciation used in the second millennium and the early part of the first millennium BC.[10] However, inscriptions from the seventh century BC on and papyri from a few centuries later demonstrate how normal—often uneducated—people thought Greek sounded, due to a huge number of phonetically-based spelling mistakes.

As Caragounis says, the letters α, ε, ι, κ, λ, μ, ν, ξ, π, ρ, ς, τ, φ, ψ are not in dispute.[11] Rather, the disputed letters are the consonants β, γ, δ, ζ, θ, χ, the vowels η, υ, ω, the diphthongs αυ, ευ, ηυ, αι, ει, οι, and υι.[12] The evidence for the disputed letters and diphthongs can be determined as follows:

> The pronunciation of each vowel and diphthong, in particular, becomes apparent from their interchange with one another witnessed in the inscriptions and the papyri. This interchange, this writing of one letter instead

---

9. Caragounis, *Development of Greek*, 350.
10. Ibid.
11. Ibid.
12. Ibid., 351.

of another, shows that the two letters (or diphthongs) in question were sounded identically or similarly and hence were confused by those not acquainted with historical *orthography* (i.e. the etymological spelling).[13]

Noticing these spelling mistakes and their relevance for understanding the practice of pronunciation is not novel. A hundred years ago, A. T. Robertson was able to make the following statements:

> As early as the fifth century B.C. the change between η and ι is seen on vases and inscriptions.[14]

> The interchange between these vowel-symbols [ι and ει] began very early (certainly by the sixth century B.C.) and has been very persistent to the present day.[15]

> As early as 150 B.C. the Egyptian papyri show evidence of the use of ι for η. By the middle of the second century A.D. the confusion between η and ι, η and ει, ηι and ει is very general. By the Byzantine period it is complete and the itacism[16] is triumphant in the modern Greek.[17]

In his monumental two-volume work, *A Grammar of the Greek Papyri of the Roman and Byzantine Periods*, Francis T. Gignac goes to great lengths to demonstrate this common interchange of Greek vowels, summarized by the following statements:

> There is a very frequent interchange of ει and ι (whether long or short etymologically) in all phonetic environments throughout the Roman and Byzantine periods.[18]

> There is a very frequent interchange of αι and ε in all phonetic environments from the beginning of the Roman period on.[19]

> There is a frequent interchange of οι with etymologically long or short υ in various phonetic environments.[20]

---

13. Ibid., 364.
14. Robertson, *Grammar*, 191.
15. Ibid., 195.
16. Regarding *itacism*, "the term specifically refers to the change of /ɛ/ (Η ēta) into /i/. However, itacism was a process of much wider scope, since it affected the vowel system as a whole, and a series of vowels and diphthongs merged with /i/" (Sven-Tage Teodorsson, "Attic," in *EAGLL*).
17. Robertson, *Grammar*, 191.
18. Francis T. Gignac, *A Grammar of the Greek Papyri of the Roman and Byzantine Periods, Volume I: Phonology* (Milano: Istituto Editoriale Cisalpino, La Goliardica, 1976), 189; see pp. 189–91 for examples.
19. Gignac, *Greek Papyri*, 191; see pp. 192–93 for examples.
20. Ibid., 197; see pp. 197–99 for examples.

There is a frequent interchange of ου with ω and with ο, and an occasional interchange of ου with υ and its orthographic equivalent οι, in various phonetic environments, including in accented as well as unaccented syllables.[21]

The process of itacism, which resulted in the eventual identification of the sounds originally represented by ι, ει, η, ηι, οι, υ, and υι in /i/, was well advanced in Egypt by the beginning of the Roman period.[22]

This interchange [of η and ι] occurs very frequently in all phonetic conditions throughout the Roman and Byzantine periods.[23]

This interchange [of η and ει] likewise occurs very frequently in all phonetic conditions throughout the Roman and Byzantine periods.[24]

This interchange [of υ and η] occurs frequently in all phonetic conditions throughout the Roman and Byzantine periods.[25]

There is an occasional interchange of η with οι, the phonetic equivalent of υ.[26]

This interchange [of υ and ι] occurs occasionally throughout the Roman and Byzantine periods.[27]

This [interchange of ω and ο] occurs very frequently in all phonetic conditions throughout the Roman and Byzantine periods.[28]

As Gignac's multiple examples attest, there is a plethora of material in the papyri to demonstrate that many vowels and diphthongs were interchangeable in the way they sounded, but it's worth exhibiting a text to further bring this reality home to the reader.

In this somewhat entertaining letter found in Oxyrhynchus (P.Oxy. 119) to a father from his young son, we see a good dose of teenage angst as well as a few phonetically based spelling mistakes.[29] Note the spellings marked out:

---

21. Ibid., 208; see pp. 208–15 for examples.
22. Gignac, *Greek Papyri*, 235.
23. Ibid.; see pp. 235–39 for examples.
24. Ibid., 239; see pp. 239–41 for examples.
25. Ibid., 262; see pp. 262–65 for examples.
26. Ibid., 265; see pp. 265–67 for examples.
27. Ibid., 267; see pp. 267–71 for examples.
28. Ibid., 275; see pp. 276–77 for examples.
29. Taken from Bernard P. Grenfell and Arthur S. Hunt, *The Oxyrhynchus Papyri: Part I* (Egypt Exploration Society, 1898), 185–86. Grenfell and Hunt offer the following translation: *Theon to*

CXIX. A Boy's Letter

10 x 13.5 CM. Second or third century

A letter to a father from his youthful son, who begs to be taken to Alexandria. The letter is written in a rude uncial hand, and its grammar and spelling leave a good deal to be desired.

Θέων Θέωνι τῷ πατρὶ χαίρειν.
καλῶς ἐποίησες οὐκ ἀπένηχές με μετὲ
σοῦ εἰς πόλιν. ἡ οὐ θέλις ἀπενέκκειν μετὲ σοῦ εἰς Ἀλεχανδρίαν οὐ μὴ γράψω σε ἐ-
5 πιστολὴν οὔτε λαλῶ σε οὔτε υἰγέτω σε,
εἶτα ἂν δὲ ἔλθῃς εἰς Ἀλεχανδρίαν οὐ
μὴ λάβω χεῖραν παρὰ [σ]οῦ οὔτε πάλι χαίρω
σε λυπόν. ἄμ μὴ θέλης ἀπενέκαι μ[ε]
ταῦτα γε[ί]νετε. καὶ ἡ μήτηρ μου εἶπε Ἀρ-
10 χεκλάῳ ὅτι ἀναστατοῖ μὲ ἄρρον αὐτόν.
καλῶς δὲ ἐποίησες δῶρα μοι ἔπεμψες
μεγάλα ἀράκια πεπλανηκανημωσκετε[.
τῇ ἡμέρᾳ ιβ ὅτι ἔπλευσες. λύρον πέμψον εἰς
με παρακαλῶ σε. ἄμ μὴ πέμψῃς οὐ μὴ φά-
15 γω, οὐ μὴ πείνω. ταῦτα.

ἐρῶσθε σε εὔχ(ομαι).

Τῦβι ιη

On the *verso*

ἀπόδος Θέωνι [ἀ]πὸ Θεωνᾶτος υἱῶ.

Line 3: ἡ for εἰ / θέλις for θέλεις
Line 4: σε for σοι[30]
Line 5: υἰγένω for ὑγιαίνω
Line 8: λυπόν for λοιπόν
Line 15: πείνω for πίνω

---

his father Theon, greeting. It was a fine thing of you not to take me with you to the city! If you won't take me with you to Alexandria I won't write you a letter or speak to you or say goodbye to you; and if you go to Alexandria I won't take your hand nor ever greet you again. That is what will happen if you won't take me. Mother said to Archelaus, "It quite upsets him to be left behind (?)." It was good of you to send me presents ... on the 12th, the day you sailed. Send me a lyre, I implore you. If you don't, I won't eat, I won't drink; there now! It is noted that, since Grenfell and Hunt's publication of this letter, the papyrus has been reread and improved, making their translation a little out of date in various places (according to John Lee, via personal correspondence).

30. This could be a syntactical use of the accusative for dative (John Lee).

The consonants in question are the *mediae* B, Γ, Δ, the aspirates Θ, Φ, X, as well as Z.[31] There is limited evidence of interchange between consonants, unlike vowels, such that it is difficult to determine much by way of their pronunciation. So Randall Buth says, "Consonants are trickier to evaluate than the vowels because they tended to remain phonemic and are often preserved with a correct spelling regardless of how they were pronounced."[32] Caragounis suggests the principle of *syllabification* as a way forward; "the rule that these consonants build syllables together with the vowel following them, and this determines their sound."[33] He argues that, while we may not be sure of the exact quality of each of these letters, there is sufficient evidence "to know that the present Greek pronunciation was in all essentials establishing itself already in the Vth and IVth c. B.C."[34]

The evidence strongly suggests that a pronunciation that is essentially the same as that of modern Greek today was in place by the time the New Testament was written. Some scholars, such as Caragounis and John Lee, have therefore simply adopted the pronunciation of modern Greek for the Koine period. Other scholars, such as Randall Buth, prefer a slightly tweaked version of the modern pronunciation. Drawing on Gignac's papyrological evidence, Buth concludes that the letter η had not yet merged with the other *i* sounds (ι, υ, ει, οι, υι): "It appears to have still had popular phonemic status in the early Roman period," but merges with the *i* vowels in the late second century A.D.[35] For Buth, η retains an *e* sound, like ε and αι, but apart from that his approach is essentially the same as the pronunciation of modern Greek.

John A. L. Lee is one of those scholars for whom the modern Greek pronunciation is regarded as more or less accurate for the Koine period, and his pronunciation guide is reproduced below.

31. Caragounis, *Development of Greek*, 377.
32. Randall Buth, "Ἡ Κοινὴ Προφορά: Notes on the Pronunciation System of Koiné Greek." www.biblicallanguagecenter.com/koine-greek-pronunciation/, 222.
33. Caragounis, *Development of Greek*, 377.
34. Ibid., 391.
35. Buth, "Pronunciation," 221–22.

9.4 Guide to Pronunciation of Koine Greek

By John A. L. Lee.[36] 22 May 2014

The following pronunciation, which is essentially that of Modern Greek, is recommended even though it involves some anachronism. The phonetic developments involved were completed at different times in the Koine period, and a small number not until the end of, or even after it. But the arguments in favour of following the model of the modern language are: 1) It is less anachronistic than the Classical pronunciation of say 400 BC, which underwent rapid change in the Koine period. By I AD the pronunciation was closer to that of Modern Greek than to Classical. 2) It accords with the non-standard phonetic spellings frequently encountered in Koine Greek documents and is indispensible to reading them. 3) It is the same as a living system of pronunciation, i.e., the modern language, which can be accessed orally and used as a model. 4) To attempt a fully accurate synchronic pronunciation would involve producing different pronunciations for different dates in the 900-year history of Koine Greek.

VOWELS		
Letter	Sound	Examples
α	like *a* in *a*way, or *u* in l*u*ck	λάβετε = lávete
	(NOT like *a* in c*a*t)	παραλαμβάνω = paralamváno
ε	like *e* in g*e*t, *e*gg	πατέρα = patéra
αι	"	λύεται = líete
ι	like *i* in sp*i*t	τιμή = timí
ει	"	γράφει = ghráfi
οι	"	σοι = si οἰκεῖ = ikí
υ	"	θυσία = thisía
η	"	γραφή = ghrafí ἤδη = ídi
υι	"	υἱός = iós ὑγιαίνω = iyéno
ο	like *o* in *o*n	σόν = son ἄνθρωπος = ánthropos
ω	"	πάντων = pándon παντός = pandós
ου	like *oo* in s*oo*n, or *ou* in y*ou*	σου = soo οὗτος = óotos
αυ, ευ	→ consonants	

---

36. The guide was provided by John Lee via personal correspondence and is used with permission. It should be noted that, while Lee recommends a modern pronunciation for Koine Greek, he regards Allen's reconstructed pronunciation system to be accurate for Classical Greek (see Allen, *Vox Graeca*).

Consonants		
Letter	**Sound**	**Examples**
β	like *v* in *v*an	βλέπω = vlépo
γ	1) before e or i sound: like *y* in *y*et	γίνομαι = yínome ἐγένετο = eyéneto
	2) before a, o, or u sound, or a consonant: a sound not found in English, similar to *g*, but with vibration. One kind of French *r* is the same.	μέγα = mégha γόνυ = ghóni γέγονα = yéghona
δ	like *th* in *th*is, o*th*er	δύναμις = dhínamis
ζ	like *z* in gaze	ζωή = zo-í κράζω = krázo
θ	like *th* in *th*ing	θέλω = thélo
κ	like *k* in *k*ick	καί = ke κάππα = káppa
λ	like *l* in *l*ick	ἔλεος = éleos
μ	like *m* in *m*e	ἐμοῦ = emóo
ν	like *n* in *n*ot	ἐνύπνιον = enípnion νῦν = nin
ξ	like *x* in si*x*, or *ks*	δόξα = dhóxa ξένος = ksénos
π	like *p* in *sp*ot	πόλις = pólis
ρ	like *r* in th*r*ill	θύρα = thíra
σ, ς	like *s* in *s*it (*not* like *z*, except before m or r → σμ, σρ)	εἰς = iss στάσις = stásis
τ	like *t* in s*t*ill	τήν = tin τέταρτος = tétartos
φ	like *f* in *f*ill	σοφία = sofía
χ	1) before e or i sound: like *h* in *h*uge, or *ch* in German i*ch*	χεῖρα = hyíra χαίρετε = hyérete
	2) before a, o, or u sound or consonant: like *ch* in Scottish lo*ch*, or *ch* in German a*ch*	χάρις = háris χοῦς = hoos
ψ	like *ps* in a*ps*e	ψυχή = psihyí
ντ	like *nd* in a*nd*	πάντες = pándes ὄντως = óndos
μπ	like *mb* in ti*mb*er	ἄμπελος = ámbelos εἰς τὴν πόλιν = istimbólin
γκ	like *ng* in fi*ng*er	ἄγκυρα = ángira εἰσενέγκῃς = isenéngis
γγ	"	ἄγγελος = ángelos

γχ	like *ng* + χ	συγχωρῶ = sinhoró	
γξ	like *nx* in sphi*nx*	σφίγξ = sfinx	
σμ	like *sm* in spa*sm*odic	ἐσμέν = ezmén	πρός με = prózme
		σμύρνα = zmírna	
σρ	like *sr* in I*sr*ael	Ἰσραήλ = Izraíl	
αυ	1) before unvoiced sound: like *uff*	αὐτός = aftós	αὐξάνω = afxáno
	2) before voiced sound: like *uvv*	σταυρός = stavrós	αὔριον = ávrion
ευ	1) before unvoiced sound: like *ef*	εὐχαριστῶ = efharistó	
		ἐλευθερία = elefthería	
	2) before voiced sound: like *ev*	κελεύω = kelévo	πνεῦμα = pnévma
ηυ	1) before unvoiced sound: like *if*	ηὔξατο = ífxato	
	2) before voiced sound: like *iv*	ηὐδόκησε = ivdhókise	
ου	sometimes like *w*	Οὐαλέριος = Walérios	
ι	sometimes like *y*	Ἰωσήφ = Yosíf	
		Ἰουλιανός = Youlianós	

Diacritical marks

Breathings and **iota subscript**. These have no effect on the pronunciation and are ignored.

Iota adscript. This iota is often found written, but in pronunciation it is treated the same as iota subscript, i.e., ignored. So αι = a, ηι = i, ωι = o. But note in the case of αι the need to distinguish αι = ᾳ (= a) from αι (= e). E.g., τῆι αἰτίαι (dat.) = ti etía, but αἱ αἰτίαι (nom.) = e etíe.

Accents. Stress the syllable marked with an accent, whether a circumflex, acute, or grave (but some graves are not stressed). Placing the accent correctly is an essential part of the pronunciation. When a word has two accents on different syllables, the second has the main stress if they are in this pattern: τὸ ὄνομά σου = to onomá soo. But if the pattern is τὸν οἶκόν σου, the first is stressed and the second not, i.e., ton íkon soo.

Diaeresis. Indicates that the vowel so marked is not to be combined with the preceding vowel. E.g., λαϊκός = la-ikós (not lekós).

9.5 An Argument for the Erasmian Pronunciation of New Testament Greek

It is difficult to mount a serious argument in favor of the Erasmian pronunciation of New Testament Greek, at least as far as its accuracy goes. In modern times, I doubt there is a serious Greek scholar who thinks that the Erasmian system reflects the way people actually spoke Greek in the first century. Erasmus may have been largely correct about the pronunciation of Classical Greek, but the papyrological evidence demonstrates how Koine Greek was pronounced.

Yet the Erasmian pronunciation of Koine Greek remains dominant among universities and seminaries, is commonly heard at scholarly conferences, and is still taught in the majority of Greek grammars. Some of this is simply due to the fact that things can move slowly in the academic world. Even if everyone agrees that a modern pronunciation is more accurate for the Koine period, that is not how modern scholars know how to speak Greek. It's not the way they learned Greek, it's not the way they're used to teaching, and it's not the way they're comfortable reading out loud. Something that is ingrained so deeply at the level of habit is difficult to overturn.

Then there are others who defend the Erasmian pronunciation of New Testament Greek. At the 2011 Society of Biblical Literature conference in San Francisco, the Biblical Greek Language and Linguistics section cohosted a session on Greek pronunciation with the Applied Linguistics for Biblical Languages Group. The presenters were Oliver Simkin, Daniel Wallace, Randall Buth, and Michael Theophilos. Simkin simply offered an overview of Greek phonology. Buth presented his reconstructed Koine pronunciation, and Theophilos argued for a "modern" pronunciation for the Koine period. Wallace, however, defended Erasmus.

Wallace did not attempt to defend the accuracy of the Erasmian system, though he did reveal that he finds the usual criteria for determining pronunciation (such as we have explored in this chapter) inconclusive and would rather remain agnostic regarding first-century pronunciation. His main argument in defense of the Erasmian system was pedagogical. Its chief advantage is that all the vowel and diphthong sounds are distinct. This means that phonetic spelling is easier to achieve, memorization is theoretically simpler, and confusion between letters that otherwise would sound the same is minimized if not eliminated. In addition, the vast majority of Greek classes around the world use the Erasmian pronunciation, and that reality is unlikely to be overturned. In other words, adopting a modern pronunciation (or a version of it, like Buth's Koine system) would make life more difficult for the student both in terms of their learning of the language and their interaction with others who study Koine Greek.

These SBL conference papers, and responses to them, will be published in a forthcoming volume edited by Randall Buth.

9.6 Evaluation

It ought to be clear that I regard the Erasmian system of pronunciation to be inaccurate for Koine Greek. While Erasmus was most likely correct for Classical Greek pronunciation, his accuracy is not the real issue. What matters is the abundant evidence from papyri and inscriptions that reveal how people thought the language sounded. There is so much evidence (see Gignac's copious examples) pointing in the same direction that it is difficult to conceive of a sensible argument for the accuracy of Erasmus on Koine Greek. The evidence allows some wriggle room on one or two sounds, so that there is a slight distinction between Buth's Koine system and the current modern Greek pronunciation, but both are plausible options considering the evidence, and each represents a major improvement on the Erasmian system.

But what should we make of Wallace's pedagogical defense of Erasmus? Most purists will no doubt reject it out of hand—accuracy is the only thing that matters, so down with Erasmus! But many Greek teachers will sympathize with the strength of the pedagogical argument. For many students, Greek is already difficult. There is so much to be learned, memorized, and absorbed. Do we really want to add to that burden the fact that six or seven vowels and diphthongs now sound exactly the same? The pedagogical case should not be dismissed quickly; it is a live issue in a day when fewer and fewer students are bothering with Greek, with fewer universities and seminaries demanding its acquisition.

Nevertheless, we might wonder: Would anyone deliberately invent a system of pronunciation simply for pedagogical reasons? Maybe that would be acceptable to some who regard Greek a "dead" language. But surely a modern pronunciation would reinforce the fact that Greek is *not* a dead language! It is a changed language, to be sure, but one that has been spoken continuously for four thousand years. Furthermore, use of the Erasmian system may lead to unforseen negative consequences, especially in the field of textual criticism. Misunderstanding how certain letters sounded could have a serious effect on one's ability to understand scribal errors and corrections, not to mention any sense of rhyme, tonality, and cadence of Greek sentences and poetry.

Another question to ask is how serious are the negative pedagogical consequences of abandoning the Erasmian pronunciation system? After all, when it comes to learning languages, having a distinct phonology for each letter is an incredible luxury. It's not the case for Hebrew, and it's certainly not the case for English. But then it might be countered that those are both difficult languages to learn, and this is partly why. But then again, most students are learning to *read* Greek, not speak it. And they are often not required to write it either. Reading the Greek on the page means that you are not trying to guess which *i* is being used this time, because the ι, ει, υ, or η is right there in the correctly spelled word you are reading.

Also on the pedagogical side, it can be argued that abandoning Erasmus could have several positive outcomes. The students to whom I have taught a modern pronunciation (after they already knew the Erasmian system) often comment that they feel more connected to a real language; it *sounds* like a real language. There is a connection with a living people and culture who call this language their own, and they need not be embarrassed if they ever pronounce Greek in front of a live Greek speaker. They will certainly save themselves from immediate chastisement from such people! To be able to pick out a word here or there on the Greek news on television or in a Greek newspaper is a great thrill for the Greek student. They can practice Greek pronunciation with their Greek grandmother, neighbor, or local fish and chip storeowner. In my view, these experiences far outweigh any difficulty that may or may not be added by using a modern Greek pronunciation.

9.7 Conclusion

It is rather ironic that ancient misspelling is the means by which we might put our mispronunciation to death. But from an academic point of view, that is precisely what has happened. Thousands of phonetically based spelling mistakes in the papyri demonstrate beyond doubt that the Erasmian system of pronunciation was not how Koine Greek was pronounced in the first century. Unfortunately, that error has persisted in the study of Greek for nearly five hundred years. Now, at last, a growing consensus among Greek scholars against Erasmus is taking hold.

The pedagogical issues may keep the Erasmian pronunciation alive for some time yet to come in classrooms around the world, but I predict that as it becomes clearer to all that Erasmus represents a misstep and puts Greek pedagogy increasingly out of step with Greek scholarship, this will eventually be corrected too. A positive sign in this direction is the publication of two new major Greek grammars.

Porter, Reed, and O'Donnell's *Fundamentals of New Testament Greek* presents both the Erasmian and the modern systems of pronunciation and allows the student (or teacher, as the case may be) to choose which will be adopted.[37] Rodney Decker's *Reading Koine Greek* likewise presents two systems of pronunciation, but alongside the Erasmian is Buth's Reconstructed Koine system. Decker freely acknowledges that the Erasmian system is inaccurate for Koine Greek and is only useful from a pedagogical point of view.[38] Following the publication of these two Greek grammars, it is likely that any subsequently published Koine grammar that promotes only the Erasmian pronunciation system will be seen to be out of step with current trends. We still await a New Testament Greek grammar that completely abandons Erasmus, but no doubt that day will come.

In the meantime, my preference is to see the teaching of Koine Greek adopt one of the "modern" systems of pronunciation, whether that is straight from Modern Greek or from Buth's Reconstructed Koine system. As for institutions that are not yet willing to move fully in that direction, there is some benefit in adopting a compromise position if possible. For the past several years, I have taught some students the modern pronunciation of Greek. These students had all learned Greek with the Erasmian system, so the modern system represented a number of changes and some adjustment was required. Contrary to popular expectation, they have always coped with the transition well. Generally, students have enjoyed the

---

37. Porter, Reed, and O'Donnell, *Fundamentals of New Testament Greek*, 2–5.
38. Decker, *Reading Koine Greek*, xxi-xxii, 13-14

experience of pronouncing Greek in this way, and they share with me in the sense that the modern pronunciation treats Greek like a real language. It sounds like something that might be heard in a café or on Greek TV.

A by-product of this is that my students learn to pronounce Greek two ways. Since they begin by learning the Erasmian approach, they do not quickly forget it. In fact, once they have learned the modern pronunciation, they are able to switch between the two approaches (as am I). While this was not my original intention—since I would prefer all students to learn the modern pronunciation from the beginning—I now see that there are some benefits this way. First, students are able to understand and "converse" with all "Erasmian–pronouncers," which is still virtually everyone. If they study or teach in other institutions, they will be able to use the Erasmian pronunciation if need be. Second, any pedagogical advantage in using an Erasmian approach is maintained. In the long term, I would prefer to see all Greek students and teachers using a modern pronunciation, but it may take some time for that to become a reality. In the meantime, we find ourselves in an intermediate period—the age of the now and the not yet. As such, it is not a bad thing for students to be proficient in both Erasmian and modern pronunciations.

9.8 Further Reading

Allen, W. Sidney. *Vox Graeca: A Guide to the Pronunciation of Classical Greek*. Third edition. Cambridge: Cambridge University Press, 1987.

Buth, Randall. "Ἡ Κοινὴ Προφορά: Notes on the Pronunciation System of Koiné Greek." Available at www.biblicallanguagecenter.com/koine-greek-pronunciation.

Caragounis, Chrys. *The Development of Greek and the New Testament: Morphology, Syntax, Phonology, and Textual Transmission*. Grand Rapids: Baker, 2006 [Tübingen: Mohr Siebeck, 2004].

Gignac, Francis T. *A Grammar of the Greek Papyri of the Roman and Byzantine Periods*. Volume I: *Phonology*. Milano: Istituto Editoriale Cisalpino, La Goliardica, 1976.

CHAPTER 10

TEACHING AND LEARNING GREEK

Greek and pedagogy are two topics of behemoth proportion, and at their intersection lies double trouble. —Jonathan M. Watt

10.1 Introduction

This chapter differs from previous chapters in that it does not address issues about Greek per se, but rather the *teaching and learning* of the language. It is all very well to apprehend the significant (and some *very* significant) changes in our understanding of the Greek language, but what will be the point if no one wants to study the language in the first place?

It is commonplace to hear the concerns of Greek professors about decreasing numbers of students interested in studying Greek, seminaries and universities that are decreasing their commitment to biblical languages in a competitive race to the bottom, and all too many celebrity preachers who don't know a word of Greek—which occasionally becomes evident to those who *do* know Greek, by their exegesis of the New Testament. If we fail to teach Greek well, in a way that engages the student and makes the acquisition of the language as pain-free as possible, it is little wonder that potential students weigh up if it is all worth it. Bad teaching simply cannot be tolerated in a climate in which the margins for error are already thin.

Add to those concerns the real issue of language retention and the alarming number of Greek students who fail to keep their Greek over the long haul, and we see that Greek pedagogy is an incredibly important topic. You might be the best Greek teacher in the world, but if most of your students forget most of what you taught them, how useful is that? I always cringe when a pastor either embarrassingly admits, or (perversely) proudly declares to me, that he or she has lost the knowledge of Greek; it always causes me to wonder whether I am completely wasting my time. Greek instructors who do not want to waste their time and the time of their students *must* pay attention to pedagogy, and their pedagogy must include a strategy for retention.

This chapter will explore some innovations within the traditional mode of Greek pedagogy, offer a discussion of immersion learning, and briefly address the subject of Greek retention.

10.2 Fresh Ideas for Traditional Methods

The traditional grammatical-translation method of teaching and learning Greek needs no introduction, since virtually everyone reading this book will have learned Greek according to its pattern. Typically, it involves a grammar book, the learning of grammatical rules, noun and verb paradigms, basic translation, and lists of vocabulary. There is an emphasis on rote memorization, the fundamentals of grammar and some basic syntax, and gloss translation. The only really significant alternative to this approach currently is the immersion method, which will be explored in §10.3. But there have been some innovations within the older method that are also worth pondering.

10.2.1 Reading Greek

Probably the most significant variable within the traditional method is how soon beginning students are encouraged to read Greek. Older versions of the traditional method tended to leave translation until most of the grammar had already been learned. The reasons for this are understandable. How can a student be expected to read a real text when all they've learned so far are, say, nouns and twenty-five Greek words? A well-known example is J. W. Wenham's *The Elements of New Testament Greek*.[1] While Wenham's streamlined approach has certain strengths, the student is never encour-

---

1. J. W. Wenham, *The Elements of New Testament Greek* (Cambridge: Cambridge University Press, 1965).

aged to read even a paragraph of the Greek New Testament. The grammar includes several exercises, including translation exercises, but these are all fragmentary clauses or isolated sentences. That is decidedly not the same thing as reading Greek text, in which each clause and sentence is understood in light of its context, and through which the student may gain an appreciation of how clauses relate one to another and how wider units of text shape our overall understanding of Greek.

Rodney Decker's new grammar, *Reading Koine Greek*, however, includes the reading of paragraphs of the Greek New Testament from as early as the second chapter (John 1:1–8).[2] Each subsequent chapter includes at least a paragraph (often three or four) of text from the Greek New Testament, the Septuagint, or the Apostolic Fathers. These set readings come with notes and other helps based on where the student is up to in the grammar, so that knowledge not yet acquired does not prevent the reading experience.[3]

There are great strengths to Decker's model. While his grammar still belongs to the traditional grammatical-translation pedagogy, this one characteristic alone makes a significant break with many other Koine grammars. Right from the beginning, the student is experiencing the text of the Greek New Testament, which progressively becomes a more fulfilling experience as the student is able to understand more and more of each text. This enhances one's ability to digest the "vibe" of the language in a way that other expressions of the grammatical-translation pedagogy are not able to convey, because there is no substitute for reading Greek text.

My own experience, first as a student, then as a teacher of Greek, has been under the model set by my former colleague at Moore College, Richard Gibson. Similar to Decker's approach, students begin reading and translating Greek text almost from the beginning of their instruction. Working through the first few chapters of Mark's gospel, students spend between a third and a half of class hours in small translation groups, engaging the text together, while the instructor would "hover," answering questions and

---

2. Decker, *Reading Koine Greek*.
3. An important forerunner to this approach is William D. Mounce, *Basics of Biblical Greek Grammar* (Grand Rapids: Zondervan; 1st ed., 1993; 2nd ed., 2003; 3rd ed., 2009), which, together with Mounce's workbook (*Basics of Biblical Greek Workbook* [Grand Rapids: Zondervan, 1993, 2003, 2009]), represents a significant break with previous pedagogy. The workbook encourages Greek reading from an early stage with the help of study notes. Mounce's grammar is also complemented by software tools, such as ParseWorks and FlashWorks, and eventually by a continually updated website.

providing assistance as needs be.[4] I remember my own enjoyment of learning Greek under this model and the sense of satisfaction of being able to read the Greek New Testament very early in the process. I also knew satisfaction as a teacher seeing my students come under the same experience of enjoyment and wonder at encountering the Greek New Testament from an early stage in their learning.

10.2.2 Technology

Many Greek instructors already make good use of technology in their teaching, and there are at least two aspects to this topic. The first is how technology can be utilized for presentation purposes, as it may be so utilized in the teaching of virtually anything. The second is how interaction with Bible software tools can aid (or, possibly, hinder) Greek learning.

As for the use of technology for presentation purposes, there is a range of possibilities that no doubt belong to the domain of general knowledge among most teachers today, and they do not require comment here, except to agree with Decker:

> It should be noted at the outset that the use of technology is not to be regarded as a pedagogical panacea. It has some unique advantages, but it also comes with inherent complexities, some of which can be counterproductive.[5]

Using PowerPoint presentations, video, smart boards, and the like ought to help to keep classrooms engaged with content. Generally, however, they do not address the heart of pedagogy, which involves the strategy of how knowledge is imparted and learned. In other words, technology can be used to dress up nineteenth-century pedagogy into twenty-first century garb, but it is still nineteenth-century pedagogy underneath. Keeping students' attention is one thing; successfully imparting the language is another.

The second use of technology involves the ways in which software packages such as Accordance, BibleWorks, and Logos impact Greek teach-

---

4. When three hours per week were assigned, two would be spent on grammar, with one hour in reading groups. When two hours per week were allocated, one hour would be spent on grammar and one in reading groups.

5. Rodney J. Decker, "Adapting Technology to Teach Koine Greek," in *The Linguist as Pedagogue: Trends in the Teaching and Linguistic Analysis of the Greek New Testament* (ed. Stanley E. Porter and Matthew Brook O'Donnell; Sheffield: Sheffield Phoenix, 2009), 27.

ing and learning. Most serious students of the Greek New Testament will at some stage engage with such platforms, and rightly so since they are incredibly useful tools. Software relates to the issue of *retention* of the language, addressed briefly below (§10.4), but it can also be a factor in the classroom.

Given that many students will interact with such software, it has become incumbent on the Greek teacher to offer some guidance in their use. Students will welcome some basic instruction as to how software can assist with Greek exegesis and how to harness their power in searching and studying syntactical constructions, vocabulary, idiolect, and so forth. The multiplicity of platforms means that it is unlikely that every member of a class will be using the same software package; hence, instruction in software either requires competence across the leading platforms, or it must remain nonspecific in *how* to accomplish certain tasks. A possibility here is that the Greek teacher may offer classroom instruction as to the kinds of uses that will be beneficial, while technical guidance is reserved for tutorial instruction outside class time, according to platform—perhaps offered by specialists in each software package.[6] Another option is for an institution to decide on the platform that students will use. Calvin Theological Seminary, for example, requires students to purchase Logos as one of their "textbooks."

Moreover, Bible software programs can be implemented in the actual teaching of the language. Say, for example, the lesson is on the Greek article. Students could be asked to conduct a search for all the articles in a chapter of the New Testament. Then, without using the instant parsing function of the software, students can be asked to parse each occurrence of the article and, depending on the level of instruction, they can reflect on each use of the article in context. There are endless possibilities for this kind of interaction with software in the classroom.

Bringing together these two elements of technology makes good sense too. The instructor can easily use Bible software and a projector in partnership to instantly generate examples of Greek text, search for certain parts of speech, and examine a variety of syntactical constructions. This is also a sensible way to introduce major reference tools, such as BDAG. The class

---

6. Accordance and BibleWorks offer "in person" instruction at seminaries by arrangement. Logos provides assistance through a variety of online instructional tools (as does Accordance).

can observe the layout of a lexical entry while the instructor discusses how to navigate BDAG's various headings, definitions, and examples of usage.

In a different mode, some language classes aim to teach basic Greek grammar with the view that the student will rely on software tools rather than learn the morphology and vocabulary for themselves. Indeed, students of any type of Greek class may well harbor the thought: Why learn all these paradigms when my computer can instantly parse everything for me? There is probably a place for this, and it's better than nothing—if nothing is the only other option. But there should be no illusion: this is a severely impoverished approach to engaging the Greek of the New Testament.

Knowing Greek is not simply a matter of being able to parse and translate. Having your machine do the hackwork for you does not replicate the ability to read Greek for yourself. As with any language, communication depends on a complex of factors that go well beyond a 1+1=2, formulaic computation. Idiom, idiolect, aspectual pragmatics, and depth of linguistic perception—to name but a few concepts—cannot be parsed. Without the ability to *read* Greek, rather than simply *compute* Greek, the student will never achieve competency in Greek exegesis. Software tools are immensely helpful, but they *do not* replace the need to learn the language properly.

10.2.3 Learning Styles

One more way in which the grammatical-translation pedagogy can be tweaked is through attention to differing learning styles. Jonathan Watt comments, "The old adage about the necessity of 'memorization' is unhelpful, in my opinion, because it is nondescript: *how* one memorizes is more important, because it is idiosyncratic to the learner."[7] He thus explores auditory, visual, tactile, and kinesthetic strategies for learning and memorization, and he encourages students to discover which learning modalities work best for them.[8] Interestingly, however, Watt's research about second language (L2) acquisition points in the direction of immersion learning:

---

7. Jonathan M. Watt, "Linguistics and Pedagogy of Hellenistic Greek," in *The Linguist as Pedagogue: Trends in the Teaching and Linguistic Analysis of the Greek New Testament* (ed. Stanley E. Porter and Matthew Brook O'Donnell; Sheffield: Sheffield Phoenix, 2009), 19.
8. Ibid. 18–19.

Dulay, Burt and Krashen show that L2 acquisition depends heavily on environmental and subjective factors, and that "mechanical or manipulative practice," e.g. manual translation, and frequent repetition alone, are of limited value. Instead, "full, two-way communication" is the optimal mode for effective language learning.[9]

Clearly, "full, two-way communication" in Koine Greek is generally not possible through the grammatical-translation approach to teaching and learning. Rather, the topic of learning capabilities segues to that of immersion learning, which represents a significant break from traditional pedagogies. To this subject we now turn.

10.3 Immersion Methods

A topic of interest and frequent discussion at academic conferences over the past few years has been the rise of immersion language learning for Koine Greek. Immersion learning is a method of teaching a second language (L2) in which that language is itself used for the classroom instruction. In other words, the language you are attempting to learn is also the language used for the *instruction* in the language. The goal of immersion is to produce bilingualism in L2, that is, to achieve "communicative competence" or "language proficiency" in the second language. Communicative competence refers to a language user's grammatical knowledge — understanding of phonology, morphology, syntax, and cohesion.[10] Language proficiency refers to the ability to speak in the acquired language.

Classroom immersion techniques were first developed in Canada in the 1960s in order for English-speaking Canadians to become fluent in French.[11] There are now a variety of classroom immersion methods, spanning different student age ranges and differing levels of immersion. Early immersion is the most effective, with students beginning to learn L2 from ages five or six. Middle immersion is for students who begin learning L2 from ages nine or ten. Late immersion students begin between the ages of eleven and fourteen. And adult immersion students begin learning L2 at

---

9. Ibid., 22.
10. Dell H. Hymes, "Two Types of Linguistic Relativity," in *Sociolinguistics* (ed. W. Bright; The Hague: Mouton, 1966), 114–58.
11. Colin Baker, *Foundations of Bilingual Education and Bilingualism* (5th ed.; Bristol: Multilingual Matters, 2011).

seventeen or older. There is also a spectrum of levels of immersion, ranging from complete immersion, in which virtually 100 percent of class time is spent in the target language, through to differing levels of partial immersion, in which anywhere between 15 and 50 percent of class time is spent in L2.

Classroom immersion can be supplemented by (or conducted in the context of) location immersion, in which the language student spends time in a country or region in which the target language is predominant. For Canadian Anglophones, this may mean spending a few months in Quebec; for Hebrew students, it might involve attending an *ulpan* in Israel; German students may attend the Goethe-Institut in Berlin. Location immersion is the most "authentic" immersion experience, since the student's whole experience is immersed in the target language throughout every waking hour. The language learner is simply forced to grapple with everyday linguistic functionality, cultural-linguistic phenomena, and the vicissitudes of the language habits of individual native speakers.

That is all very well, but what about learning Koine Greek through immersion?

10.3.1 Randall Buth

The pioneer and foremost figure in immersion for Koine Greek is Randall Buth. In 1996, after twenty years working in Africa as a Bible translator and translation consultant with Wycliffe Bible Translators and United Bible Societies, Buth, based in Israel, began to develop new classroom methodologies for teaching biblical languages. His Living Biblical Languages method is the first to apply immersion techniques to learning biblical Greek.[12]

The vision of Buth's Biblical Languages Center is "to promote and develop a living knowledge of Hebrew, Greek, and Aramaic, so that anyone can fluently read and understand the Bible in its original languages, being capable of conversing in the languages, and that there may be teachers who can reproduce these skills in others."[13]

The immersion courses offered by the Biblical Languages Center spend more than 90 percent of classroom time with the spoken biblical language, with the goal of internalization of the language and communicative com-

---

12. See www.biblicallanguagecenter.com/randall-buth-biography/ (accessed July 10, 2014).
13. See www.biblicallanguagecenter.com/blc-vision/ (accessed July 10, 2014).

petence. Each BLC course is led by two instructors, who employ a variety of teaching techniques. One such technique is known as Total Physical Response, in which students respond to commands that require physical movement. Another technique is Teaching Proficiency through Reading and Storytelling, which "builds language proficiency in the use of grammatical structures through reading and telling stories."[14] There are also a variety of audio-lingual materials, such as books with related audio content, that are used for review and homework. The results, it is claimed, include a much faster acquisition rate, better retention of the language, and an internalized fluency in reading and speaking Greek.

To date there are no formal studies to prove the effectiveness of Buth's immersion approach, but by all reports it is very good. Though anecdotal evidence, every person I have spoken to who has learned Greek or Hebrew through BLC has been enthusiastic about their experience and its results. Could immersion be the way of the future for Greek pedagogy?

10.3.2 Other Voices

Buth may be the pioneer and leader, but there are now others promoting Greek immersion. Michael Halcomb's Conversational Greek Institute is a good example.[15] The Conversational Greek Institute offers immersion classes in person and online, as well as a host of resources, including *Speak Koine Greek: A Conversational Phrasebook*.[16] Another example is The Academy of Classical Languages, which offers courses in Biblical Greek, Classical Greek, Latin, and Slavonic, all through immersion learning.[17] A distinguishing feature of the academy is that *all* its courses are conducted online through live interaction with an instructor.

On his blog καὶ τὰ λοιπά, Daniel Streett has written an insightful nine-post series on Greek pedagogy, in which he puts forward the case for immersion learning.[18] Of particular interest are his reflections on the challenges of using an immersion approach in seminaries. Some of his comments on this subject are included in the following section.

---

14. See www.biblicallanguagecenter.com/methodology/ (accessed July 10, 2014).
15. See www.conversationalkoine.com/ (accessed July 10, 2014).
16. T. Michael W. Halcomb and Fredrick J. Long, *Speak Koine Greek: A Conversational Phrasebook* (n.p.: GlossaHouse, 2014).
17. http://academyofclassicallanguages.com/ (accessed July 11, 2014).
18. http://danielstreett.com/tag/basics-of-greek-pedagogy/ (accessed July 11, 2014).

10.3.3 Evaluation

Immersion may well hold the key to solving many of the problems facing Greek pedagogy. But there are also a number of hurdles in its path. The obvious challenge is that it is difficult, if not impossible, to maintain the immersive experience. Once the immersion class is concluded, how will the Greek student maintain conversational fluency? While they may, of course, read copious amounts of Greek text (which is highly recommended for everyone else anyway), there are no native speakers of Koine Greek alive today. Time spent in Greece will be of some benefit, especially for pronunciation, but Modern Greek is sufficiently different from Koine such that it will not achieve the desired outcome. My mother was fluent in Modern Greek, but could only pick out a few words here or there from a page in the Greek New Testament. Being immersed in Modern Greek will not achieve linguistic competency in Koine.

The next most obvious challenge is the paucity of teachers of immersion learning. The vision statement of Buth's Biblical Languages Center includes the training of "teachers who can reproduce these skills in others," but so far few Greek instructors in seminaries and universities are thus equipped. Unless hundreds of Greek professors are willing to take Buth's courses, our institutions are not likely to be able to adopt an immersion method even if they wanted to.

One shortcut around this problem is raised on Daniel Streett's blog, in which he discusses the possibility of outsourcing immersion instruction to a school that specializes in it.[19] With the right accreditation, such schools could enable seminaries to embrace immersion learning without the difficult, expensive, and time-consuming process of retraining their Greek faculty. Randall Buth has offered such a school for years, but he is based in Israel.[20] As Streett says, "We need language centers in Boston, LA, Chicago, and Dallas!"[21] An encouraging sign is the fact that Asbury Theological Seminary has partnered with the Conversational Greek Institute

---

19. http://danielstreett.com/2011/09/24/greek-immersion-in-the-seminary-curriculumpractical-suggestions-basics-of-greek-pedagogy-pt-8/ (accessed July 11, 2014).

20. However, the Biblical Languages Center has recently offered its first summer intensive course in the United States; see www.biblicallanguagecenter.com/immersion-courses/summer-session-2014-in-north-carolina/ (accessed July 11, 2014).

21. See danielstreett.com/2011/09/24/greek-immersion-in-the-seminary-curriculumpractical-suggestions-basics-of-greek-pedagogy-pt-8/ (accessed July 11, 2014).

for their Greek Certificate Program. This certificate can achieve advanced standing for enrollment in one of Asbury's Masters degree programs.[22]

A lack of qualified instructors is not the only problem institutions face in implementing immersion methods; there's also the question of *time*. Immersion learning generally requires a significant time commitment, or at least a decent block of intensive time — time that seminaries generally do not have to spare. Nevertheless, Streett compares the average MDiv language requirement with a language course in a university:

> Seminary requirements for Greek/Hebrew pale in comparison, as modern language programs a) require 50 credits worth of immersive classes, b) enjoy a support structure that includes student clubs and language labs, and c) often include a year spent abroad in a country where the target language is spoken.[23]

Streett offers some suggestions as to how seminaries might be able to incorporate immersion practices into their timetable. He points out that in a modern language major, only two or three semesters of class will focus on the language itself. The other credits in the major are literature and history courses taught *in the language*. If this is applied to a seminary curriculum, after establishing a basic level of fluency in Greek, all subsequent Greek grammar and New Testament classes could be taught in Greek, thus steadily increasing students' fluency.[24] Another practical suggestion that might be realistic for some seminaries is the idea of a block intensive course conducted over summer:

> There's a reason missionary organizations, foreign exchange programs, and government language training centers all use intensive immersion programs where students are focused on acquiring the language and nothing else: they work!... Groups like the Goethe Institut specialize in intensive courses that last 8 weeks and meet 5 days a week for 4–5 hours a day, resulting in upper-intermediate level fluency. So, what if seminaries just required an 8-week language immersion during the summer, before students began their MDiv? Then, once the degree started, the student could take Biblical studies courses that would be conducted in the language and thereby continue to advance in fluency.[25]

---

22. See www.conversationalkoine.com/p/greek-certificate/ (accessed July 11, 2014).
23. See danielstreett.com/2011/09/24/greek-immersion-in-the-seminary-curriculumpractical -suggestions-basics-of-greek-pedagogy-pt-8/ (accessed July 11, 2014).
24. Ibid.
25. Ibid.

Streett also suggests some ideas for the creation of supportive structures that a seminary could fairly easily implement. One example is a dedicated Greek language lab with props, Greek games, phrasebooks, easy Greek reading, lexical resources including picture dictionaries, flashcards, audio resources, and a few computer stations with Greek keyboards and useful software.[26] Another example is a Greek club, which would enable students to "gather together regularly for extracurricular activities to provide them a chance to use the language in a relaxed atmosphere." The club could host dinners, game nights, or even plan to perform a Greek play.[27]

Finally, one of those "good problems." Immersion learning aims at fluency in the language, and for Koine Greek that includes being able to read Greek almost as quickly and easily as English (or whatever the student's primary language is). If that is achieved, there is a risk that the ability to read *slowly* could be compromised. Yes, it's a bit of a hollow point—would that we all had that problem! But the point is that for most of us, the goal is not simply to read Greek quickly and easily, but to do serious exegesis of the Greek New Testament text, engaging closely with the details of Greek syntax and vocabulary, clause construction, and discourse features. It is not unusual for interpreters of the New Testament to be better exegetes of *Greek* text than *English* text for the simple reason that the "old school" grammatical approach of learning Greek has caused them to be much more acutely aware of the details in the Greek text than they would an English text, which they might read quickly and easily. Some have even said to me that they are thankful to be *slow* readers of Greek for that very reason.

I assume there is not an inherent reason why a *fast* reader of Greek should not be able to slow down as required. But in our time-poor society, with its attendant call for efficiency and speed, reading quickly will no doubt be the preferred default mode if it is available. I have no interest, however, in advocating a "speed cap" for Greek students, but merely to offer a caution about an unintended consequence should the day come when we are all able to read Greek too quickly.

---

26. See danielstreett.com/2011/09/29/immersion-greekdeveloping-the-necessary-support-structure
-basics-of-greek-pedagogy-pt-9/ (accessed July 11, 2014).
27. Ibid.

10.4 Greek Retention

My short book, *Keep Your Greek: Strategies for Busy People*, is aimed directly at the issue of Greek retention and, I hope, is helpful with its range of practical suggestions.[28] Aimed in particular at pastors and other former students of Greek, there is a chapter addressed to first-time Greek students, called "Get It Right the First Time."[29] The premise is simple, based on the proverb, "A stitch in time saves nine": "The more capable you become with Greek when you first learn it, the easier it will be to keep your Greek in the future."[30] Current students have a unique opportunity to be immersed in the language-learning process, and if competency is achieved during that time, retention will be less difficult, because it will be easier to continue to read Greek.

As for those whose formal Greek learning is in the past, there is a range of retention techniques that revolve around the fundamental principle of reading Greek on a regular basis. Similar to the immersion method of learning Greek, in which the student is saturated with Greek, reading Greek regularly is the most effective way to remind, refresh, and reinforce one's capacity with the language. Reading Greek everyday increases confidence, as your subconscious mind is triggered regularly to reinforce learning and knowledge.[31]

In addition to being encouraged to burn your interlinear in chapter 2, the topic of using software tools wisely is addressed in chapter 3. Software tools, such as Accordance, BibleWorks, and Logos, are incredible tools, but they can misused in a way that compromises one's ability to (learn and) retain Greek. Because they make it possible to look up the gloss definition of a word with a small move of the mouse, the process of strengthening memory connections in the mind is short-circuited. Thus, software tools have the potential to weaken, rather than strengthen, Greek retention.[32] Of course, this need not necessarily occur, but some discipline is required in order to avoid the powerful shortcuts that software offers, in order to strengthen the memory.

---

28. Constantine R. Campbell, *Keep Your Greek: Strategies for Busy People* (Grand Rapids: Zondervan, 2010).
29. Ibid., 81–86.
30. Ibid., 82.
31. Ibid., 15.
32. Ibid., 28–29.

Keep Your Greek includes tips for remembering vocabulary and parsing in chapters 4 and 5, the value of reading quickly and slowly in chapters 6 and 7, using your senses in chapter 8, and getting your Greek back and putting it all together in chapters 9 and 10.

10.5 Conclusion

As fewer and fewer students elect to study Greek, as more institutions lessen their emphasis on languages, and as nearly all students struggle to retain what they've learned, Greek pedagogy has probably never been more important. It is essential that Greek instructors and professors everywhere consider how to teach Greek in the most effective manner possible. This may mean tweaking long-held practices. It may mean completely rethinking one's pedagogical approach. While we tend to cling to methods we know—which may be comfortable and safe—good teachers ought to be willing to adapt and change for the sake of their students. Ultimately, what is good for Greek students will be good for Greek, and good for the exegesis, teaching, and preaching of the Greek New Testament.

In an ideal world, we would all teach and learn Greek through immersion. Indeed, some institutions and teachers are up to the challenge of adopting immersion techniques, and they ought to do so. For other institutions and teachers, this may be a step too far considering their resources and adaptability. Even so, there are ways to innovate within traditional pedagogies that will make them more effective at engaging students, imparting information, and increasing skill. And the cultivation of good habits aimed at long-term retention of Greek ought to be a factor in all teaching, regardless of pedagogical approach.

10.6 Further Reading

Buth, Randall. *Living Koiné Greek. Part One: Ἡ Ἑλληνικὴ Σχολή* (Fresno, CA: Biblical Language Center, 2007).

Campbell, Constantine R. *Keep Your Greek: Strategies for Busy People.* Grand Rapids: Zondervan, 2010.

Decker, Rodney J. *Reading Koine Greek: An Introduction and Integrated Workbook.* Grand Rapids: Baker, 2014.

————. "Adapting Technology to Teach Koine Greek." Pages 25–42 in *The Linguist as Pedagogue: Trends in the Teaching and Linguistic Analysis of the Greek New Testament*. Edited by Stanley E. Porter and Matthew Brook O'Donnell; Sheffield: Sheffield Phoenix, 2009.

Streett, Daniel R. "Basics of Greek Pedagogy," http://danielstreett.com/tag/basics-of-greek-pedagogy/.

Watt, Jonathan M. "Linguistics and Pedagogy of Hellenistic Greek." Pages 11–24 in *The Linguist as Pedagogue: Trends in the Teaching and Linguistic Analysis of the Greek New Testament*. Edited by Stanley E. Porter and Matthew Brook O'Donnell; Sheffield: Sheffield Phoenix, 2009.

CONCLUSION

There is no such thing as Greek exegesis that does not involve Greek.

This book began with two laments. Those within Greek scholarship lament that students, pastors, professors, and New Testament commentators seem out of touch with Greek studies. Those outside Greek scholarship lament that they don't know what's going on, nor do they know how to get up to speed. In this book, I have sought to answer these twin laments. It is hoped that this introduction to the advances in the study of Greek will facilitate a greater degree of interaction between those in the guild and those who are not.

Future exegesis and translation of the New Testament, whether performed by student, pastor, or professor, must reflect consideration of the insights and arguments of Greek scholarship. To ignore Greek scholarship represents a missed opportunity at best and irresponsibility at worst. The simple reason is that there is no such thing as Greek exegesis that does not involve Greek. And whenever Greek is involved, our understanding of the language determines how well we will handle Greek text.

Thus, Greek cannot be regarded a peripheral issue for New Testament studies, since the entire New Testament is written in Greek. This means that New Testament studies can no longer afford to hold Greek scholarship at arm's length, for there is no area of New Testament interest that does not involve Greek in some capacity. It affects the entire guild. This is fact; the only question is whether or not we will be responsible with that fact. For bad Greek is like a poisoned water stream in a village; its ill effects touch everyone.

Before concluding, I reiterate my several hopes for this book. First, I hope the reader will be properly introduced to the issues of greatest importance for current Greek studies. Second, I hope the reader will become better equipped to handle Greek text with linguistic sophistication, both on a methodological and practical level. Third, I hope the reader will feel competent to engage further with Greek scholarship. Fourth, I hope the reader will engage further with Greek scholarship. Fifth, I hope that the teaching of Greek will be well informed of current issues. Sixth, I hope that the wider world of New Testament scholarship will become more engaged with Greek scholarship. Seventh, I hope that some readers will be inspired to become Greek scholars themselves. Eighth, I hope that future editions of this book will need to include the contributions of some of those aforementioned readers.

The study of New Testament Greek is probably more exciting now than at any time since the discovery of the Oxyrhynchus Papyri in 1897. So much substantial work is being conducted, some of which has huge implications for our understanding of Greek, and all of which has bearing on the exegesis of the New Testament. A world of discovery and insight await those who heed its call.

BIBLIOGRAPHY

Allan, Rutger J. "The Middle Voice in Ancient Greek: A Study in Polysemy," Dissertation presented to the University of Amsterdam, 2002. http://dare.uva.nl/record/108528.

———. "Towards a Typology of the Narrative Modes in Ancient Greek. Text Type and Narrative Structure in Euripidean Messenger Speeches." Pages 171–204 in *Discourse Cohesion in Ancient Greek.* Edited by Stephanie Bakker and Gerry Wakker.

Allen, W. Sidney. *Vox Graeca: A Guide to the Pronunciation of Classical Greek.* Third edition. Cambridge: Cambridge University Press, 1987.

Baker, Colin. *Foundations of Bilingual Education and Bilingualism.* Fifth edition. Bristol: Multilingual Matters, 2011.

Bakker, Egbert J. "Voice, Aspect and Aktionsart Middle and Passive in Ancient Greek." Pages 23–47 in *Voice: Form and Function.* Edited by Barbara Fox and Paul J. Hopper. Amsterdam: John Benjamins, 1994.

Bakker, Stéphanie J. "On the Curious Combination of the Particles γάρ and οὖν." Pages 41–62 in *Discourse Cohesion in Ancient Greek.* Edited by Stephanie Bakker and Gerry Wakker.

Bakker, Stephanie, and Gerry Wakker, eds. *Discourse Cohesion in Ancient Greek.* Amsterdam Studies in Classical Philology 16. Leiden: Brill, 2009.

Barr, James. *The Semantics of Biblical Language.* Eugene: Wipf & Stock, 2004 [Oxford: Oxford University Press, 1961].

Basset, Louis. "The Use of the Imperfect to Express Completed States of Affairs. The Imperfect as a Marker of Narrative Cohesion." Pages 205–20 in *Discourse Cohesion in Ancient Greek.* Edited by Stephanie Bakker and Gerry Wakker.

Beneš, E. "Die Verbstellung im Deutschen, von der Mitteilungsperspektive her betrachtet." *Philologica Pragensia* 5 (1962): 6–19.

Bentein, Klaas. "Tense and Aspect from Hellenistic to Early Byzantine." In *Encyclopedia of Ancient Greek Language and Linguistics*. Edited by Georgios K. Giannakis et al. Brill Online, 2014.

Black, David Alan. *Linguistics for Students of New Testament Greek: A Survey of Basic Concepts and Applications*. Second edition. Grand Rapids: Baker, 1995.

Blass, Friedrich. *Grammatik des neutestamentlichen Griechisch*. Göttingen: Vandenhoeck & Ruprecht, 1896.

———. *Pronunciation of Ancient Greek*. Translated by Purton. Cambridge: Cambridge University Press, 1890.

Blass, Friedrich, Albert Debrunner, and Robert W. Funk. *A Greek Grammar of the New Testament and Other Early Christian Literature*. Chicago: University of Chicago Press, 1961.

Bonifazi, Anna. "Discourse Cohesion through Third Person Pronouns. The Case of κεῖνος and αὐτός in Homer." Pages 1–20 in *Discourse Cohesion in Ancient Greek*. Edited by Stephanie Bakker and Gerry Wakker.

Bopp, Franz. *Vergleichende Grammatik des Sanskrit, Zend, Armenischen, Griechischen, Lateinischen, Litthauischen, Altslawischen, Gothisehen und Deutschen*. Second edition. Berlin: Ferd. Dümmler's Verlagsbuchhandlung, 1857.

Bortone, Pietro. *Greek Prepositions from Antiquity to the Present*. Oxford: Oxford University Press, 2010.

Brown, Gillian, and George Yule. *Discourse Analysis*. Cambridge: Cambridge University Press, 1983.

Brugmann, Karl, and Berthold Delbrück. *Grundriß der vergleichenden Grammatik der indogermanischen Sprachen*. Strassburg: Karl J. Trübner, 1886–1900.

Bubenik, Vit. "Compound Tenses (Hellenistic Greek)." In *Encyclopedia of Ancient Greek Language and Linguistics*. Edited by Georgios K. Giannakis et al. Brill Online, 2014.

Burridge, Richard A. *What Are the Gospels? A Comparison with Graeco-Roman Biography*. SNTSMS 70. Cambridge: Cambridge University Press, 1992.

Burton, Ernest de Witt. *Syntax of the Moods and Tenses in New Testament Greek*. Third edition. Grand Rapids: Kregel, 1976 (orig. Boston, 1888).

Buth, Randall. "Ἡ Κοινὴ Προφορά: Notes on the Pronunciation System of Koiné Greek." www.biblicallanguagecenter.com/koine-greek-pronunciation.

———. *Living Koiné Greek. Part One: Ἡ Ἑλληνικὴ Σχολή.* Fresno, CA: Biblical Language Center, 2007.

Butler, Christopher S. *Structure and Function: A Guide to Three Major Structural-Functional Theories.* 2 volumes. Amsterdam: Benjamins, 2003.

Caffarel, Alice, J. R. Martin & Christian M. I. M. Matthiessen, eds. *Language Typology: A Functional Perspective.* Amsterdam: Benjamins, 2004.

Callow, Kathleen. *Discourse Considerations in Translating the Word of God.* Grand Rapids: Zondervan, 1974.

Campbell, Constantine R. *Basics of Verbal Aspect in Biblical Greek.* Grand Rapids: Zondervan, 2008.

———. *Keep Your Greek: Strategies for Busy People.* Grand Rapids: Zondervan, 2010.

———. *Paul and Union with Christ: An Exegetical and Theological Study.* Grand Rapids: Zondervan, 2012.

———. *Verbal Aspect, the Indicative Mood, and Narrative: Soundings in the Greek of the New Testament.* SBG 13; New York: Peter Lang, 2007.

———. *Verbal Aspect and Non-Indicative Verbs: Further Soundings in the Greek of the New Testament.* SBG 15. New York: Peter Lang, 2008.

Caragounis, Chrys. *The Development of Greek and the New Testament: Morphology, Syntax, Phonology, and Textual Transmission.* Grand Rapids: Baker, 2006 [Mohr Siebeck, 2004].

Chantraine, Pierre. *Histoire du parfait grec.* Collection linguistique. Paris: Honoré Champion, 1927.

Chomsky, Noam. *Aspects of the Theory of Syntax.* Cambridge: M.I.T., 1965.

———. *Current Issues in Linguistic Theory.* The Hague: Mouton, 1964.

———. *Language and Mind.* Cambridge: Cambridge University Press, 1968.

———. *New Horizons in the Study of Language and Mind.* Cambridge: Cambridge University Press, 2000.

———. *Syntactic Structures.* The Hague: Mouton, 1957.

Cirafesi, Wally V. *Verbal Aspect in Synoptic Parallels: On the Method and Meaning of Divergent Tense-Form Usage in the Synoptic Passion Narratives.* LBS 7. Leiden: Brill, 2013.

Conrad, Carl. "New Observations on Voice in the Ancient Greek Verb." Unpublished paper, 2002. www.artsci.wustl.edu/~cwconrad/docs/NewObsAncGrkVc.pdf.

Cotterell, Peter, and Max Turner. *Linguistics and Biblical Interpretation.* Downers Grove, IL: InterVarsity Press, 1989.

Coulthard, M. *An Introduction to Discourse Analysis.* Second edition. London: Longman, 1985.

Crusius, Timothy W. *Discourse: A Critique and Synthesis of Major Theories.* New York: Modern Language Association, 1989.

Crystal, David. *A Dictionary of Linguistics and Phonetics.* Sixth edition. Malden: Blackwell, 2008.

———. *Linguistics.* Middlesex: Penguin, 1971.

Curtius, Georg. *Das Verbum der grichischen Sprache.* Leipzig: S. Hirzel, 1873.

———. *Die Bildung de Tempora und Modi im Griechischen und Lateinischen sprachvergleichend dargestellt.* Berlin: Wilhelm Besser, 1846.

———. *Erläuterungen zu meiner griechischen Schulgrammatick.* Prague: F. Tempsky, 1863.

Danker, Frederick William. "Lexical Evolution and Linguistic Hazard." Pages 1–31 in *Biblical Greek Language and Lexicography: Essays in Honor of Frederick W. Danker.* Edited by Bernard A. Taylor et al.

———. "Review of *Lexical Semantics of the Greek New Testament*, by E. A. Nida and J. P. Louw, 1992." *JBL* 113 (1994): 532–33.

Danker, Frederick William, with Kathryn Krug. *The Concise Greek-English Lexicon of the New Testament.* Chicago: University of Chicago Press, 2009.

Decker, Rodney J. "Adapting Technology to Teach Koine Greek." Pages 25–42 in *The Linguist as Pedagogue: Trends in the Teaching and Linguistic Analysis of the Greek New Testament.* Edited by Stanley E. Porter and Matthew Brook O'Donnell.

———. *Reading Koine Greek: An Introduction and Integrated Workbook.* Grand Rapids: Baker, 2014.

———. *Temporal Deixis of the Greek Verb in the Gospel of Mark with Reference to Verbal Aspect.* SBG 10. New York: Peter Lang, 2001.

Deissmann, G. Adolf. *Bibelstudien: Beiträge, zumeist aus den Papyri und Inschriften, zur Geschichte der Sprache, des Schrifttums und der Religion des hellenistischen Judentums und des Urchristentums.* Marburg: N. G. Elwert, 1895.

———. *Licht vom Osten. Das Neue Testament und die neuentdeckten Texte der hellenistisch-römischen Welt.* Tübingen: Mohr, 1908.

———. *Light from the Ancient East: The New Testament Illustrated by Recently Discovered Texts of the Graeco-Roman World.* Translated by Lionel R. M. Strachan. New York: Hodder & Stoughton, 1910.

———. *Neue Bibelstudien. Sprachgeschichtliche Beiträge, zumeist aus den Papyri und Inschriften, zur Erklärung des Neuen Testaments.* Marburg: N. G. Elwert, 1897.

Delbrück, Berthold. *Introduction to the Study of Language: A Critical Survey of the History and Methods of Comparative Philology of the Indo-European Languages.* Translated by E. Channing. Leipzig: Breitkopf and Härtel, 1882.

van Dijk, Teun A. *Text and Context: Explorations in the Semantics and Pragmatics of Discourse.* London: Longman, 1977.

Dillon, Matthew. "Erasmian Pronunciation." In *Encyclopedia of Ancient Greek Language and Linguistics.* Edited by Georgios K. Giannakis et al. Brill Online, 2014.

Dooley, Robert and Stephen H. Levinsohn. *Analyzing Discourse: A Manual of Basic Concepts.* Dallas: SIL International, 2001.

Dressler, Woflgang. *Einführung in die Textlinguistik.* Tübingen: Niemeyer, 1972.

Drummen, Annemieke. "Cohesion." In *Encyclopedia of Ancient Greek Language and Linguistics.* Edited by Georgios K. Giannakis et al. Brill Online, 2014.

———. "Discourse Cohesion in Dialogue. Turn-Initial ἀλλά in Greek Drama." Pages 135–54 in *Discourse Cohesion in Ancient Greek.* Edited by Stephanie Bakker and Gerry Wakker.

Dryer, Matthew S. "On the Six-Way Word Order Typology." *Studies in Language* 21.1 (1997): 69–103.

Dryer, Matthew S., and Martin Haspelmath. *The World Atlas of Language Structures Online.* http://wals.info/.

Duhoux, Yves. *Le verbe grec ancient: Éléments de morphologie et de syntaxe historiques.* Second edition. Bibliothèque des cahiers de l'Institut de linguistique de Louvain 114. Leuven: Peeters, 2000.

van Erp Taalman Kip, A. Maria. "Καὶ μήν, καὶ δή and ἤδη in Tragedy and Comedy." Pages 111–34 in *Discourse Cohesion in Ancient Greek.* Edited by Stephanie Bakker and Gerry Wakker.

Evans, T. V. *Verbal Syntax in the Greek Pentateuch: Natural Greek Usage and Hebrew Interference.* Oxford: Oxford University Press, 2001.

Fanning, Buist M. *Verbal Aspect in New Testament Greek.* Oxford Theological Monographs. Oxford: Clarendon, 1990.

Fantin, Joseph D. *The Greek Imperative Mood in the New Testament: A Cognitive Approach.* SBG 12. New York: Peter Lang, 2010.

Ferguson, C.A. "Diglossia Revisited." *Southwest Journal of Linguistics* 10 (1991): 227–29.

Fernández, Paula Lorente. *L'aspect verbal en grec ancien: le choix des themes verbaux chez Isocrate.* Bibliothèque des cahiers de l'Institut de linguistique de Louvain 111. Bern: Peeters, 2003.

Firbas, Jan. "Thoughts on the Communicative Function of the Verb in English, German and Czech." *BRNO Studies in English* 1 (1959): 39–63.

Firbas, Jan, and K. Pala. "Review of Ö. Dahl, *Topic and Comment: A Study in Russian and General Transformational Grammar.*" *Journal of Linguistics* 7 (1971): 91–101.

Firth, J. R. *Papers in Linguistics 1934–1951.* Oxford: Oxford University Press, 1957.

George, Coulter H. "Greek Particles: Just a Literary Phenomenon?" Pages 155–70 in *Discourse Cohesion in Ancient Greek.* Edited by Stephanie Bakker and Gerry Wakker.

———. "Lexical Aspect (Aktionsart)." In *Encyclopedia of Ancient Greek Language and Linguistics.* Edited by Georgios K. Giannakis et al. Brill Online, 2014.

Giannakis, Georgios K., Vit Bubenik, Emilio Crespo, Chris Golston, Alexandra Lianeri, Silvia Luraghi, and Stephanos Matthaios, eds. *Encyclopedia of Ancient Greek Language and Linguistics.* Brill Online, 2014.

Gignac, Francis T. *A Grammar of the Greek Papyri of the Roman and Byzantine Periods.* Volume I: *Phonology.* Milano: Istituto Editoriale Cisalpino, La Goliardica, 1976.

Greenberg, Joseph H. *Universals of Language.* Cambridge: MIT, 1963.

Grimes, Joseph E. *The Thread of Discourse.* The Hague: Mouton, 1975.

Guthrie, George H. *The Structure of Hebrews: A Text-Linguistic Analysis.* NovTSup 73. Leiden: Brill, 1994.

Halcomb, T. Michael W., and Fredrick J. Long. *Speak Koine Greek: A Conversational Phrasebook.* N.p., GlossaHouse, 2014.

Halliday, M. A. K. *An Introduction to Functional Grammar.* Second edition. London: Edward Arnold, 1994.

———. "Categories of the Theory of Grammar." *Word* 17 (1961): 241–92.

———. *Language as Social Semiotic: The Social Interpretation of Language and Meaning.* London: Edward Arnold, 1978.

Halliday, M. A. K., and Ruqaiya Hasan. *Cohesion in English.* London: Routledge, 1976.

———. *Language, Context, and Text: Aspects of Language in a Social-Semiotic Perspective.* Oxford: Oxford University Press, 1989.

Halliday, M. A. K., and Christian M. I. M. Matthiessen. *Halliday's Introduction to Functional Grammar.* Fourth revised edition. London: Routledge, 2014.

Harris, Murray J. *Prepositions and Theology in the Greek New Testament: An Essential Reference Resource for Exegesis.* Grand Rapids: Zondervan, 2012.

Hatina, Thomas R. "The Perfect Tense-Form in Colossians: Verbal Aspect, Temporality and the Challenge of Translation." Pages 224–52 in *Translating the Bible: Problems and Prospects.* Edited by Stanley E. Porter and Richard S. Hess. JSNTSup 173. Sheffield: Sheffield Academic, 1999.

———. "The Perfect Tense-Form in Recent Debate: Galatians as a Case Study." *Filologia Neotestamentaria* 15.8 (1995): 3–22.

Hellholm, D. *Das Visionenbuch des Hermas als Apokalypse: Formgeschichtliche und texttheoretische Studien zu einer literarischen Gattung. I. Methodologische Vorüberlegungen und makrostrukturelle Textanalyse.* ConBNT 13.1. Lund: Gleerup, 1980.

Herbig, Gustav. "Aktionsart und Zeitstufe: Beiträge zur Funktionslehre des indogermanischen Verbums." *Indogermanische Forschungen* 6 (1896): 157–269.

Holt, Jens. *Études d'aspect.* Acta Jutlandica Aarsskrift for Aarhus Universitet 15.2. Copenhagen: Munksgaard, 1943.

Hopper, Paul J. "Aspect and Foregrounding in Discourse." Pages 213–41 in *Discourse and Syntax.* Edited by Talmy Givón. Syntax and Semantics 12. New York: Academic Press, 1979.

Huffman, Douglas S. *Verbal Aspect Theory and the Prohibitions in the Greek New Testament.* SBG 16. New York: Peter Lang, 2014.

Hymes, Dell H. "Two Types of Linguistic Relativity." Pages 114–58 in *Sociolinguistics.* Edited by W. Bright. The Hague: Mouton, 1966.

Isačenko, A.V. *Grammaticheskij stroj russkogo jazyka v sopostavlenii s slovatskim: Morfologija.* Bratislava: The Slovak Academy of Sciences Press, 1960.

Jipp, Joshua W. "Paul's Areopagus Speech of Acts 17:16–34 as *Both* Critique *and* Propaganda." *JBL* 131.3 (2012): 567–88.

Johanson, B. C. *To All the Brethren: A Text-Linguistic and Rhetorical Approach to 1 Thessalonians.* ConBNT 16; Stockholm: Almqvist & Wiksell, 1987.

Koerner, E. F. K. *Practicing Linguistic Historiography: Selected Papers.* Amsterdam: John Benjamins, 1989.

Labov, William. *Sociolinguistic Patterns.* Philadelphia: University of Philadelphia Press, 1972.

Ladewig, Stratton, L. "Defining Deponency: An Investigation into Greek Deponency of the Middle and Passive Voices in the Koine Period." Unpublished doctoral dissertation. Dallas Theological Seminary, 2010.

Lamb, S. M. *Outline of Stratificational Grammar.* Washington: Georgetown University Press, 1966.

Lee, John A. L. *A History of New Testament Lexicography.* SBG 8. New York: Peter Lang, 2003.

———. "The Present State of Lexicography of Ancient Greek." Pages 66–74 in *Biblical Greek Language and Lexicography: Essays in Honor of Frederick W. Danker.* Edited by Bernard A. Taylor, et al.

Levinsohn, Stephen H. "Adverbial Participial Clauses in Koiné Greek: Grounding and Information Structure." Paper presented at the International Conference on Discourse and Grammar. Universeit Ghent, Belgium, May 2008 (www.sil.org/levinsohns/papers).

―――. "Aspect and Prominence in the Synoptic Accounts of Jesus' Entry into Jerusalem." *Filología Neotestamentaria* 23 (2010): 161–74.

―――. *Discourse Features of New Testament Greek: A Coursebook on the Information Structure of New Testament Greek.* Second Edition. SIL International, 2000.

―――. "Is ὅτι an Interpretive Use Marker?" Pages 163–82 in *The Linguist as Pedagogue: Trends in the Teaching and Linguistic Analysis of the Greek New Testament.* Edited by Stanley E. Porter and Matthew Brook O'Donnell. Sheffield: Sheffield Phoenix, 2009.

―――. "Self-Instruction Materials on Narrative Discourse Analysis." www.sil.org/~levinsohns/.

―――. "Self-Instruction Materials on Non-Narrative Discourse Analysis." www.sil.org/~levinsohns/.

―――. "Some Constraints on Discourse Development in the Pastoral Epistles." Pages 316–33 in *Discourse Analysis and the New Testament: Approaches and Results.* Edited by Stanley E. Porter and Jeffrey T. Reed.

―――. "Preliminary Observations on the Use of the Historic Present in Mark." *Notes on Translation* 65 (1977): 13–28.

―――. *Textual Connections in Acts.* Atlanta: SBL, 1987.

―――. "The Groupings and Classification of Events in Mark 14." *Notes on Translation* 66 (1977): 19–28.

―――. "The Relevance of Greek Discourse Studies to Exegesis." *Journal of Translation* 2.2 (2006): 11–21.

―――. "'Therefore' or 'Wherefore': What's the Difference?." Pages 349–68 in *Reflections on Lexicography.* Edited by Richard A. Taylor and Craig E. Morrison. Perspectives on Linguistics and Ancient Languages 4. Piscataway, NJ: Gorgias, 2013.

―――. "Towards a Typology of Story Development Marking." Pages 143–51 in *Bantu Languages: Analyses, Description and Theory.* Edited by Karsten Legère and Christina Thornell. Köln: Rudiger Köppe Verlag, 2010.

———. "Towards a Unified Linguistic Description of οὗτος and ἐκεῖνος." Pages 206–19 in *The Linguist as Pedagogue: Trends in the Teaching and Linguistic Analysis of the Greek New Testament*. Edited by Stanley E. Porter and Matthew Brook O'Donnell. Sheffield: Sheffield Phoenix, 2009.

Longacre, Robert E. "Mark 5.1–43: Generating the Complexity of a Narrative from its Most Basic Elements." Pages 169–96 in *Discourse Analysis and the New Testament: Approaches and Results*. Edited by Stanley E. Porter & Jeffrey T. Reed. JSNTSup 170. Sheffield: Sheffield Academic Press, 1999.

Louw, Johannes P. "A Semantic Domain Approach to Lexicography." Pages 157–97 in *Lexicography and Translation: With Special Reference to Bible Translation*. Edited by J. P. Louw. Cape Town: Bible Society of South Africa, 1985.

———. *A Semantic Discourse Analysis of Romans*. Pretoria: University of Pretoria, 1987.

———. "Discourse Analysis and the Greek New Testament." *BT* 24 (1973): 101–18.

———. *Semantics of New Testament Greek* . Philadelphia: Fortress Press, 1982.

Louw, Johannes P., and Eugene A. Nida. *Greek-English Lexicon of the New Testament Based on Semantic Domains*. New York: United Bible Societies, 1989.

Lyons, John. *Chomsky*. Revised edition. Glasgow: Fontana, 1977.

———. "Firth's Theory of 'Meaning.'" Pages 288–302 in *In Memory of J. R. Firth*. Edited by C. E. Bazell, C. J. Catford, M. A. K. Halliday, and R. H. Robins. London: Longmans, 1966.

———. *Language and Linguistics: An Introduction*. Cambridge: Cambridge University Press, 1981.

———. *Semantics: Volume I*. Cambridge: Cambridge University Press, 1977.

———. *Semantics: Volume II*. Cambridge: Cambridge University Press, 1977.

Mathewson, David L. *Verbal Aspect in the Book of Revelation: The Function of Greek Verb Tenses in John's Apocalypse*. LBS 4. Leiden: Brill, 2010.

McKay, K. L. *A New Syntax of the Verb in New Testament Greek: An Aspectual Approach.* SBG 5. New York: Peter Lang, 1994.

———. "The Use of the Ancient Greek Perfect Down to the Second Century A.D." *Bulletin of the Institute of Classical Studies* 12 (1965): 1–21.

Miller, Neva F. "A Theory of Deponent Verbs." Pages 423–30, Appendix 2, in *Analytical Lexicon of the Greek New Testament.* Edited by Barbara Friberg, Timothy Friberg, and Neva F. Miller. Grand Rapids: Baker, 2000.

Moo, Douglas J. *The Epistle to the Romans.* NICNT. Grand Rapids: Eerdmans, 1996.

Moulton, James Hope. *A Grammar of New Testament Greek: Prolegomena.* Volume I. Edinburgh: T&T Clark, 1906.

Mounce, William D. *Basics of Biblical Greek Grammar.* Third edition. Grand Rapids: Zondervan, 2009.

———. *Basics of Biblical Greek Workbook.* Third edition. Grand Rapids: Zondervan, 2009.

Nida, Eugene A. *Toward a Science of Translating: With Special Reference to Principles and Procedures Involved in Bible Translating.* Leiden: Brill, 1964.

Nida, Eugene A., and Johannes P. Louw. *Lexical Semantics of the Greek New Testament: A Supplement to the Greek-English Lexicon of the New Testament Based on Semantic Domains.* Atlanta: Scholars Press, 1992.

O'Donnell, Matthew Brook. *Corpus Linguistics and the Greek New Testament.* New Testament Monographs 6. Sheffield: Sheffield Phoenix Press, 2005.

———. "Designing and Compiling a Register-Balanced Corpus of Hellenistic Greek for the Purpose of Linguistic Description and Investigation." Pages 225–97 in *Diglossia and Other Topics in New Testament Linguistics.* Edited by Stanley E. Porter.

———. "Designing and Compiling a Register-Balanced Corpus of Hellenistic Greek for the Purpose of Linguistic Description and Investigation." Pages 255–97 in *Diglossia and Other Topics in New Testament Linguistics.* Edited by Stanley E. Porter.

Ogden, C. K., and I. A. Richards. *The Meaning of Meaning.* New York: Harcourt, Brace & Co., 1945.

238 • Advances in the Study of Greek

Olsen, Mari Broman. *A Semantic and Pragmatic Model of Lexical and Grammatical Aspect.* Outstanding Dissertations in Linguistics. New York: Garland, 1997.

Orriens, Sander. "Involving the Past in the Present: The Classical Greek Perfect as a Situating Cohesion Device." Pages 221–40 in *Discourse Cohesion in Ancient Greek.* Edited by Stephanie Bakker and Gerry Wakker.

Pearson, Brook W. R., and Stanley E. Porter. "The Genres of the New Testament." Pages 131–65 in *Handbook to Exegesis of the New Testament.* Edited by Stanley E. Porter. Leiden: Brill, 2002.

Pennington, Jonathan T. "Deponency in Koine Greek: The Grammatical Question and the Lexicographical Dilemma." *TJ* 24 (2003): 55–76.

———. "Setting Aside 'Deponency': Rediscovering the Greek Middle Voice in New Testament Studies." Pages 181–203 in *The Linguist as Pedagogue: Trends in the Teaching and Linguistic Analysis of the Greek New Testament.* Edited by Stanley E. Porter and Matthew Brook O'Donnell. New Testament Monographs 11. Sheffield: Sheffield Phoenix, 2009.

Perdicoyianni-Paleologou, Helene. "Discourse Analysis and Greek." In *Encyclopedia of Ancient Greek Language and Linguistics.* Edited by Georgios K. Giannakis et al. Brill Online, 2014.

Peters, Ronald D. *The Greek Article: A Functional Grammar of ὁ-items in the Greek New Testament with Special Emphasis on the Greek Article.* LBS 9. Leiden: Brill, 2014.

Pike, Kenneth L. *Language in Relation to a Unified Theory of the Structure of Human Behavior.* The Hague: Mouton, 1967.

———. *Linguistic Concepts: An Introduction to Tagmemics.* Nebraska: University of Nebraska Press, 1982.

Porter, Stanley E. "Discourse Analysis and New Testament Studies: An Introductory Survey." Pages 14–35 in *Discourse Analysis and Other Topics in Biblical Greek.* Edited by Stanley E. Porter and D. A. Carson.

———. "Greek Linguistics and Lexicography." Pages 46–54 in *Understanding the Times: New Testament Studies in the 21st Century.* Edited by Andreas J. Köstenberger and Robert W. Yarbrough. Wheaton: Crossway, 2011.

———. *Idioms of the Greek New Testament.* Second edition. Sheffield: Sheffield Academic, 1994.

———. "New Testament." In *Encyclopedia of Ancient Greek Language and Linguistics.* Edited by Georgios K. Giannakis et al. Brill Online, 2014.

———. "Prominence: An Overview." Pages 45–74 in *The Linguist as Pedagogue: Trends in the Teaching and Linguistic Analysis of the Greek New Testament.* Edited by Stanley E. Porter and Matthew Brook O'Donnell. Sheffield: Sheffield Phoenix, 2009.

———. "Septuagint." In *Encyclopedia of Ancient Greek Language and Linguistics.* Edited by Georgios K. Giannakis et al. Brill Online, 2014.

———. "The Functional Distribution of Koine Greek." Pages 53–75 in *Diglossia and Other Topics in New Testament Linguistics.* Edited by Stanley E. Porter.

———. "Verbal Aspect and Discourse Function in Mark 16:1–8: Three Significant Instances." Pages 123–37 in *Studies in the Greek Bible: Essays in Honor of Francis T. Gignac, S. J.* Edited by Jeremy Corley and Vincent Skemp. CBQMS 44. Washington: Catholic Biblical Association of America, 2008.

———. *Verbal Aspect in the Greek of the New Testament with Reference to Tense and Mood.* SBG 1. New York: Peter Lang, 1989.

Porter, Stanley E., ed. *Diglossia and Other Topics in New Testament Linguistics.* JSNTSup 193. Sheffield: Sheffield Academic, 2000.

Porter, Stanley E., and D. A. Carson, eds. *Discourse Analysis and Other Topics in Biblical Greek.* JSNTSup 113. Sheffield: Sheffield Academic, 1995.

Porter, Stanley E., Buist M. Fanning, and Constantine R. Campbell. *The Perfect Volume: Critical Discussion of the Semantics of the Greek Perfect Tense under Aspect Theory.* Introduction by D. A. Carson. SBG 17. New York: Peter Lang, 2015.

Porter, Stanley E., Jeffrey T. Reed, and Matthew Brook O'Donnell. *Fundamentals of New Testament Greek.* Grand Rapids: Eerdmans, 2010.

Reed, Jeffrey T. "Cohesive Ties in 1 Timothy: In Defense of the Epistle's Unity." *Neot* 26 (1992): 131–47.

———. "Discourse Analysis." Pages 189–217 in *Handbook to Exegesis of the New Testament*. Edited by Stanley E. Porter. Leiden: Brill, 2002.

———. *Discourse Analysis of Philippians: Method and Rhetoric in the Debate over Literary Integrity*. JSNTSup 136. Sheffield: Sheffield Academic, 1997.

———. "The Cohesiveness of Discourse: Towards a Model of Linguistic Criteria for Analyzing New Testament Discourse." Pages 28–46 in *Discourse Analysis and the New Testament: Approaches and Results*. JSNTSup 170. Edited by Stanley E. Porter and Jeffrey T. Reed. Sheffield: Sheffield Academic Press, 1999.

———. "To Timothy or Not: A Discourse Analysis of 1 Timothy." Pages 90–118 in *Biblical Greek Language and Linguistics: Open Questions in Current Research*. Edited by Stanley E. Porter and D. A. Carson. JSNTSup 80. Sheffield: Sheffield Academic, 1993.

Revuelta Puigdollers, Antonio R. "The Particles αὖ and αὖτε in Ancient Greek as Topicalizing Devices." Pages 83–110 in *Discourse Cohesion in Ancient Greek*. Edited by Stephanie Bakker and Gerry Wakker.

Rijksbaron, Albert. "Discourse Cohesion in the Proem of Hesiod's *Theogony*." Pages 241–66 in *Discourse Cohesion in Ancient Greek*. Edited by Stephanie Bakker and Gerry Wakker.

Roberts, Terry. "A Review of BDAG." Pages 53–65 in *Biblical Greek Language and Lexicography: Essays in Honor of Frederick W. Danker*. Edited by Bernard A. Taylor et al.

Robertson, A. T. *A Grammar of the Greek New Testament in the Light of Historical Research*. Fourth Edition. Nashville: Broadman, 1934.

Ruipérez, Martín S. *Estructura del Sistema de Aspectos y Tiempos del Verbo Griego Antiguo: Análisis Funcional Sincrónico*. Theses et Studia Philologica Salmanticensia 7. Salamanca: Colegio Trilingüe de la Universidad, 1954.

Runge, Steven E. *Discourse Grammar of the Greek New Testament: A Practical Introduction for Teaching and Exegesis*. Bellingham: Lexham Press, 2010.

———. "Now and Then: Clarifying the Role of Temporal Adverbs as Discourse Markers." Pages 327–48 in *Reflections on Lexicography*. Edited by Richard A. Taylor and Craig E. Morrison. Perspectives on Linguistics and Ancient Languages 4. Piscataway, NJ: Gorgias, 2013.

———. *The Lexham Discourse Greek New Testament*. Bellingham: Logos Bible Software, 2008 (available only as an electronic product as part of the Logos Bible Software system).

———. "The Verbal Aspect of the Historical Present Indicative in Narrative." Pages 191–223 in *Discourse Studies & Biblical Interpretation: A Festschrift in Honor of Stephen H. Levinsohn*. Edited by Steven E. Runge. Bellingham: Logos, 2011.

Rydbeck, L. "On the Question of Linguistic Levels and the Place of the New Testament in the Contemporary Language Milieu." Pages 191–204 in *The Language of the New Testament: Classic Essays*. JSNTSup 60. Sheffield: Sheffield Academic, 1991.

Sampson, Geoffrey. *Schools of Linguistics: Competition and Evolution*. London: Hutchison, 1980.

Sauge, André. *Les degrés du verbe: Sens et formation du parfait en grec ancient*. Bern: Peter Lang, 2000.

Saussure, Ferdinand de. *Course in General Linguistics*. Edited by Charles Bally and Albert Sechehaye. Translated by Wade Baskin. New York: Fontana, 1974.

Schenk, W. *Der Philipperbrief des Paulus*. Stuttgart: Kohlhammer, 1984.

Shopen, Timothy. *Language Typology and Syntactic Description*. 3 volumes. 2nd edition. Cambridge University Press, 2007.

Silva, Moisés. *Biblical Words and Their Meaning: An Introduction to Lexical Semantics*. Revised edition. Grand Rapids: Zondervan, 1994.

———. "Discourse Analysis and Philippians." Pages 102–6 in *Discourse Analysis and Other Topics in Biblical Greek*. Edited by Stanley E. Porter and D. A. Carson. JSNTSup 113. Sheffield: Sheffield Academic Press, 1995.

———. *God, Language, and Scripture: Reading the Bible in the Light of General Linguistics*. Grand Rapids: Zondervan, 1990.

Stamps, Dennis L. "Interpreting the Language of St Paul: Grammar, Modern Linguistics and Translation Theory." Pages 131–39 in *Discourse Analysis and Other Topics in Biblical Greek*. Edited by Stanley E. Porter and D. A. Carson.

Streett, Daniel R. "Basics of Greek Pedagogy." http://danielstreett.com/tag/basics-of-greek-pedagogy/.

Taylor, Bernard A. "Deponency and Greek Lexicography." Pages 167–76 in *Biblical Greek Language and Lexicography: Essays in Honor of Frederick W. Danker.* Edited by Bernard A. Taylor et al.

Taylor, Bernard A., John A. L. Lee, Peter R. Burton, and Richard E. Whitaker, eds. *Biblical Greek Language and Lexicography: Essays in Honor of Frederick W. Danker.* Grand Rapids: Eerdmans, 2004.

Teodorsson, Sven-Tage. "Attic." In *Encyclopedia of Ancient Greek Language and Linguistics.* Edited by Georgios K. Giannakis et al. Brill Online, 2014.

Thumb, Albert. *Die griechische Sprache im Zeitalter des Hellenismus: Beiträge zur Geschichte und Beurteilung der ÊÏÉÇ.* Strassburg: Verlag von Karl J. Trübner, 1901.

Vossii, Gerardi Ioannis. *Aristsarchus, sive de arte Grammatica libri septem* etc. Amstelædami: I. Blaev 1635. Editio secunda 1662.

Wackernagel, Jakob. "Studien zum griechischen Perfectum." Pages 3–24 in *Programm zur akademischen Preisverteilung.* N.p. 1904. Reprinted in *Kleine Schriften.* Göttingen: Vandenhoeck & Ruprecht, 1953, 1000–1021.

Wakker, Gerry C. " 'Well I Will Now Present My Arguments': Discourse Cohesion Marked by οὖν and τοίνυν in Lysias." Pages 63–82 in *Discourse Cohesion in Ancient Greek.* Edited by Stephanie Bakker and Gerry Wakker.

———. "Text Linguistics and Greek." In *Encyclopedia of Ancient Greek Language and Linguistics.* Edited by Georgios K. Giannakis et al. Brill Online, 2014.

Wallace, Daniel B. *Granville Sharp's Canon and Its Kin: Semantics and Significance.* SBG 14. New York, Peter Lang, 2009.

Watt, Jonathan M. "Linguistics and Pedagogy of Hellenistic Greek." Pages 11–24 in *The Linguist as Pedagogue: Trends in the Teaching and Linguistic Analysis of the Greek New Testament.* Edited by Stanley E. Porter and Matthew Brook O'Donnell. Sheffield: Sheffield Phoenix, 2009.

Welo, Eirik. "Null Anaphora." In *Encyclopedia of Ancient Greek Language and Linguistics.* Edited by Georgios K. Giannakis et al. Brill Online, 2014.

Wenham, J. W. *The Elements of New Testament Greek.* Cambridge: Cambridge University Press, 1965.

Westfall, Cynthia Long. *A Discourse Analysis of the Letter to the Hebrews: The Relationship between Form and Meaning.* JSNTSup 297. New York: T&T Clark, 2005.

Whaley, Lindsay J. *Introduction to Typology: The Unity and Diversity of Language.* Thousand Oaks, CA: SAGE, 1997.

Wifstrand, Albert. "Language and Style of the New Testament." Pages 71–77 in *Epochs and Styles: Selected Writings on the New Testament, Greek Language and Greek Culture in the Post-Classical Era.* Edited by Lars Rydbeck and Stanley E. Porter. Translated from the Swedish originals by Denis Searby. WUNT 179. Tübingen: Mohr Siebeck, 2005.

———. "Luke and Greek Classicism." Pages 17–27 in *Epochs and Styles: Selected Writings on the New Testament, Greek Language and Greek Culture in the Post-Classical Era.*

———. "Luke and the Septuagint." Pages 28–45 in *Epochs and Styles: Selected Writings on the New Testament, Greek Language and Greek Culture in the Post-Classical Era.*

Winer, Georg Benedict. *Grammatik des Neutestamentliches Sprachidioms.* Leipzig: Friedrich Christian Wilhelm Vogel, 1822.

INDEX OF SUBJECTS AND NAMES

2015. 07. 28   34. 99 (18.15)